Analysis for Marketing Planning

McGraw-Hill/Irwin Series in Marketing

Alreck & Settle
The Survey Research Handbook
Second Edition

Anderson, Hair & Bush
Professional Sales Management
Second Edition

Arens
Contemporary Advertising
Eighth Edition

Arnould, Price & Zinkhan
Consumers
First Edition

Bearden, Ingram & Laforge
Marketing: Principles & Perspectives
Third Edition

Belch & Belch
Introduction to Advertising & Promotion: An Integrated Marketing Communications Approach
Fifth Edition

Bernhardt & Kinnear
Cases in Marketing Management
Seventh Edition

Berkowitz, Kerin, Hartley and Rudelius
Marketing
Sixth Edition

Bowersox and Closs
Logistical Management
First Edition

Bowersox and Cooper
Strategic Marketing Channel Management
First Edition

Boyd, Walker & Larreche
Marketing Management: A Strategic Approach with a Global Orientation
Fourth Edition

Cateora & Graham
International Marketing
Eleventh Edition

Churchill, Ford, Walker, Johnston, & Tanner
Sales Force Management
Sixth Edition

Churchill & Peter
Marketing
Second Edition

Cole & Mishler
Consumer and Business Credit Management
Eleventh Edition

Cravens
Strategic Marketing
Seventh Edition

Cravens, Lamb & Crittenden
Strategic Marketing Management Cases
Sixth Edition

Crawford & Di Benedetto
New Products Management
Sixth Edition

Duncan
IMC: Building Relationships that Build Brands
First Edition

Dwyer & Tanner
Business Marketing
Second Edition

Dolan
Marketing Management: Text and Cases
First Edition

Eisenmann
Internet Business Models: Text and Cases
First Edition

Etzel, Walker & Stanton
Marketing
Twelfth Edition

Futrell
ABC's of Relationship Selling
Sixth Edition

Futrell
Fundamentals of Selling
Seventh Edition

Hair, Bush & Ortinau
Marketing Research
First Edition

Hasty and Rearden
Retail Management
First Edition

Hawkins, Best & Coney
Consumer Behavior
Eighth Edition

Hayes, Jenster & Aaby
Business To Business Marketing
First Edition

Johansson
Global Marketing
Second Edition

Lambert & Stock
Strategic Logistics Management
Fourth Edition

Lambert, Stock & Ellram
Fundamentals of Logistic Management
First Edition

Lehmann & Winer
Analysis for Marketing Planning
Fifth Edition

Lehmann & Winer
Product Management
Third Edition

Levy & Weitz
Retailing Management
Fourth Edition

Mason & Perreault
The Marketing Game
Second Edition

McDonald
Direct Marketing: An Integrated Approach
First Edition

Meloan & Graham
International and Global Marketing Concepts and Cases
Second Edition

Mohammed, Fisher, Jaworski, & Cahill
Internet Marketing
First Edition

Monroe
Pricing
Second Edition

Patton
Sales Force: A Sales Management Simulation Game
First Edition

Pelton, Strutton, Lumpkin
Marketing Channels: A Relationship Management Build Brands Approach
Second Edition

Perreault & McCarthy
Basic Marketing: A Global Managerial Approach
Thirteenth Edition

Perreault & McCarthy
Essentials of Marketing: A Global Managerial
Eighth Edition

Peter & Donnelly
A Preface to Marketing Management
Eighth Edition

Peter & Donnelly
Marketing Management: Knowledge and Skills
Sixth Edition

Peter & Olson
Consumer Behavior and Marketing Strategy
Sixth Edition

Rangan
Business Marketing Strategy: Cases, Concepts & Applications
First Edition

Rangan, Shapiro & Moriaty
Business Marketing Strategy: Concepts and Applications
First Edition

Rayport, Jaworski & Breakaway Solutions
Introduction to e-Commerce
First Edition

Rayport & Jaworski
Cases in e-Commerce
First Edition

Rayport & Jaworski
e-Commerce
First Edition

Stanton & Spiro
Management of a Sales Force
Tenth Edition

Sudman & Blair
Marketing Research: A Problem Solving Approach
First Edition

Ulrich & Eppinger
Product Design and Development
Second Edition

Walker, Boyd and Larreche
Marketing Strategy: Planning and Implementation
Third Edition

Weitz, Castleberry and Tanner
Selling: Building Partnerships
Fourth Edition

Zeithaml & Bitner
Services Marketing
Second Edition

Analysis for Marketing Planning

Fifth Edition

Donald R. Lehmann
Columbia University

Russell S. Winer
University of California—Berkeley

Boston   Burr Ridge, IL   Dubuque, IA   Madison, WI   New York   San Francisco   St. Louis
Bangkok   Bogotá   Caracas   Kuala Lumpur   Lisbon   London   Madrid   Mexico City
Milan   Montreal   New Delhi   Santiago   Seoul   Singapore   Sydney   Taipei   Toronto

McGraw-Hill Higher Education

A Division of The **McGraw-Hill** Companies

ANAYLSIS FOR MARKETING PLANNING
Published by McGraw-Hill, an imprint of The McGraw-Hill Companies, Inc. 1221 Avenue of the Americas, New York, NY, 10020. Copyright © 2002, 1997, 1994, 1991, 1988, by The McGraw-Hill Companies, Inc. All rights reserved. No part of this publication may be reproduced or distributed in any form or by any means, or stored in a data base or retrieval system, without the prior written consent of The McGraw-Hill Companies, Inc., including, but not limited to, in any network or other electronic storage or transmission, or broadcast for distance learning. Some ancillaries, including electronic and print components, may not be available to customers outside the United States.

This book is printed on acid-free paper.

1 2 3 4 5 6 7 8 9 0 FGR/FGR 0 9 8 7 6 5 4 3 2 1

ISBN 0-07-027547-5

Publisher: *John Biernat*
Executive editor: *Linda Schreiber*
Developmental editor: *Nina McGuffin*
Editorial Assistant: *Scott Becker*
Marketing manager: *Kim Kanakes Szum*
Project manager: *Jean R. Starr*
Production supervisor: *Debra R. Sylvester*
Designer: *Matthew Baldwin*
Cover design: *Joanne Schopler*
Cover Image: ©*Image Bank / Roy Wiemann*
Supplement producer: *Kate Boylan*
Printer: *Quebecor World Fairfield Inc*
Typeface: *10 / 12 Century Schoolbook*
Compositor: *Carlisle Communications, Ltd*

Library of Congress Cataloging-in-Publication Data

Lehmann, Donald R.
    Analysis for marketing planning / Donald R. Lehmann, Russell S. Winer.—5th ed.
      p. cm.— (The McGraw-Hill/Irwin series in marketing)
    Includes bibliographical references and index.
    ISBN 0-07-027547-5 (alk. paper)
    1. Marketing—United States—Management. I. Winer, Russell S. II. Title. III.
Series

    HF5415.13 .L395 2002
    658.8'02—cd21

                          2001030305

www.mhhe.com

To
our families, colleagues,
and students

Preface

Rationale

Many marketing books deal with marketing on the strategy level, addressing issues such as what business to be in. Others focus on operating-level product/brand management decisions involving the marketing mix or its individual elements (e.g., price, advertising/communications) whether the focus is strategic or tactical. In either case, sound decisions generally stem from sound analysis. This book focuses on the analysis needed for marketing decisions. It is structured around the basic planning document, the marketing plan.

This book evolved from a course given at the Columbia Business School called Marketing Planning and Strategy. In the mid-1970s, the marketing faculty at Columbia realized that traditional marketing management courses in business school curricula were fine for preparing MBA students for senior-level marketing positions, but did not equip them with the tools necessary for first jobs with titles such as "assistant brand manager" or "product manager." It was felt that students needed a "hands-on" course that would prepare them for the data collection and analysis tasks that often fall to junior-level managers. Interestingly, having a basic template for analysis proved beneficial for strategy-based courses as well.

The exercise of actually developing a marketing plan is highly integrative as it brings together concepts learned from marketing research, marketing strategy, finance, operations, and policy courses. Despite the advent of the Internet and the resulting development of new job titles, terminology, and technology, the need to develop sound analysis and planning is as important as ever.

This book does not attempt to cover all aspects of the marketing plan. We focus on the analysis of information pertaining to a product's environment, customers, and competitors. Chapter 1 contains an overview of an operating marketing plan. As such, the book can be used as a companion text to books on strategic marketing management, which tend to focus more on what to do after the type of analysis treated in this book has been completed, as part of a product/brand management course, or as a general reference for practitioners. Over the previous four editions of the book, we have been surprised and gratified at the wide variety of courses and contexts for which the book has been adopted.

Outline of the Book

The book has seven chapters. The first six provide specific analytical methods and data sources that can be useful for each of the analyses discussed in the chapters. Perhaps as important, they also provide some useful formats for summarizing the information. Chapter 7 then relates the concepts to the development of marketing strategy. The chapters are:

1. **Overview of Marketing Planning.** In this chapter, we present the rationale for planning, pitfalls that should be avoided, and an outline of a complete marketing plan.
2. **Defining the Competitive Set.** One of the most challenging decisions faced by marketing managers is that of defining the competition since the set of competitors can usually be constructed as narrowly or as broadly as desired. This chapter discusses methods for defining different levels of competition.
3. **Industry Analysis.** Fundamental criteria for evaluating a product's position in the market are aggregate factors such as market growth rate, industry factors such as barriers to entry, and environmental factors such as regulation.
4. **Competitor Analysis.** Monitoring strategies of key competitors and anticipating their likely moves are key to the development of successful marketing strategy. This chapter covers how to analyze competition in terms of competitors' objectives, strategies, and capabilities, and most important, how to predict future actions.
5. **Customer Analysis.** At the core of modern thinking about marketing is a customer orientation. In this chapter, we discuss the key information required to monitor customer behavior.
6. **Market Potential and Sales Forecasting.** In this chapter, we describe methods for estimating the potential size of a market and predicting future levels of sales and/or market share.
7. **Developing Product Strategy.** Rather than leaving the reader "hanging" after the discussion of the situation analysis, we have

included a chapter outlining how the concepts developed earlier in the book can be used to develop a marketing strategy.

We have incorporated several changes into this fifth edition:

- We have expanded the chapter on customer analysis (Chapter 5). Since customers are both the key to a successful business and at the core of marketing, we felt some additional material was warranted. This includes some newer material such as the lifetime value of a customer.

- We also expanded the discussion of marketing strategy (Chapter 7). We present a measure of brand equity based on sales and prices and discuss customer-based strategy (acquisition, retention, expansion, and deletion).

- Of course, in the year 2001, any marketing book has to include the Internet. Although the core of a product manager's job has not changed, the Internet has certainly affected a number of activities. The outline of the marketing plan, for example, now has sections for Web site design.

- One of the features readers liked best about the earlier editions is the pair of running examples. The two examples in the third edition are super-premium ice cream and personal digital assistants (PDAs).

Acknowledgements

We would like to acknowledge our former students at Columbia, Vanderbilt, and Berkeley who have stimulated our thoughts and given us incentive to improve our understanding of marketing planning. Over the years, we have received valuable comments from the reviewers and colleagues at our current schools and other universities. We also want to thank our team at McGraw-Hill—Linda Schreiber, Nina McGuffin, Scott Becker, and Jean Starr. As always, we thank our families for their patience. A special thanks also goes to Kris Lehmann for her outstanding editorial and word processing assistance.

We hope you find the book useful.

Donald R. Lehmann
drl2@columbia.edu
Russell S. Winer
winer@haas.berkeley.edu

About the Authors

Donald R. Lehmann

Donald R. Lehmann is George E. Warren Professor of Business at the Columbia University graduate School of Business. He has a B.S. degree in mathematics from Union College, Schenectady, New York, and an M.S.I.A. and Ph.D. from the Krannert School of Purdue University.

His research interests include modeling individual and group choice and decision making, empirical generalizations and meta-analysis, the introduction and adoption of new products and innovations, and measuring the value of marketing assets such as brands and customers. He has taught courses in marketing, management, and statistics at Columbia, and has also taught at Cornell, Dartmouth, New York University, and the University of Pennsylvania. He has published in and served on the editorial boards of *Journal of Consumer Research, Journal of Marketing, Journal of Marketing Research, Management Science,* and *Marketing Science,* and was founding editor of *Marketing Letters.* In addition to numerous journal articles, he has published four books: *Market Research and Analysis, Analysis for Marketing Planning, Product Management,* and *Meta Analysis in Marketing.* Professor Lehmann has served as Executive Director of the Marketing Science Institute and as President of the Association for Consumer Research.

Russell S. Winer

Russell S. Winer is the J. Gary Shansby Professor of Marketing Strategy, and the Chair of the marketing group at the Haas School of Business, University of California at Berkeley. He received a B.A. in Economics from Union College (N.Y.) and has an M.S. and Ph.D. in Industrial Administration from Carnegie Mellon University. He has been on the faculties of Columbia and Vanderbilt universities and has been a visiting faculty member at M.I.T., Stanford University, the Helsinki School of Economics, the University of Tokyo, and École Nationale des Ponts et Chausées. He has written three books, *Marketing Management, Analysis for Marketing Planning* and *Product Management,* and has authored over 50 papers in marketing on a variety of topics including consumer choice, marketing research methodology, marketing planning, advertising, and pricing. He is a past editor of the *Journal of Marketing Research,* the current co-editor of the *Journal of Interactive Marketing,* and is on the editorial boards of the *Journal of Marketing,* the *Journal of Consumer Research,* and the *California Management Review.* Winer is the academic director of the Fisher Center for the Strategic Use of Information Technology at the Haas School and co-director of the Center for Marketing and Technology. He has participated in executive education programs around the world, and is currently a director of Round Table Pizza, Inc. and an advisor to a number of startup companies.

Contents

1 Overview

Overview

Mention the term *marketing* and many people immediately think of catchy advertising slogans, price promotions, or the dreaded phone solicitation during dinner. While both important and salient, however, these and other tactics are simply manifestations of strategies that in turn are, or at least should be, developed consistently with an analysis of the world outside the firm: industry trends and competitor and customer behavior. This book focuses on the analyses that guide strategy selection and the tactics of advertising, pricing, distribution, product design, and service. It is organized around the development of a marketing plan, with particular emphasis on annual marketing plans.

The marketing plan provides a format useful for both organizing discussion and aiding the systematic development of marketing strategy. This chapter provides a brief overview of marketing planning and a general format for constructing a plan. Recognize, however, that planning is not an end in itself (although to someone preparing a plan, it seems to be), but rather a means for improving the chances of selecting a sound and profitable strategy.

Definition and Objectives of Plans

Marketing planning is a major activity in most large firms. One survey (Hulbert, Lehmann, & Hoenig, 1987) found over 90 percent of marketing executives engaged in formal planning. The executives spent an average of 45 days a year in planning, and they relied most heavily on information from the sales force, management information systems, and internal marketing research. Moreover, marketing plans are also crucial for small firms and emerging markets. The development of plans, which are generally annual in nature and focus on product/product line or market, is thus an important function for marketers, one that improves both coordination and performance.

The marketing plan can be divided into three general parts: the situation analysis, the objectives and strategy, and programs that direct the firm's actions. While most books and the popular press concentrate on the latter, incorrect or inadequate analysis often leads to poor decisions about pricing, advertising, and the like. Therefore, this book is devoted to the mundane but critical and surprisingly interesting task of providing the analysis on which to base an action plan—-in short, the marketing homework. Moreover, since our objective is to produce a short book, we consciously leave out some important topics. Specifically, we do not cover detailed financial analysis (e.g., of profitability by product or channel) because it requires very specific, and often faulty, internal data and promotes to some extent an inward rather than outward orientation. Also, we consider the firm's strengths and weaknesses as part of competitor analysis rather than on their own. We also do not focus on program implementation and the important area of control procedures since these vary substantially depending on objectives and data availability, and because they are applied after a plan and strategy are selected.

More specifically, the purpose of this book is to provide guidelines for preparing the central parts of the background analysis necessary to develop a marketing plan: customer, competitor, and industry analysis, plus planning assumptions and forecasting. Thus the book follows a niche strategy rather than trying to be all things to all people.

What is a formal **marketing plan?** A working definition is:

> A marketing plan is a *written* document containing the guidelines for the *business unit's* marketing programs and allocations over the *planning period.*

Several parts of the above definition have been emphasized and merit further explanation.

First, note that a formal plan is a *written document,* not something stored in a manager's head. This characteristic of marketing plans produces multiple benefits. It encourages disciplined thinking. It ensures that prior experiences with strategies that succeeded or failed are not lost. It provides a vehicle for communication among functional areas of the firm, such as manufacturing, finance, and sales, which is vital to the successful implementation of a plan. The marketing plan also helps pinpoint responsibility for achieving results by a specified date. Finally, a written plan provides continuity when there is management turnover and helps indoctrinate new employees to the situation facing the business.

A second noteworthy aspect of a marketing plan is that it is usually written at the *business unit level.* This is purposely vague because the precise level at which plans are written varies from organization to organization. For example, in a typical brand-management-organized company, a marketing plan is written for each brand since it is (at least nominally) a profit center. Alternatively, some companies write plans for groups of brands or services,

FIGURE 1–1   **Time Horizons for Marketing Plans**

Time Period	Consumer Products	Industrial Products	Services
1 year	62%	45%	65%
3 years	5	5	8
5 years	15	17	3
Long term	4	3	6
Indefinite	0	2	2
Other	14	28	16

Source: Sutton, *The Marketing Plan in the 1990s,* p. 25.

particularly when direct fixed costs are difficult to allocate by individual product.

For example, General Foods developed a separate marketing plan for each brand of cereal marketed by the Post Division, such as Raisin Bran and Grape Nuts. At the same time, McDonald's had one overall marketing plan for its fast-food operations, with perhaps some regional differences, since separate menu items such as Chicken McNuggets and the McLean sandwich (a nonsuccess) were tightly integrated into the menu and not viewed as distinct brands. In this case, the menu is the "product" and menu items are product features.

Note that the *planning period* or horizon varies from product to product. Retailing traditionally has short planning cycles to match the seasonality and vagaries of fashion trends. Automobiles, however, have longer planning cycles since lead times for product development and/or modifications are longer. Other factors contributing to variation in the length of planning horizons are rates of technological change, intensity of competition, and frequency of shifts in the tastes of relevant groups of customers. The typical horizon, however, has been annual as supported by data reported in Figure 1–1, although one impact of the Internet has been to shorten planning cycles.

Often, there is confusion between what is termed *strategic* planning and *marketing* planning. We make a distinction in the following ways. First, strategic planning is usually performed at a higher level in the organization. Using Figure 1–2 as a guide, strategic planning takes place at the corporate, group, or strategic business unit levels. At these levels, objectives are broad (e.g., return on investment or assets) and strategies are general (e.g., divesting manufacturing appliances and investing in financial services). At the business center level, marketing plans have specific objectives (e.g., market share) and strategies (e.g., pursuing the small business segment). A second difference is that due to the long-term nature of strategy, strategic plans usually have a longer time horizon than marketing plans; three to five years or more with annual updates is not uncommon.

In summary, the marketing plan is an operational document. While it contains strategies for the business center, it is more short-term oriented than

FIGURE 1–2

Hierarchy of planning

Corporate
strategic planning

Group or
sector planning

SBU
planning

Annual marketing
(business) plan

what might be called a strategic plan. Marketing plans are specific statements of how to achieve short-term results.

The objectives of a marketing plan are to:

1. Define the current business situation (and how we got there).
2. Define problems and opportunities facing the business.
3. Establish objectives.
4. Define the strategies (e.g., target market) and programs necessary to achieve the objectives.
5. Pinpoint responsibility for objectives.
6. Establish timetables and metrics for achieving objectives.
7. Encourage careful and disciplined thinking.
8. Establish an outward (customer/competitor) orientation.

This last objective is particularly relevant for this book. Today most managers are aware of the *marketing concept* popularized in the 1960s, which dictates that marketers maintain a customer orientation in their strategies. This customer orientation was reinforced during the early 1980s by Peters and Waterman's book *In Search of Excellence* and the total quality movement

(TQM). A competitor orientation, especially in today's business environment, is equally important. Books with titles incorporating the word *warfare* have focused on the competitive nature of marketing. The vast majority of products and services are not monopolies; competitors often determine a brand's profits as much as any action taken by the marketing manager. By emphasizing the importance of having both a customer and competitor orientation, this book focuses on the two most important components of the strategy development process.

Issues in the Planning Process

Unfortunately, not all organizations attempting to develop marketing plans have been pleased with the process. The Strategic Planning Institute identified common mistakes and issues in strategic planning that seem relevant to marketing planning as well.

The Speed of the Process
The process can either be so slow that it seems to go on continuously or so fast that there is an extreme burst of activity to rush out a plan. In the former case, managers become "burned out" by constantly filling out forms that can distract them from operational tasks. In the latter case, a quickly developed plan can easily lead to critical oversights.

The Amount of Data Collected
It is important to collect sufficient data to properly estimate customer needs and competitive trends. However, the law of diminishing returns quickly sets in on the data collection process. A small percentage of the available data usually produces a large percentage of the insights obtainable. We hope this book will be useful in describing the most essential data.

Who Does the Planning?
In the late 1960s, strategic planning models developed by the Boston Consulting Group, McKinsey, General Electric, and others led to the formation of formal strategic planning groups in many major corporations. Essentially, the planning process was delegated to professional planners, while implementation of the plans was left to line managers. Naturally, line managers resented this process; they thought that the planners had no "feel" for the markets for which they were planning and were managing totally by the numbers rather than including any market intuition gleaned from experience. As a result, hostility grew between staff planners and line managers to the point where recommended strategies were either poorly implemented or ignored. Currently, due to both poor results from staff-directed planning efforts and downsizings (a.k.a. reengineering), which led to large cuts in corporate staffs, line managers are much more

involved with planning, both strategic and marketing (*Business Week*, 1984). In general line managers should indeed develop marketing plans with staff assistance.

The Structure

Any formal planning effort involves some structure. The advantage of structure is that it forces discipline on the planners; that is, certain data must be collected. Interestingly, many executives believe that the most important result of planning is not the plan itself but rather the process of structuring thought about the strategic issues facing the business. However, an apparent danger is that the structure could take precedence over the content so planning becomes mere form filling or number crunching, with little thought given to the purposes of the effort. Thus, while the process should not be too bureaucratic, there must be enough structure to force thorough analysis. A good solution to the dilemma is to consider the plan format as a guide but with a rigid timetable. Flexibility in format helps prevent the plan from becoming mindless paper shuffling.

Length of Plan

The length of a marketing plan must be balanced between being so long it is ignored by both line and senior managers and so brief that it ignores key details. Many organizations have formal guidelines for the optimal lengths of documents (e.g., Procter & Gamble's one-page limit on memos); what is long for one firm is optimal for another. Median length, however, is about 20 to 30 pages.

Frequency of Planning

A common mistake made in planning is to plan either more frequently or less frequently than necessary. Overly frequent reevaluation of strategies can lead to erratic firm behavior and makes the process more burdensome than necessary. However, when plans are not revised frequently enough, the business may not adapt quickly enough to changes in the environment (e.g., due to the Internet) and may thus suffer a deterioration in its competitive position. Environmental conditions such as tax returns and reporting requirements tend to favor an annual plan.

Number of Alternative Strategies Considered

Either too few alternatives may be discussed, raising the likelihood of failure, or too many, which increases the time and cost of the planning effort. It is important to have diversity in the strategic options (e.g., both growth and hold strategies) since discarded strategies often prove useful as contingency plans.

Cross-Functional Acceptance

The successful implementation of a marketing plan requires a broad consensus including other functional areas. For example, a strategy that emphasizes high quality is difficult to implement if manufacturing does not simultaneously exert high-quality control. On the other hand, growth objectives may be achievable only through the relaxation of credit policies. A common mistake is to view the plan as a proprietary possession of the marketing department. Of course, plan acceptance is greatly enhanced by both senior management support and compensation systems tied to performance versus the plan.

Using the Plan as a Sales Document

A major but often overlooked purpose of a plan and its presentation is to generate funds from either internal sources (e.g., to gain budget approval) or external sources (e.g., to gain a partner for a joint venture). To state it differently, the plan and its proponents compete with other plans and their proponents for scarce resources. Therefore, the more appealing the plan and the better the track record of its proponents, the better the chance of budget approval.

The Planning Process

Approaches to Planning

Two general approaches to planning have developed. "Top-down" planning refers to a process where the marketing plans are formulated either by senior or middle management with the aid of staff and implemented by lower-echelon personnel such as sales representatives. An alternative to such top-down approaches are "bottom-up" methods where the lower ranks are actively involved with the planning process in terms of forecasts and collecting competitor and customer information. Information and plans are subject to higher-level review, but in such a planning system, the lower-level personnel play a key role in the process.

Both systems have some commendable characteristics. The rationale often used for top-down planning is that the higher the level the person occupies in the organization, the better the perspective that person has of the context of problems facing the business. Field salespeople, for example, tend to consider the competitive battleground as their sales territory and not necessarily the national or international market. Bottom-up planning systems are consistent with the current trend toward employee empowerment and are often characterized by better implementation than top-down approaches since the people primarily charged with executing the plan are involved in its development.

FIGURE 1–3

Marketing planning sequence

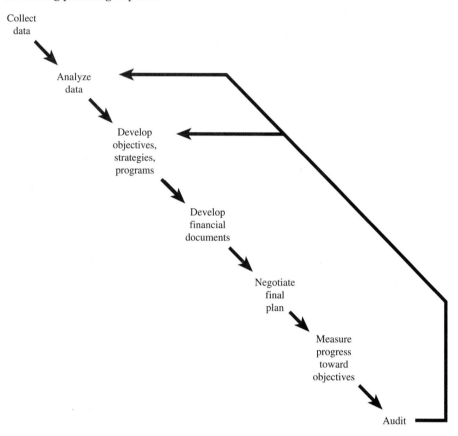

Steps in the Planning Process

In most organizations, the need to collect information and the structure of the marketing plan suggest a sequence of activities. The planning process involves a programmed sequence of events. These generally follow the order of steps one through seven shown in Figure 1–3, but the process may start at any point (e.g., customer analysis) and then iterate until it converges in a consistent document.

Step 1. Collecting Background Data

The data collection effort focuses on information available on the past and current situations. Data collected for marketing planning are often either provisional or estimated. For example, in planning for 2002, actual market size data for 2001 may not be available. However, forecasts for 2001 developed in 2000 may be. For example, preliminary estimates of the gross domestic product (GDP) may exist but not final figures.

Step 2. Analyzing Historical and Background Data
Existing data are analyzed to forecast competitors' actions, customers' behavior, economic conditions, and so forth. Such an analysis, termed the *situation analysis*, need not be quantitative; in fact, much of the analysis, as will be seen in later chapters, is qualitative and draws implications from non-numerical data. This analysis leads to the delineation of key opportunities and threats to the business.

Step 3. Developing Objectives, Strategies, Action Programs
The implications drawn from analyzing the background data (see Step 2) are used to formulate product objectives, strategies, and marketing mix decisions. This is, in fact, the critical activity of the planning process because it outlines what will be done with the product during the year (or appropriate planning period).

Objectives, strategies, and mix decisions are constrained by company mission, objectives and strategy, company policy and resources, and legal considerations, among other factors. Thus, this part of the process generally involves (*a*) setting objectives; (*b*) developing strategies and programs to achieve the objectives; (*c*) comparing the programs in terms of their ability to achieve objectives such as profit *and* to be acceptable in terms of company policy and legal constraints; and (*d*) selecting a basic objective, strategy, and program combination.

Step 4. Developing Pro Forma Financial Statements
Such statements typically include budgets and profit and loss (income) figures. As such they become the key sales document for the plan itself.

Step 5. Negotiating
Rarely, if ever, is the market plan generated from Steps 1 to 4 implemented without several rounds of negotiations with senior management. In a brand management organizational structure, the plans themselves must be marketed as managers vie for their desired portions of corporate resources. In large organizations, this negotiation phase can last as long as all the prior steps.

Step 6. Measuring Progress
In order to make necessary corrections to the plan as the environment changes within the planning period, the progress of the plan toward the

stated objectives must be monitored. Thus marketing research and other information relevant to measuring the objectives (e.g., market share and sales) must be collected on an interim basis.

Step 7. Auditing

After a planning period, it is customary to review the results to determine the variances of planned versus actual results and sources of the variances. This audit provides important diagnostic information for both current and future planning efforts and thus acts as a source of feedback.

The planning sequence is therefore a logical flow of events leading from data collection and analysis to strategy formulation to auditing the performance.

Components of the Marketing Plan

While nearly every firm has its own format (see Hopkins, 1981, and Sutton, 1990, for examples), most marketing plans do have a common set of elements. A sample of a complete marketing plan outline is provided as an appendix to this chapter and is summarized in Figure 1–4. This outline describes the major areas of analysis and data collection required for a typical marketing plan. The rationale and a brief description of each major component of the plan are offered below to give an overview of the plan and a context for the rest of this book.

The Executive Summary

A senior manager often reviews multiple marketing plans. In such situations, a brief summary of the marketing plan focusing on the objectives,

FIGURE 1–4 **Marketing Plan Summary**

  I. Executive summary
 II. Situation analysis
     A. Industry analysis
     B. Sales analysis
     C. Competitor analysis
     D. Customer analysis
     E. Planning assumptions
     F. Forecasts
III. Marketing objectives
 IV. Marketing strategy
  V. Marketing programs
 VI. Financial documents
VII. Monitors and controls
VIII. Contingency plans

strategies, and expected financial performance is mandatory. This summation provides a quick overview of the major elements of the plan and simplifies comparison between plans.

Situation Analysis

A. Industry/Category Analysis identifies long-term trends and short-term changes in the market. This section applies to past data; that is, if we are planning for 2002 in 2001, historical data will include 2000 and older information. The major areas of interest include general market data, such as sales and market shares; market activity information, such as advertising and pricing histories; historical cost and profit data; and facts related to changes in technology, regulations, or other general environmental conditions. Since these data become voluminous over time, they are often stored in a separate document called a Product Fact Book.

The Product Fact Book is a separate but related part of the overall marketing plan comprising the statistical and permanent record of product and market results, activities, conditions, and characteristics. Its purpose is to:

1. Provide a ready reference for all necessary information that forms the basis of the marketing plan.
2. Permit the basic part of the marketing plan to be relatively brief in form and operational in usage.
3. Provide a fast and easy way for new personnel to become acquainted with the product and market. (This is especially pertinent given the high turnover in many companies.)

Primary responsibility for preparation and maintenance of the Product Fact Book is usually assumed by the senior marketing manager for a product/product line.

The *Industry Analysis* also identifies factors that can be used to assess the attractiveness of an industry in which the firm is competing at a given point in time. Since all markets are dynamic in that competitors, customers, technology, and sales growth rates change, the underlying attractiveness of an industry as a target for investment also changes.

B. Sales Analysis is an intensive study of a brand's sales records intended to uncover tendencies that are hidden by aggregate numbers. For example, an overall sales increase of a line of shoes may be hiding the fact that the sales of a particular size or color are dropping or unprofitable.

C. Competitor Analysis addresses the question: What are the key competitors in the market likely to do in the future? Since virtually all markets are competitive, this is a vital section. Analysis includes engineering-based comparison of both competitors' product capabilities and their sales levels. Also relevant is a competitor analysis of the product for which the plan is being written. In other words, strengths and weaknesses of the product of interest are determined by comparison to those of the major competitors.

D. Customer Analysis guarantees a customer orientation. It is vital to understand not only who the customers are but also how and why they behave as they do.

E. Planning Assumptions involve a wide variety of quantities. For example, market potential for the product is a key number since it affects expected future category growth and resource allocation. Assumptions are also made about uncontrollable factors, such as raw material prices or labor supply.

F. Forecasts of both industry and product sales are crucial since they drive decisions and profit and loss statements.

The situation analysis thus forms the "homework" part of the plan necessary before marketing objectives and strategies can be properly formulated. While it is perhaps more enjoyable to develop concepts of where a business should go during the next planning horizon unencumbered by facts, up-front data collection and analysis are the most vital part of the plan; time spent drawing implications from the background data often makes the optimal strategies relatively apparent.

The Marketing Strategy Section

It is logical that the situation analysis precedes the strategy portion of the plan. The strategy part actually comprises three sections: a statement of marketing objectives (Where do we want to go?), the marketing strategy itself (Generally, how are we going to get there?), and the marketing programs consisting of the marketing mix elements (Exactly what do we do in what order?).

The Rest of the Plan

The final three parts of the marketing plan do not form a cohesive unit but are vital components. The financial documents report the budgets and *pro forma* profit and loss (income) statements. Senior managers, naturally, inspect expected financial outcomes with extreme care. In fact, the P&L statements are often the key "sales document" in securing approval for the plan. The monitors and controls section specifies the type of marketing research and other information necessary to measure the progress toward achieving stated objectives. The kind of information usually collected depends on the objectives; for example, if a market share increase is the objective, then share information must be collected in a timely manner to check for possible shortfalls. Finally, contingency plans are helpful, particularly in dynamic markets where either new products or competitors often create the need for strategy changes before the end of the plan's horizon. Often, these contingencies are strategies previously considered and discarded for some reason.

Summary

A marketing plan can thus be seen as a cohesive device intended to act as a guideline for the allocation of resources for a product. While there are many good references for the development of strategy, relatively few sources exist for a description of the background analysis necessary prior to strategy formulation. This book thus emphasizes the homework part of marketing planning activities.

We aim to be as complete as possible with each topic in taking a how-to orientation. In other words, we discuss the steps necessary to conduct the analyses, provide illustrations of approaches taken, and describe some sources of information typically used to perform the analyses. In doing so, we often use examples from consumer packaged goods. This does not indicate that the material applies primarily to consumer goods; it applies as well to industrial goods and services. Our choice of examples is dictated by the desire to be understandable to most readers; hence food or clothing serves our pedagogical purposes better than oil well drilling equipment or financial hedging instruments.

Since much of the situation analysis presumes a definition of the industry in which a product is competing, we begin by describing methods employed for defining the competitive set. Once that has been established, Chapter 3 discusses industry analysis. Chapter 4 describes how competitors can be analyzed with an eye toward predicting their likely future strategies. In Chapter 5, we describe approaches for analyzing customers, including methods for identifying market segments. The role of planning assumptions, market potential, and forecasting are detailed in Chapter 6, while in the concluding chapter, we describe the results of putting together all the data, developing marketing strategies.

References

Cohen, William (1997) *The Marketing Plan,* 2nd ed. New York: Wiley.

Hopkins, David (1981) *The Marketing Plan.* New York: The Conference Board.

Hulbert, James M., Donald R. Lehmann, and Scott Hoenig (1987) "Practices and Impacts of Marketing Planning," working paper, Graduate School of Business, Columbia University.

"The New Breed of Strategic Planner" (1984) *Business Week,* September 17, 62–66, 68.

Peters, Thomas J., and Robert H. Waterman, Jr. (1982) *In Search of Excellence.* New York: Warner Books.

Sutton, Howard (1990) *The Marketing Plan in the 1990s.* New York: The Conference Board.

APPENDIX 1
MARKETING PLAN OUTLINE

The following is a possible outline for developing a marketing plan. The upcoming chapters provide more detail on the situation analysis and objectives and strategies sections.

    I. *Executive Summary.* A one- to three-page synopsis of the plan providing highlights of the current situation, objectives, strategies, principal action programs, and financial expectations.

    II. *Situation Analysis.*

        A. Industry analysis.

            1. Market.

                a. Size, scope, and share of the market; sales history of producers and their market shares.

                b. Market potential and major trends in supply and demand of this and related products.

                c. Distribution channels.

                d. Selling policies and practices.

                e. Advertising and promotion.

            2. Industry attractiveness.

                a. Market factors.

                    1) Size.

                    2) Growth.

                    3) Cyclicity.

                    4) Seasonality.

                    5) Stage in life cycle.

                b. Industry factors.

                    1) Capacity.

                    2) New product entry prospects.

                    3) Threat of substitutes.

                    4) Power of suppliers.

                    5) Power of buyers.

                    6) Rivalry.

    c. Environmental factors.
        1) Social.
        2) Political.
        3) Demographic.
        4) Technological.
        5) Regulatory.
B. Sales analysis.
    1. Market area performance versus company average.
    2. Trends of sales, costs, and profits by products.
    3. Performance of distributors, end-users, key customers.
    4. Past versus current results by area, product, channel, and so on.
C. Competitor and company analysis.
    1. Behavior.
        a. Product features.
        b. Objectives.
        c. Strategies.
        d. Marketing mix.
        e. Profits.
        f. Value chain.
    2. Resources.
        a. Ability to conceive and design new products.
        b. Ability to produce or manufacture.
        c. Ability to market.
        d. Ability to finance.
        e. Ability to manage.
        f. Will to succeed in this business.
    3. Expected future marketing strategies.
D. Customer analysis.
    1. Who are the customers?
    2. What do they buy?
    3. Where do they buy?
    4. When do they buy?
    5. How do they choose?
    6. Why do they select a particular product?
    7. How do they respond to marketing programs?
    8. Will they buy again? (loyalty)
    9. Long-term value of customers.
    10. Segmentation.

E. Planning assumptions and forecasts.
  1. Market potential.
  2. Projections, predictions, and forecasts.

III. *Objectives.*
  A. Corporate objectives (if appropriate).
  B. Divisional objectives (if appropriate).
  C. Overall marketing objectives.
    1. Sales volume and profit (sales, share, and so on).
    2. Market acceptance (brand equity; customer acquisition, retention, expansion, deletion).
  D. Program objectives.
    1. Pricing.
    2. Advertising/promotion.
    3. Sales/distribution.
    4. Product.
    5. Service.

IV. *Marketing Strategy.* How the objectives will be achieved.
  A. Customer targets.
  B. Competitor targets.
  C. Core strategy.
  D. Strategic alternative(s) considered.

V. *Marketing Programs.*
  A. Product development.
  B. Advertising/communication.
  C. Pricing/promotion.
  D. Distribution.
  E. Sales.
  F. Direct marketing and customer management.
  G. Internet.
  H. Service.
  I. Partnerships/alliances.
  J. Market research.

VI. *Financial Documents.*
  A. Budgets.
  B. *Pro forma* statements.

VII. *Monitors and Controls.* Specific research information to be used:
 A. Secondary data.
   1. Sales reports.
   2. Orders.
   3. Informal sources.
 B. Primary data.
   1. Sales records (Nielsen, IRI).
   2. Specialized consulting firms.
   3. Customer panel.
VIII. *Contingency Plans and Other Miscellaneous Documents.*
 A. Contingency plans.
 B. Alternative strategies considered.
 C. Miscellaneous.

2 Defining the Competitive Set

Overview

Market analysis principally focuses on customers, competitors, and the general environment for the industry (e.g., growth prospects, suppliers, regulation). These three components are inevitably interrelated: Who the competitors are helps define the industry and customers, analysis of customers helps define who the competitors are, and industry characteristics suggest likely competitive strategies. Consequently analyses of the customers, competitors, and industry are interdependent, and which comes first is a bit of a "chicken and egg" issue. Here we begin somewhat nontraditionally with a focus on the industry and competition and then discuss customer analysis. One benefit of this approach is that it leads to a broad view of customers, in essence a minor guarantee against a myopic view of the world.

More specifically, we begin with a discussion of how to define the firm's product/ service competitors. Essentially, we address the "who do we or will we compete with" question to better understand what industry we are in, to select which competitors to analyze (i.e., in terms of financial strength), and to inform our customer analysis. For short-run plans in a mature market, most of the focus is usually on competitors with similar offerings targeted to the same customers, or what we later define as product form and product category competitors. This chapter takes a broader, more long-run view to help avoid being caught by a major technological shift (e.g., computers substituting for typewriters) and to encourage a more long-run orientation.

A distinct precondition to both analyzing competitors' capabilities and developing competitive strategy is the assessment of the sources of competitive threat. The purpose of this chapter is to make marketing managers determine the identity of the "enemy."

Consider the following quote from *Advertising Age* attributed to a copywriter at Ted Bates:

> A Bates writer can't write until someone points out the enemy. . . . If your share goes up, somebody else's share must go down. I want to know that somebody else. . . . Many categories have stopped growing so it's more important than ever to know where you're going to get your customers.

In one sense, everything competes with everything else. The key question, therefore, is not whether products or services compete but the extent to which they do. Defining competition requires a balance between identifying too many competitors, and therefore complicating instead of simplifying decision making, and identifying too few, and overlooking one or more key competitors.

Although the competitive arena usually involves the fight for customers, competitors tangle on other bases as well. For example, Amazon.com and Emerson Electric, noncompetitors in terms of customers, compete for computer programmers from the same labor supply. Kodak and jewelers compete for silver, that is, raw materials. Avon and Tupperware compete for home demonstration sales and salespeople: the same channel of distribution. Palm, Nokia, and Motorola compete for components such as memory chips and liquid crystal displays. Similarly, all manufacturers that sell through supermarkets and department stores compete for shelf space. Geographically based competition is important for both local retailers, such as hardware stores, and multinational firms, such as Ericsson (Sweden), NEC (Japan), Lucent (USA), and NorTel (Canada) in the telecommunications equipment market. More generally, there are several different types of competition listed in Figure 2–1.

As this figure suggests, competitors can be defined using several criteria. Competition can exist for customers in terms of their budgets (disposable income: vacations versus financial products), when they use a product

---

FIGURE 2–1   Bases of Competition

    I. Customer-oriented
          Who they are—competition for same budget
          When they use it
          Why they used it—benefits sought
   II. Marketing-oriented: advertising and promotion
          Theme/copy strategy
          Media
          Distribution
          Price
  III. Resource-oriented
          Raw materials
          Employees
          Financial resources
   IV. Geographic

(evenings: a basketball game versus a personal improvement seminar), and benefits sought (cancer treatments: bioengineered drugs versus chemotherapy and radiation). Competition is also related to marketing activities such as advertising (time on network television programs) and distribution (shelf space). The battle for shelf facings in supermarkets has led to a variety of manufacturer concessions to retailers to obtain desirable shelf positions, and the struggle for shelf space occurs across as well as within traditional product category boundaries.

Perhaps the most crucial competition occurs *within* a company, when different units in an organization ask for funds. In this competition, the plan acts mainly as a sales document, and its financial projections often become the key to the sale. This competition is often intentional as it puts pressure on product managers to develop sound and ambitious marketing plans.

Misidentification of the competitive set can have a serious impact on the success of a marketing plan, especially in the long run. One problem is that an important competitive threat can be overlooked. For example, the Swiss controlled the market for premium watches and Timex the market for inexpensive watches for many years. When Japanese firms developed electronic watches in the 1970s, they were not viewed as a threat or serious competition to either business. History, of course, tells a different story; Timex was forced to develop electronic watches, while the Swiss added lines using electronic works such as Swatch.

Similarly, steelmakers only slowly reacted to the intrusion of plastics into the automobile market. Recognizing the threat years ago would have produced new products with the lighter weight advantage of plastics and, perhaps, prevented or at least slowed the steel industry's decline.

As another example, consider the coffee industry (Yip and Williams, 1986). During 1977–78 sales dropped 20 percent partly due to increased competition from other beverages, particularly in the morning segment. Orange juice manufacturers have spent increasing sums on advertising and product development. Pepsi developed its brand Pepsi A.M. to compete squarely (if not effectively) with the coffee brands. Finally, notice the slow initial reaction of "bricks and mortar" firms to Internet-based competitors. From Chrysler, Ford, and GM (versus Autobytel, CarPoint, and Cars Direct) to Barnes and Noble versus Amazon.com, companies are often slow to recognize competitive threats.

Of course, ambiguous definition of the competition creates uncertainty in market definition and, therefore, market-related statistics such as market share. This leaves open the possible manipulation of market boundaries, particularly when compensation or allocation decisions are at stake. For example, assume an objective for a notebook computer (weighing four pounds with a hard disk drive but no floppy disk drive or CD-ROM) is to gain 10 percent market share. The ability to achieve this objective depends on whether the "market" is defined as all similarly-configured notebook products, all portable computers including those with floppy and CD-ROM drives, all portable Windows-based computers, all desktop computers plus portables, and so on.

A chocolate-covered granola bar could have a large share if measured in the snack bar category or a very small share if considered in the snack food category. Recently, to combat complacency, General Electric required redefining the markets in which it competes so its share was 15 percent or less. Thus, deciding in which market you wish to compete is important for both developing and controlling marketing effort.

In this chapter, therefore, we take the view that the definition of the competitive set ultimately affects what strategy is pursued. Not all authors subscribe to this approach. Abell (1980), for example, feels that the corporate mission or business definition selected affects the set of competitors against which a firm fights. Unfortunately, competitors usually do not care how a company chooses to define itself, and a company can compete against a firm's brands even if that firm does not define the company or its brands as competitors.

Here, we describe several levels of competition that can help identify the competitive set. In addition, we discuss methods that can be employed to determine the competition at the various levels. Finally, the notion of enterprise competition—firms competing against each other—is described.

Levels of Market Competition

One way to delineate the set of competitors facing a brand is to consider other products in terms of their proximity to the physical attributes of the brand. As Figure 2–2 shows, the problem of defining competition can be viewed as defining a set of concentric circles with the brand in question at the center.

The narrowest perspective one can take of competition is called *product form*. This reflects the view that the main competitors are those brands in the product category that are going after the same segment with essentially the same product features. As Figure 2–2 shows, from Diet Coke's perspective, a narrow view of competition would include only the diet colas such as Diet-Rite and Diet Pepsi. Similarly, Windows-based computers might not include Apple's iMac as a product form competitor. Thus, product form competition is a narrow view of competition that focuses mainly on what competitors' current offerings are and not what could happen in the (possibly near) future.

The second level of competition is based on those products or services with similar features. This type of competition, called *product category,* is what managers typically think of as a definition for the competitive set. For example, all firms producing personal computers, regardless of the target market, are competitors. All soft drinks (see Figure 2–2) form a "market" as well. Firms specializing in the collection of retail sales data, such as A. C. Nielsen and IRI, define product subcategories or markets based on the similarity of physical attributes such as diet soft drinks or instant oatmeal.

FIGURE 2–2

Levels of competition

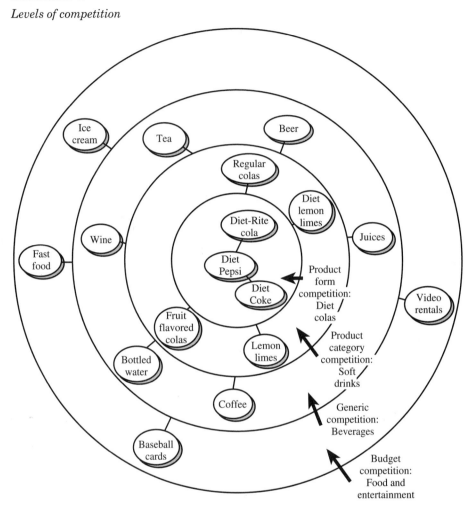

While somewhat broader than product form competition, a product category definition of competition still takes a short-run view of the market definition problem.

The third level of competition is more long-term oriented and focuses on substitutable product categories. Termed *generic competition* by Kotler (2000), it defines the competition, and therefore the market, as those products or services fulfilling the same customer need. Thus, soft drinks compete with orange juice in the "thirst-quenching" market, fast-food outlets compete against frozen entrees in the "convenience" eating market, and so on.

This need-based perspective is essential if a manager wishes to avoid both overlooking threats and ignoring opportunities. It is well described in

Levitt's (1960) classic article that admonishes several industries for defining their businesses too narrowly. Railroads viewed themselves as providing rail-based rather than general transportation services and lost business to trucks and airlines. Steel companies thought they were providing steel rather than general structural material; automobile manufacturers wanted the latter so they substituted plastics in some areas of the cars. Some firms take this generic perspective. Federal Express, for example, saw its competitors as not only Purolator, UPS, and the U.S. Postal Service, but also other companies providing quick transmission of information. As a result, Federal Express tried to develop a facsimile business as an alternative to overnight package and small letter delivery. Interestingly, recently FedEx has reemphasized package delivery for Internet-based firms.

An even more general level of competition, termed *rivalry* by Kotler (2000), is *budget* competition. This is the broadest view of competition; it considers all products and services competing for the same customer dollar as forming a market. For example, a consumer who has $500 in discretionary disposable income could spend it on a vacation, a ring, a money market instrument, or a variety of other things. *The Wall Street Journal* (1986) noted that because of a healthy U.S. economy, people had been spending money on consumer durables rather than at fast-food chains such as Wendy's or McDonald's. Competition for dollars is even tighter when the economy is not so healthy, as the early 1990s demonstrated. While a budget level view of competition is conceptually useful, it is very difficult to implement strategically as it implies an enormous number of competitors.

A crucial difference between generically defined competitors and either product form or product category competition is that the former is *outward* oriented while the latter two are *inward*. Product form and product category competitors are defined by products that look like those we are producing. Generic competitors are defined by looking outside the firm to the customers. After all, who really defines competition, the firm or the customer? It is the customer who determines what alternative products and services solve the problem at hand. Although in some cases there may be a limited number of ways to solve the same problem or provide the same benefit, in most instances focusing on the physical product alone ignores viable competitors.

Southwest Airlines used this outward perspective on competition very successfully to build what is generally considered to be the most successful U.S. airline (Kim and Mauborgne, 1999). The reasons for its success are well-documented: It focuses on short-haul flights, it does not serve meals or in-flight films and the like, but it does offer extraordinary value with fares often 60 percent below competition, on-time flights, and airports with less congestion. When developing its concept, instead of focusing on rivals in the airline industry, Southwest realized that for short-haul destinations, surface transportation like cars and trains were substitutes for flying. By concentrating on the factors that lead people to drive versus fly and eliminating or reducing everything else, the company's value proposition was established.

FIGURE 2–3   **Federal Express Competitors, Circa 1995**

Level of Competition	Definition	Competing Companies	Need Satisfied
Product form	Overnight air delivery	Emery, DHL	Exact form transmission of material overnight picked up and delivered
Product category	Small package delivery, facsimile	American Airlines, UPS, U.S. Post Office	Rapid transmission of exact form
Generic	Transportation and transmission of information	AT&T, IBM, MCI, Telex, Southwest Airlines (people movement), America On-Line, libraries	Movement of information
Budget	Provision of parts	Parts wholesalers and dealers	Provision of parts

What competition does the marketing manager for a line of low-priced stereo components such as Pioneer face? First, there are the competitors fighting for the same segment of the stereo market. Second, there are other, higher-priced component manufacturers. Third, manufacturers of other entertainment products such as television sets and videocassette recorders must be considered. Finally, alternative ways to spend the money, such as on a vacation, could be relevant. These different sets of competitors create multiple marketing tasks. First, the manager's brand must be shown to have advantages over competitors' brands in the low-price segment. Second, the advantages of the low-price components over more expensive ones (e.g., Bank and Olufsen, McIntosh) must be established. Third, customers must be convinced to buy stereos rather than, say, VCRs. Finally, prospects have to be informed about the benefits of buying stereos instead of going on vacation or buying stocks. Thus, market definition has implications not only for defining the market but for the strategy employed as well.

Consider the problem facing the product manager for Diet Pepsi. Clearly it competes with other diet colas such as Diet Coke, but also with other soft drinks, especially nondiet colas and diet lemon-lime drinks that differ in only one aspect from diet colas. Further, Diet Pepsi competes with most food and beverages (wines, fruit juice, tea, coffee, and bottled waters as a drink with a meal, ice cream as a treat, etc.). Finally, to some extent, it competes with other low-ticket entertainment products such as baseball cards and video rentals.

A similar approach can be used to define competitors for Federal Express in the overnight package delivery market circa 1995. Such a delineation might be that shown in Figure 2–3. The fact that it would be different now (e.g., including e-mail providers) points to the need to update the definition of the competitive set.

FIGURE 2–4   **Super-Premium Ice Cream Competitors**

Level of Competition	Definition	Competitors
Product form	Super-Premium	Häagen-Dazs Starbuck/Godiva Ben & Jerry's
Product category	Ice cream	Breyer's Dreyer's Private labels
Generic	Snacks Desserts Novelties	Frito Lay Nabisco Nestlé Mrs. Fields Yoplait
Budget	Other supermarket, convenience store products	Many

We now can apply these concepts to two categories that serve as running examples in this book: Dreyer's Dreamery super-premium ice cream and Handspring's Visor personal digital assistant.

Super-Premium Ice Cream

Figure 2–4 shows the competitive structure of the super-premium ice cream category. The narrowest form of competition for Dreamery is other super-premium brands like Häagen-Dazs and Ben & Jerry's. These are the direct, day-to-day competitors that the Dreamery product manager would typically worry about. However, there is also the job of "selling" the super-premium category to those simply interested in ice cream. This is the product category competition problem. As a result, the super-premium managers have to convince ice cream customers that better taste and richer flavors offset the higher price. Broadening the definition further, customers interested in ice cream could also consider other desserts, snacks, or frozen novelties. (There may well be other products that substitute for ice cream. These could be uncovered using some of the approaches described later in this chapter.) This introduces a whole new set of competitors into the picture as snack food companies like Frito Lay and Nabisco and other companies making desserts become relevant. In this situation, the product manager's job is to convince snack food customers about the benefits of ice cream in terms of taste, texture, and unique properties (i.e., it's cold). Finally, budget competitors include many other items that cost about the same and are discretionary purchases.

Personal Digital Assistants

Figure 2–5 indicates the different levels of competition for the PDA category. The closest competitors are those PDAs that are high-end personal information

Figure 2–5   PDA Competition

Level of Competition	Definition	Competitors	Need Satisfied
Product form	Full-featured PDAs	Palm Pilot VII Compaq Aero Cassiopoeia	Personal information management plus integrated communications
Product category	PIMs	Palm III Royal Casio PV-100	PIM only
Generic	Notebook/subnotebook computers	IBM Toshiba Many others	Other solutions to the above
	Paper-based solutions	Rolodex	
Budget	Business items costing $100–$1,000	Day Timer Fax machines Personal copiers Cellular phones Furniture (e.g. Steelcase)	

managers (PIMs) and offer address/telephone/fax record keeping, calculators, financial calculations, and optional links to personal computers and modems via wireless communications. The major competitors to Handspring's Visor are products from Palm, Casio, and Compaq. These products are marketed as offering many functions needed by businesspeople away from the office at a moderate price. The product category also includes lower-end PDAs with more limited communications capabilities, smaller screens, less software, and a lower price. One job of the Visor product manager is to differentiate it from lower-end models, primarily on the basis of price but perhaps also by indicating that a simpler product may be all that is needed, particularly if the user also has a notebook computer. Generic competition consists of two quite different kinds of products. First, notebook and sub-notebook computers provide the benefits of PDAs, although at a larger size, a higher price, and with slower access to the information. Second, manual, paper-based solutions still exist. One can still use a Rolodex, a Day-Timer, or just paper files to obtain many of the benefits of the PDAs. Add a cellular phone and this combination matches the full-featured PDAs as well. There are many serious budget competitors. If we consider other business-related personal productivity items, portable printers, home fax machines, and similar items compete with PDAs. Of course, other durable goods may also compete for the same dollar if the purchase is not just for business purposes.

As one moves from product form toward budget competition, the customer targets change. Product form competition suggests battling for exactly the same customers in terms of who they are and why they buy. (But not necessarily where or when they buy: one soft drink manufacturer may concen-

Figure 2–6   Defining Competition Using Customer Segments

	Market Segments		
Generic Competitors	*Business Travelers*	*Tourists*	*Students*
Airlines	X	X	X
Bus		X	X
Train	X	X	X
Automobile (own)		X	X
Automobile (rent)		X	

trate on fountain sales—Coke—and another on grocery store sales—Pepsi.) As you move toward budget competition, both who the customers are and why they buy begin to differ as the needs satisfied become more general. Since the key to a business is customers, this suggests that the most crucial short-run form of competition will *generally* be product form since product form competitors compete directly for the same customers. On the other hand, generic competition can destroy entire product categories when a major innovation occurs, and thus it, too, requires attention, especially for long-run planning.

Note that those products thought of as substitutes, and therefore competitors, may also be viewed as complements, such as soda and hamburgers. When viewed this way, potential competitors can be turned into allies in various joint ventures. Thus, this delineation of competitive levels defines potential competitors and not necessarily mortal foes.

An additional and valuable way to define competitors is to consider market segments. The market for travel services is shown in Figure 2–6. We list the modes of travel on the left side of the figure. These are the generic competitors (i.e., they satisfy the benefit of providing transportation). Across the top, we list possible market segments. These could be defined in many ways depending on the benefit being analyzed.

The figure has the following interpretation. One column would be generic competitors for that segment. Consider the San Francisco to Los Angeles route. For the business traveler, the major competitors are airlines. However, for tourists, airlines, trains, buses, car rental agencies, and driving their own car would be substitutes. Students might consider buses and trains as the major competitors. Hence the level of competition across generic product forms/categories varies by customer segments.

In the short run, product form and product category competition are generally more critical. Consequently, most annual plans focus on these almost exclusively. However, it seems foolish not to at least delineate more general forms of competition. Concentrating only on product form can allow a competitor to gain a massive share quickly as a market shifts or a new technology appears (e.g., IBM's loss to Digital Equipment Company [DEC] in minicomputers and DEC's subsequent loss to Apple in microcomputers).

Methods for Determining Competitors

Existing Categories

The easiest way to define competition is to let someone else do it for you. Thus, the use of categories for frequently purchased goods as defined by Nielsen or IRI or Standard Industrial Classification (SIC) codes for industrial products is popular and quite useful for uncovering exact form competition. SIC codes assign products to two-digit major groups (e.g., 34, Fabricated Metal), three-digit groups (e.g., 342, Cutlery and Hand Tools), four-digit industries (e.g., 3423, Hand and Edge Tools), and five or more digit representations of products (e.g., 34231.11, Pliers). However, since these methods are generally based on either product form or product category, relying exclusively on these categories will overlook both generic and budget competitors.

Substitutability

Another way to define competitors is based on the *technical feasibility of substitution.* Here an engineering assessment suggests what other products could serve the same function as the one in question. This defines *potential competitors,* competitors whose products and customers may be worth targeting. However, this method does not explicitly consider customer perceptions and consequently would overlook competition between, say, ice cream and soda.

Managerial Judgment

Through experience, salesperson call reports, distributors, or other company sources, managers can often develop judgments about the sources of present and future competition. One way to structure the thought process is through the use of a tabular structure such as that shown in Figure 2–7, a variant of

---

Figure 2–7   Managerial Judgment of Competition

	Product/Services	
Markets	*Same*	*Different*
Same	A	B
Different	C	D

Ansoff's (1965) well-known growth matrix. Box A represents product form competition; that is, those products or services that are basically the same and pursuing the same customers. Box C represents product form competitors that target other customers.

The most interesting cell of Figure 2–7 is B. This cell represents potential future competitors who already have a franchise with our customers but do not offer the same product or service. In this case, the manager might try to forecast which firms in B are likely to become more direct competitors. Examples of capitalization on prior customer familiarity with a company are numerous. If we consider telecommunications, IBM had a considerable franchise with large business customers through its mainframe computer business. IBM could thus easily have moved to cell A through purchases of MCI and Rolm. If we consider the orange juice market, Procter & Gamble has perhaps the best franchise of any consumer products manufacturer with both supermarkets and consumers, which it used to develop the Citrus Hill brand of orange juice. This type of movement is common in retail businesses where companies often try to use their "brand franchise" in one category to grab sales in others that serve the same customers. Managers should assess the likelihood of such horizontal movements as well as their chances of success. (Interestingly in 1992 P&G dropped out of the 100 percent fruit juice market, indicating its Citrus Hill brand was less than totally successful.)

Cell D competitors are very difficult to predict as they currently sell different products to different markets. One example of the impact of such a competitor was Litton Industries' commercialization of microwave technology in the area of consumer durables, which created a new competitor in the kitchen appliance market for General Electric.

An unscientific but useful way to see what a product or service might compete with is to imagine the item as a prop for a stand-up comedian. The comedian, unencumbered by convention (and sometimes good taste), can create many uses for a product, therefore suggesting different competitive products.

Technology substitution is particularly relevant for technological products. Engineers, marketing managers, and other experts can often identify other products or technologies that substitute for current ones. For example, in many telecommunications and computer networking applications, infrared or wireless communications are substituting for optical fiber, which in turn substituted for wire or "twisted pair," thus producing successive technological generations of competitors. Clark and Montgomery (1999) found three major factors are positively related to whether a manager views a company as a competitor:

- Size
- Success
- Threatening behavior

Interestingly, they also found that when using judgment alone managers named relatively few competitors. Thus, due to their day-to-day focus on product form and category competitors, managers often define too small a competitive set.

Customer-Purchase-Based Measures

Two types of customer data are commonly used to assess competitive market structures: actual purchase or usage data and judgments (Day, Shocker, and Srivastava, 1979). Since the former represent actual behavior, they indicate only what customers actually have done and not what they would have preferred to do in the past or will do in the future. Thus, behavioral data are more useful for assessing current rather than future market structure.

Several measures of competition based on past behavior have been proposed. We discuss brand switching and cross-elasticity of demand in detail.

Brand Switching

Brand-switching data is widely available for frequently purchased products from Nielsen and IRI and Web-behavior site switching from firms like Mediamatrix. Probabilities of brand switching have been proposed as measures of customers' perceived similarities and, therefore, substitutability among brands (Kalwani and Morrison, 1977; Lehmann, 1972). High brand switching probabilities thus imply a high degree of competition.

Consider the three cases represented by Figure 2–8. In the first case (I), repeat rates (brand loyalties) are between 60 and 75 percent, a fairly high level. When A is not repeat purchased, however, almost all past buyers of A switch to B ($35/(35 + 2 + 3) = 87.5$ percent). Similarly, nonrepeaters of B switch to A (83.3 percent). By contrast, past buyers of C switch to D and past buyers of D switch to C (85.7 and 80 percent respectively). This suggests close competition exists between brand pairs A and B and C and D, which often occurs because A and B share a common attribute (e.g., both are diet drinks).

By contrast, in case II in Figure 2–8, brand A has a higher repeat rate (90 percent) than any other brand, suggesting its customers are more satisfied and loyal. Also when customers switch from brands B, C, and D, they tend to switch to brand A. Thus brand A is clearly strong, and in some sense a strong competitor for brand B, but B is not a strong competitor for brand A. This type of pattern tends to emerge when there is a clear leader (possibly a market pioneer) and a number of "me-too" brands that offer some lower quality at periodically lower prices (i.e., on sale).

Finally, consider case III. Here the repeat rate is below 50 percent for all four brands and nonrepeat purchasers are likely to switch to any other brand. This suggests brands don't matter very much (i.e., have little equity), perhaps because customers simply pick whatever brand the outlet they shop at carries or because they buy whatever is on promotion. There is one interesting result in case III: buyers of brand C are more likely to switch to brand D than repeat purchase and vice-versa. This could be because brands C and D alternate their promotions (and customers buy on promotion), because brands C and D are complements rather than substitutes (competitors), or

Figure 2–8   Brand-Switching Data

I. Two Clear Submarkets

		Brand Bought at Time $t+1$			
		A	B	C	D
Brand	A	.60	.35	.02	.03
Bought	B	.25	.70	.03	.02
at Time t	C	.01	.04	.65	.30
	D	.03	.02	.20	.75

II. A Dominant Brand

		Brand Bought at Time $t+1$			
		A	B	C	D
Brand	A	.90	.03	.02	.05
Bought	B	.40	.40	.10	.10
at Time t	C	.30	.05	.60	.05
	D	.40	.04	.06	.50

III. All-Weak-Brands Market

		Brand Bought at Time $t+1$			
		A	B	C	D
Brand	A	.40	.20	.18	.22
Bought	B	.20	.35	.20	.25
at Time t	C	.27	.19	.30	.34
	D	.17	.18	.35	.30

because multiple parties (e.g., family members) are making the purchases. In any event, in case III all brands seem to compete with all others fairly equally.

As with any analysis of customers, when interpreting aggregate results it is important to recognize that different customers may view a market quite differently. In case III in Figure 2–8, the apparently diffuse competition based on this aggregate switching data may mask clear markets, similar to cases I and II, which are "averaged out." Hence a word of caution: while an aggregate view of competition is an important starting point, a revised, more focused view may be needed once attention turns to particular target segments.

A major drawback to brand switching measures is that the brands under consideration must be specified a priori, which constrains the breadth of the competitive set of products. Another problem with these measures is that, as McAlister and Lattin (1985) argue, brand switches (or switches among Web sites) occur across complements as well as substitutes. Complements might be sought when consumers want variety. For example, a consumer may become bored with Coke and switch to 7UP. A researcher would only observe a brand switch from Coke to 7UP for that consumer. Depending on whether one attributed the switch to substitution or variety seeking, the competitive structure might look quite different. Still another problem with using purchase data is that most sources of it, such as consumer panel data, are at the aggregate (household) level. Thus, switching between Diet Pepsi and Heineken might indicate whether the 13-year-old daughter or the father made the purchase and not that soda and beer compete. Therefore, using actual brand switching data to define competition is useful but far from infallible.

Cross-Elasticity of Demand
The cross-elasticity of demand is the percentage change in one brand's sales with respect to a percentage change in another brand's price (or other marketing variable). If a cross-elasticity with respect to price is positive (i.e., a brand's sales decline when another brand's price drops), the two brands or products in question are considered to be competitive.

Several authors have used cross-elasticities to define markets (see Cooper, 1988). The major problem with this approach is the estimation of the cross-elasticities. It is generally assumed that (1) there is no competitive reaction to the price cut, and (2) the market is static with respect to new entrants, product design, and so forth. As with brand switching measures, the set of brands or products must be defined a priori.

In summary, behavioral measures are useful in that they represent what customers actually do; they are not mere speculation. For the most part, however, they have been applied to frequently purchased, nondurable goods. (For an exception, see an analysis of the automobile market by McCarthy, Kannan, Chandrasekharan, and Wright, 1992). In addition, they tend to be most appropriate where a product class is defined a priori and what is being sought is a set of market definitions based on product form or category competition.

Customer-Judgment

Four judgmental measures have been proposed (Shocker, 1986): (1) overall similarity, (2) similarity of consideration sets, (3) product deletion, and (4) substitution in use. Although not based on actual customer behavior, they provide insight into potential future market structures, produce broader definitions of current structures, and are applicable to all types of products and services, including industrial products and consumer durables.

FIGURE 2–9

Defining competition with perceptual mapping

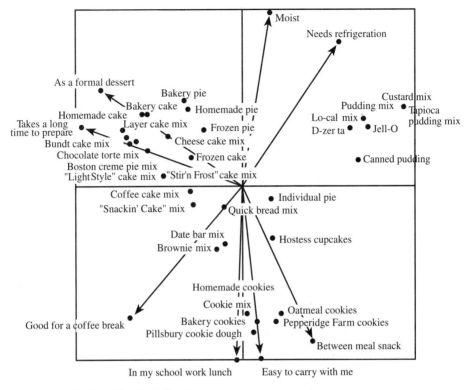

Source: *Marketing News,* May 14, 1982, p. 3.

Overall Similarity

Judged similarity measures between products or brands can be used to create geometric representations in multidimensional spaces called *perceptual maps.* Brands or products are represented by points in the space, while the dimensions represent the attributes utilized by customers in making the similarity judgments. Brands located close to each other are judged to be similar on the attributes and thus form a defined market.

For example, Figure 2–9 presents a perceptual map from the generic category of desserts. Although the analysis does (and must) begin with a pre-specified set of alternatives, the set can be developed through focus group research emphasizing products satisfying a given need. The points not attached to the vectors represent the various dessert products. Information about the competitive sets is obtained by examining clusters of points. The upper right quadrant would be very useful to, say, the brand manager for

Jell-O. From the map, it is clear that Jell-O is perceived to be quite similar to custard, pudding, tapioca, Lo-Cal, and D-zerta. The vectors help interpret the attributes defining the space.

Similarity of Consideration Sets

An approach developed by Bourgeois, Haines, and Sommers (1979) asks customers to take a large set of products and divide them into piles representing those that are thought to be substitutable, that is, that would be considered together on a purchase occasion. The frequency with which pairs of products appear in the same consideration set can be calculated and used as a measure of competition. In addition, the customers are often then asked to judge the similarity of the products within each pile. By accumulating similarity judgments across customers, a perceptual map can be developed. Thus, this approach is somewhat similar to the preceding one but collects similarity judgments after the formation of consideration sets. Other variants of this approach use verbal protocol data (with customers thinking aloud as they consider a decision).

Product Deletion

Urban, Johnson, and Hauser (1984) developed a market definition based on customer reaction to product unavailability. A set of products or brands are assumed to be substitutes and consequently form a market if, when one of them is deleted from the choice set, customers are more likely to buy from the remaining products than from a set of products outside the original set.

For example, suppose that a choice set for purchasing books included Amazon.com, Borders.com, Barnesandnoble.com, and Borders, as well as brick-and-mortar Barnes and Noble stores. If, when Barnesandnoble.com is eliminated from the set, customers are more likely to choose Amazon or Borders.com, then the three websites are assumed to be close competitors. On the other hand, if when Barnesandnoble.com is eliminated, most people go to the brick-and-mortar Barnes and Noble, most competition is within the brand with cannibalization a real issue.

Although primarily useful for partitioning product form markets into submarkets, the approach can be used in a more general setting. For example, a choice set could consist of milk, orange juice, and soft drinks. If milk were unavailable and the orange juice and soft drinks were subsequently chosen more often than tea or coffee, then milk, juice, and soft drinks apparently compete at the generic level.

Substitution in Use

Stefflre (1972) developed a procedure that has the potential to uncover broad generic market definitions. Customers are first given the target product or brand and asked to develop a list of all its possible uses. Next, they are asked to list other products or brands that provide the same uses or benefits. Since a large group of products results from these two steps, an independent sample of customers might be asked to rate the products on their appropriateness for the uses specified.

As an illustration, suppose the target product of interest is a checking account. A brief sketch of the analysis is provided below:

Checking Account Analysis			
Use	Pay bills	Transactions	Security of money
Substitutes	Pay by phone	Credit cards	Traveler's checks
Competitors	AT&T	Visa	American Express

Thus, substitution in use can produce a set of fairly diverse competitors.

Recap

The methods for determining competition are summarized in Figure 2–10 along two dimensions: (1) the usefulness of each method for determining competition at a certain level, and (2) the kind of research data typically used to implement the method. With respect to the latter, information is divided into primary sources (data collected specifically to determine competitors), and secondary sources (data collected for some general purpose other than to determine the structure of the market).

As can be seen from Figure 2–10, all the methods are useful for determining product form competition. Managerial judgment and behavior-based customer data are mainly useful for developing product form and product category markets. Customer information that is judgment based, however, can be used to assess generic competition as well. Since cross-elasticities, similarity measures, product deletion, and substitution in use either start with an a priori market definition (although possibly a very broad one) or are usage based, they cannot really be used to define budget competition, that is, those products fighting for the same customer dollar. Since the consideration-set approach has no such restrictions, it can be used to assess budget competition.

With respect to data requirements, judgment-based customer evaluations require primary data, while behavior-based methods can use secondary data. In particular, the latter methods often use consumer panel data, which are records of household purchasing from a variety of product categories. Consumer judgments might supplement purchase data with primary data, such as interviews focusing on motivations for brand switching. Managerial judgment can (and at least implicitly does) utilize both primary data (e.g., interviews with distributors) and secondary data (e.g., salesperson call reports).

FIGURE 2–10 Methods for Defining Competition

Approach	Level of Competition				Typical Data Sources	
	Product Form	Product Category	Generic	Budget	Primary	Secondary
Existing definitions	X	X				X
Technical feasibility of substitution	X	X	X		X	
Managerial judgment	X	X			X	X
Customer behavior based:						
Brand switching	X	X				X
Interpurchase times	X	X				X
Cross-elasticities	X	X	X			X
Customer evaluation based:						
Overall similarity	X	X	X		X	
Similarity of consideration sets	X	X	X		X	
Product deletion	X	X	X	X	X	
Substitution in use	X	X	X		X	

*An X indicates that either the method is useful for determining competition at that level or it employs data of a certain type.

Competitor Selection

Examining competition at four levels makes sense intuitively, and the practical implications for the market manager are substantial. As mentioned earlier, one implication is that marketing strategy must be developed with an eye toward four different problems: (1) convincing customers in your segment that your brand is best (product form competition); (2) convincing buyers that your product form is best (product category competition); (3) convincing buyers that your product category is best (generic competition); and (4) convincing buyers that the basic need your product fulfills is an important one. A manager must decide what percentage of his or her budget to expend on handling each problem.

A second implication of the four levels of competition is that a selective competitor focus must be chosen. A manager cannot focus analysis or actual strategy on each possible competitor in the market because of limited available resources. For example, the problem of the Pioneer marketing manager described earlier is the selection of which other low-priced stereos, other stereos, or other entertainment forms (and, therefore, specifically which manufacturers or service suppliers) against which to compete. Of course, if a competitor either intentionally or unintentionally targets the same customers or introduces a similar product, then there is competition whether or not it was intended.

Deciding which competitors to focus on can be facilitated through examining three factors: (1) the time horizon of the marketing plan being developed (short versus long run), (2) the stage of the product life cycle relevant for the product, and (3) the rate of change in technology.

In a one-year operating marketing plan, competition should be defined on both product form and product category bases as they reflect the short-term competitive outlook. For example, in the short run, Sanka's major competitors are primarily other decaffeinated instant coffees and secondarily other instant or regular coffees. On the other hand, for longer-term plans, all four levels of competition are relevant with special emphasis placed on the generic level (e.g., bottled teas) to identify important competitive threats, especially from new technologies.

The stage in the product life cycle is also relevant to defining competition. In the early growth stages of a product, particularly a new technology, competition should be broadly (generically) defined since a large part of the marketing task is convincing customers to substitute a new product for an existing one that was satisfying the consumers' needs. On the other hand, in mature markets the focus should generally be on product form and category competitors.

Finally, where the rate of technological change is rapid, competition should be conceived as broadly as possible. This is characteristic of the communications field as diverse products such as word processors, home computers, cellular phones, modems, fax machines, cable TV, and satellites compete for certain services. Alternatively, narrow definitions (e.g., product form) are sufficient where new technical advances occur less frequently, as with food products.

Given that the appropriate levels of competition have been selected (i.e., the market has been defined), attention shifts to choosing the relevant competitors on which to focus. This requires an initial pass at competitor analysis. The factors determining which competitors are relevant are related to the forecasts of the brands' likely strategies, or the major outputs of competitor analyses. However, the resources competitors can bring to bear in the market are also critical, thus highlighting a final perspective on competition called *enterprise competition.*

Enterprise Competition

Ultimately, brands do not compete against each other in a vacuum. The company's resources are a key determinant of its vulnerability to a marketing strategy. Thus, while we have examined competition in this chapter from the perspective of a brand or product, firm versus firm, or enterprise competition, involves selection of the competitors against which strategies are mounted. This in turn can dictate the strategy of specific brands and products; brand strategy becomes a tactic in the strategy war between enterprises.

As an illustration, consider the computer workstation market. On a product form basis, Hewlett-Packard (HP) competes against IBM, Sun, and Silicon Graphics, among others. However, not all competitors are created equal. When HP goes head to head with IBM, it competes not only in terms of product features against IBM's workstations but also against IBM's resources in terms of dollars, sales force, image, and willingness to support products.

It is often difficult to understand brand level competition without understanding the broader context in which it occurs. For example, competition in financial services is illustrated by Figure 2–11, which could easily be expanded to include Fidelity, Vanguard, and Citibank, among others, and products such as IRAs and annuities.

Enterprise competition is often characterized by asymmetries in perspective. For example, Microsoft probably views Lotus's (now IBM's) Smart-Suite the most serious competitor to Office and largely ignores others. However, Corel's Word Perfect Office has to view Microsoft's Office as a key competitor since it dominates the market. In other words, from Corel's perspective, MS Office competes against WP Office, while from Microsoft's perspective, WP Office is not a major competitor for MS Office.

Enterprise competition also often involves alliances and mergers. For example, Kimberly Clark, a fierce competitor with Procter and Gamble in the disposable diaper market, acquired Scott Paper with the intention of

FIGURE 2–11 Enterprise Competition in Financial Services

	FDIC Insured Depository	Consumer Loans	Credit/ Debit Cards	Mortgage Banking	Commercial Lending	Mutual Funds	Securities	Insurance
American Express	✓	✓	✓			✓	✓	✓
Ford	✓	✓	✓	✓	✓			✓
General Electric		✓	✓	✓	✓	✓		✓
General Motors		✓	✓	✓	✓			✓
Merrill Lynch	✓		✓	✓	✓	✓	✓	✓
Prudential	✓	✓	✓	✓	✓	✓	✓	✓

Source: "Enterprise Competition in Financial Services," *Fortune*, May 15, 1995, p. 178, using Scott's brands (e.g., toilet tissue) to compete against P&G (e.g., Charmin) in other markets to help divert its resources from the lucrative diaper category. Thus, competition at the brand or category level is often a tactic of competition at the firm level.

Summary

In this chapter, we have argued that the set of competitors posing a threat to a brand can be highly varied and come from a variety of industries. Therefore, a market is often dynamic and difficult to define. We presented a framework to conceptualize competition and methods to help form ideas about the competitive set. Finally, we discussed approaches to selecting competitors in terms of choosing the relevant levels and specific brands.

Essentially, we suggest that competitors are those companies whose products or services compete for the same customer either directly through offering similar products or services (product form or category competition), indirectly through satisfying similar basic needs (generic competition), or in terms of budget. Clearly, one can develop an essentially infinite list of competitors. In general, for a short-run plan (say, one year) most of the effort should be directed toward exact-form and similar-form competitors with relatively little attention to products that will only gradually affect sales (e.g., bottled water if you sell wine). The longer the range of the plan or the greater the pace of technological change, the more attention should turn to less similar competitors, especially those who are strong and have or are developing technologies that could threaten your business.

References

Abell, Derek F. (1980) *Defining the Business.* Englewood Cliffs, NJ: Prentice Hall.

Ansoff, H. Igor. (1965) *Corporate Strategy.* New York: McGraw-Hill.

Bourgeois, Jacques D., George H. Haines, and Montrose S. Sommers (1979) "Defining an Industry." Presented at the ORSA/TIMS Conference on Market Measurement, Stanford, CA.

Clark, Bruce H. and David B. Montgomery (1999) "Managerial Identification of Competitors," *Journal of Marketing,* 63, July, 67–83.

Cooper, Lee G. (1988) "Competitive Maps: The Structure Underlying Asymmetric Cross Elasticities," *Management Science,* 34, June, 707–23.

Day, George S., Allan D. Shocker, and Rajendra K. Srivastava (1979) "Customer-Oriented Approaches to Identifying Product Markets," *Journal of Marketing,* 43, Fall, 8–19.

"Fast-Food Slump Hits Industry Giants as More Competition Bites into Profit." (1986) *The Wall Street Journal,* April 22, 3.

Fraser, Cynthia, and John W. Bradford (1983) "Competitive Market Structure Analysis: Principal Partitioning of Revealed Substitutabilities," *Journal of Consumer Research,* 10, June, 15–30.

Kalwani, Manohar U. and Donald G. Morrison (1977) "A Parsimonious Description of the Hendry System," *Management Science,* 23, January, 467–77.

Kim, W. Chan and Renée Mauborgne (1999) "How Southwest Airlines Found a Route to Success," *Financial Times,* May 13, 20.

Kotler, Philip (2000) *Marketing Management.* 10th ed. Upper Saddle River, NJ: Prentice Hall.

Lehmann, Donald R. (1972) "Judged Similarity and Brand-Switching Data as Similarity Measures," *Journal of Marketing Research,* 9, August, 331–34.

Levitt, Theodore (1960) "Marketing Myopia." *Harvard Business Review,* 38, July–August, 45–56.

McAlister, Leigh and James M. Lattin (1985) "Using a Variety-Seeking Model to Identify Substitute and Complementary Relationships among Competing Products," *Journal of Marketing Research,* 22 August, 330–339.

McCarthy, Patrick S., P. K. Kannan, Radha Chandrasekharan, and Gordon P. Wright (1992) "Estimating Loyalty and Switching with an Application to the Automobile Market." *Management Science,* 38, October, 1371–93.

Shocker, Allan D. (1986) "A Bibliography of Recent Work in Market Definition and Structure." Working Paper, Owen Graduate School of Management, Vanderbilt University.

Shocker, Allan D., Anthony J. Zahorik, and David W. Stewart (1984) "Competitive Market Structure Analysis: A Comment on Problems," *Journal of Consumer Research,* 11, December, 836–41.

Stefflre, Volney (1972) "Some Applications of Multidimensional Scaling to Social Science Problems." In *Multidimensional Scaling: Theory and Applications in the Behavioral Sciences,* ed. A. K. Romney, R. N. Shepard, and S. B. Nerlove. Vol. III. New York: Seminar Press.

Urban, Glen L., Philip L. Johnson, and John R. Hauser (1984) "Testing Competitive Market Structures," *Marketing Science,* 3, Spring, 83–112.

Yip, George, and Jeffrey Williams (1986) "U.S. Retail Coffee Market (A)," Harvard Business School case #9-586-134.

CHAPTER

3 Industry Analysis

Overview

Analyzing a market's trends and attractiveness is important for several reasons. First, market (which we use synonymously with industry in this context) attractiveness determines whether current competitors are likely to continue in the market or exit, and whether others are likely to enter. While predicting the exact timing of a move is difficult, it was reasonable to expect GE to leave the consumer electronic and aerospace businesses, given its stated goal to be number one or two, particularly in high-margin businesses, and for DEC to belatedly enter the microcomputer business. Hence industry attractiveness provides a focus on the future rather than simply current or past competitors. Second, the state of an industry in terms of future profits and growth often determines the level of commitment (both dollars and top human resources) devoted to it by competitors, a key part of competitive analysis. Third, analysis of key trends in technology, regulation, and so on suggests major threats and opportunities. Analyzing a market is crucial to developing sound objectives and strategies. This chapter, therefore, is devoted to assessing a market's present and future characteristics.

Market attractiveness is so important that almost all strategic planning models utilize it in some form. An initial question asked before the planning process can even begin is whether the industry is sufficiently attractive to warrant investment in it, either by your company, current competitors, or potential new constraints. For example, the product portfolio of the Boston Consulting Group uses market growth rate as a proxy for attractiveness. Other models (Kerin, Mahajan, Varadarajan, 1990, Chapter 3) utilize a two-dimensional strategic grid consisting of market attractiveness and business position.

A market is an evolving entity. Sometimes dramatic changes in technology or regulation reshape it almost overnight (e.g., the breakup of AT&T), but more typically a series of less powerful forces and events leads to a seemingly smooth and gradual evolution (as in the improvement in computer speed and power). Thus it is necessary to assess the fundamentals of the industry being considered. Given that the industry has been defined (see Chapter 2), an essential component of the marketing planning process is an analysis of the potential for a firm to achieve a desired level of return on its investment.

The characteristics of an industry rarely all point in the same direction. As a result, markets that some firms find attractive will be of little interest to others. For example, most observers consider the luxury car market (over $30,000) to be overpopulated with models, particularly since the introduction of Toyota's Lexus and Nissan's Infinity. In addition, European manufacturers are very sensitive to declines in the value of the dollar, which makes their cars expensive in the important U.S. market. However, Ford purchased the British firm Jaguar, since Ford felt there was considerable brand equity in the name and the label would give the company instant entry into the luxury car field. Similarly, the fast-food industry is considered to be mature in terms of sales growth, but new concepts such as drive-up-only hamburger stands have recently been introduced. General Electric obviously found household appliances (in 1984), consumer electronics (in 1989), and aerospace (in 1992) unattractive and sold those divisions. On the other hand, the buyers—Black and Decker, Thompson, and Martin Marietta—obviously found the same markets attractive. Interestingly Thompson sold its medical products division to General Electric at the same time GE sold its consumer electronics to Thompson; in effect the two firms traded businesses. Hence attractiveness involves both industry/market factors and company factors, such as capabilities and goals.

This chapter considers three major categories of variables (Figure 3–1). First we focus on basic descriptive statistics of the industry: its size and sales patterns. Next we discuss several important aspects of the competitive and profit situation. Third, we discuss general environmental influences (technology, etc.). For each of these factors, the procedure has two important steps. First, past and current data are gathered and interpreted. That is, analysis goes beyond mere listing of facts. Then, projections are made. For example, current margins may be 20 percent. A key issue, however, is what margins will be in two years. These projections are important because they impact other analyses (e.g., if new competitors are expected, then they must be analyzed in the subsequent competitive analysis section) and provide many of the basic planning assumptions behind forecasts and profit projections.

FIGURE 3–1   **Bases for Industry Analysis**

Market Factors	*Environmental Factors*
Size	Technological
Growth	Economic
Stage in life cycle	Social
Cyclicity	Political
Seasonality	Regulatory
Marketing mix	
Profits	
Financial ratios	
Competitive Factors	
Concentration	
Power of buyers	
Power of suppliers	
Rivalry	
Pressure from substitutes	
Capacity utilization	
Entries and exits	

Aggregate Market Factors

Size

Market size, measured in both units and dollars, relates to the likelihood of a product producing sufficient revenues to support a given investment. Large markets also offer more opportunities for segmentation than small ones (see Chapter 5). Therefore, both large firms and entrepreneurial organizations find large markets attractive. Large markets, however, tend to draw competitors with considerable resources, often making them unattractive for small firms, as in the soft drink industry. Thus, absolute size is not by itself sufficient to warrant new or continuing investment.

In assessing the size of a market, it is also useful to describe the size of its major subunits. For example, the soft drink market divides into subcategories based on calories (diet versus nondiet), flavor (cola, lemon-lime, etc.), and whether real juice is included. In addition, various markets that compete with the soft drink category, such as bottled water and fruit juice, also should be tracked. This provides information and a focus on the impact of substitutes (generic competition) on the product category. Of course since Coke and Pepsi combined spent $185 million on advertising alone in the first six months of 1999, its attractiveness to new entrants may be limited.

Growth

Not only is current growth important, but, because of the product life cycle, growth projections over the horizon of the plan are also critical. Fast-growing markets are almost universally desired because they support high margins and sustain profits into future years. However, they also attract competitors. For example, while Sony developed the U.S. market for videocassette recorders, the projected high market growth rate supported the entry of other firms' marketing systems with a competing recording format (VHS), which now dominates Sony's Beta format. The high growth rate in sales of disposable diapers explains why Johnson and Johnson and Kimberly Clark aggressively followed P&G into the market.

A major factor relating to industry growth is the rate at which products become obsolete (i.e., are replaced by new products). Whether product replacement is attractive or not depends heavily on a company's ability to design and market new products of good quality in a short time. In 1994, Mosaic had 60 percent and Netscape 16 percent of the browser market while by 2000 Mosaic was gone, Netscape had 13 percent, and Microsoft's Internet Explorer had 81 percent (and a major lawsuit on its hands).

Life Cycle Stage

Two factors, market size and growth, are often portrayed simultaneously in the form of the product life cycle. This curve breaks down the sales of a product into four segments: introduction, growth, maturity, and decline. The introduction and growth phases are the early phases of the life cycle while sales are still growing, maturity represents a leveling-off in sales, while the decline phase represents the end of the life cycle.

The attractiveness of products in each of the phases of the life cycle is not always clear. Products in the growth phase, such as personal computers in the 1980s, are generally thought to be attractive. However, as Osborne, Commodore, and others found out, high rates of market growth do not ensure success. Although mature markets are often disdained, clever marketers often find new ways to segment them, which suggests opportunities. Witness the success of Miller's Lite beer and Reebok in the leisure footwear market. Finally, brands in declining product categories are also in an unfavorable position within the corporation, even though Harrigan (1980) gives several examples of strategies to turn these businesses around and the last remaining firms are often profitable.

Cyclicity

Since many firms attempt to develop products and acquire entire companies to eliminate interyear sales variation, this is clearly not an attractive characteristic of an industry unless it balances out cycles in other components of a firm's business. Capital-intensive businesses, such as automobiles, steel, and chemicals, are often dependent on general business conditions and therefore suffer through peaks and valleys of sales as gross domestic product (GDP) and/or interest rates vary.

Seasonality

As with sales cyclicity, seasonality (intrayear cycles in sales) is generally not viewed positively. Most industries are seasonal to some extent, but some are extremely so (e.g., ice cream, skis, travel services). The toy industry has tried to reduce its reliance on the Christmas period to generate most of its sales, and ski resorts have been promoted as four-season vacation destinations. Seasonal businesses tend to generate price wars since demand drops substantially as the season ends.

Marketing Mix

The general trends in terms of *distribution, pricing,* and *promotion* provide useful background for competitive and customer analysis as well as strategy formulation. For example, the trend toward direct marketing of PCs has major implications for the computer market. Similarly the attempt by P&G to decrease trade promotion and use an "everyday low pricing" approach could smooth sales, thus improving production efficiency and increasing profits. Similarly, the use of "no-haggle" car pricing by Saturn and others could be an important trend or a short-run fad. Particularly important, especially for new products, is the quality of suppliers and their willingness and ability to service a firm. Likewise, downstream elements of the supply chain (distributors, retailers) play an important role in shaping an industry.

Profits

While there is certainly variability in profits, margins, and cash flows across products in an industry, there are also interindustry differences. For example, the profit margins for the soft drink, drug, machine tool, and tire industries in 1985 were 15.1 percent, 22.7 percent, 6.6 percent, and 7.6 percent, respectively (Standard & Poor's, 1986), and are similar in relative profit margin today.

Differences in profitability can be due to a number of factors of production including labor versus capital intensity, raw materials, manufacturing technology, and competitive rivalry. Suffice it to say the industries that are chronically low in profitability are less attractive than those that offer higher returns.

A second aspect of profitability to consider is variability over time. Variance in profitability is often used as a measure of industry risk; semiconductors offer abnormally high return when demand is good but concomitant poor returns when demand slumps. Food-related businesses, on the other hand, produce steady if unspectacular profits. As is usually the case, there is a risk-return trade-off that must be made where the expected returns are evaluated against their variability.

Performance Ratios

Like profits, financial ratios vary substantially across competitors in an industry and hence are considered separately in a competitive analysis. Still there are substantial interindustry differences as well (see, for example, *Forbes Annual Review*). Most ratios are expressed as returns (e.g., return on assets [ROA], return on equity [ROE], return on capital [ROC], and return on annual marketing expenditures). These ratios provide indications of both the rewards for successful performance and the requirements for participation (e.g., capital intensity).

Competitive Factors

This section discusses factors that economists use (Porter, 1980) to analyze an industry (the power of buyers and suppliers, competitive rivalry/pressure and the threat of new entrants, and the pressure from substitutes), plus industry concentration and capacity.

Concentration

One simple indicator of the competition in an industry is its concentration, the market share controlled by a few top firms. Various simple measures are used, such as:

1. The share of the largest firm.
2. The combined shares of the largest three or four firms.
3. The number of firms with at least x percent of the market (e.g., 1 percent).
4. The share of the largest firm divided by the share of the next three largest competitors.

A slightly more complex measure is the Herfindahl Index, the sum of the squared shares of the firms in the industry. This index goes from a high of one (when one firm has 100 percent share) to close to zero (when there are many firms with similar, small shares). Interestingly, in stable markets the shares of the largest brand, next largest brand, and so on often decline approximately exponentially. This suggests that markets where two or more firms have nearly equal shares are likely to be most competitive. In general, the more competitive the industry, the greater the requirements for marketing expenditures and the lower the profits for small players.

Power of Buyers

Buyers are people or institutions who receive goods or a service. These could be distributors, original equipment manufacturers (OEMs), retail stores, or end customers. Suppliers are institutions that supply the industry with factors of production, such as labor, capital, components, and machinery.

High buyer bargaining power is negatively related to industry attractiveness. In such circumstances, buyers can force down prices and play competitors against each other for other benefits, such as service. Some conditions when buyer bargaining power is high include the following.

When the Buyer Accounts for a Large Percentage of the Industry's Output. The more important a buyer is to an industry's well-being in terms of sales and profits, the more power the buyer has.

When the Product Is Undifferentiated. If the industry views what it sells as a commodity, buyers will have a great deal of power. A good example of this is the leverage held by customers of commodity chemicals or basic semiconductors.

When the Buyers Earn Low Profits. Ailing industries such as farm equipment can extract better terms from supplier industries than can healthy industries such as food processing.

When There Is a Threat by the Buyer to Backward Integrate. Among other pressures felt by semiconductor manufacturers is the constant threat by computer manufacturers to make their own chips. IBM's purchase of part of Intel is such an example. Consumers also backward integrate, as the growth of do-it-yourself hardware and building products stores indicates.

When the Buyer Has Full Information. Consumers can exert more power in retail stores if they are fully aware of competitive offerings. For example, car dealers may be more willing to negotiate on price if the buyer signals that he or she is knowledgeable.

In general, consumers are limited in their buying power on an individual basis. (Notable exceptions exist, of course, such as the U.S. government as a purchaser of military equipment.) However, if consumers can be motivated as a group, they become a more important customer and thus exert more power than would otherwise be the case. For example, the highly desired dual-income couples in their 30s are considered to have large power since they are consumption oriented and may thus constitute a large portion of a seller's sales. Similarly, buying cooperatives have increased power. Perhaps most strikingly, the Internet has increased the potential knowledge and hence power of buyers, particularly in terms of price.

Power of Suppliers

This is really just the mirror image of the buying power assessment. High supplier power is clearly not an attractive situation, as it allows suppliers to dictate price and other terms such as delivery dates to the buying industry. Some conditions when supplier bargaining power will be high include:

When Suppliers Are Highly Concentrated, That Is, They Are Dominated by a Few Firms.   Industries in need of supercomputers face strong suppliers since there are very few in the world.

When There Is No Substitute for the Product Supplied.   The supercomputer falls into this category as well. By contrast, the power of the Organization of Petroleum Exporting Countries (OPEC) temporarily diminished when many industries converted plants to use both oil and coal.

When the Supplier Has Differentiated Its Product and/or Built-In Switching Costs.   Armco Inc. increased its power with the automobile industry by offering General Motors a delayed payment plan for its steel, a guarantee of no work stoppages, a demonstration of how cheaper steel could be substituted in certain areas, and extra service by supplying steel already prepared with adhesives. Sole-source suppliers have more power than multiple-source ones. The leaner a company runs in terms of inventory and production capacity, the more it depends on its suppliers.

When Supply Is Limited.   Scarcity leads to price increases; oversupply to price wars and losses.

Rivalry

Industries characterized by intensive combat between the major participants are not as attractive as those where the rivalry is more sedate. Often, a high degree of rivalry results in escalated marketing expenditures, price wars, employee raids, and other related activities. Such actions can go beyond what is considered to be "normal" market competition and can result in decreased welfare for both consumers and competitors.

Several examples highlight the negative aspects of rivalry. In the fast-food industry, Burger King and McDonald's periodically replay their "Battle of the Burgers." Advertising expenditures are increased, promotions and contests are run, but market shares remain fairly constant; only profits are affected—usually negatively. A similar scenario exists in airline battles with frequent flyer and other promotional programs. Several years ago, American offered triple mileage credit for program members; this was quickly copied by other airlines. Similar promotions such as "fly three—get one free" were introduced and then offered almost immediately by competitors. The result has been major losses by all airlines, and the bankruptcy of several (Pan Am, Eastern, TWA, Continental, America West). Intense rivalries exist in many industries including AT&T, MCI, and Sprint in long distance telephone service; Intel, AMD, and Cyrix in chips; Coke and Pepsi in soft drinks; and Boeing and Airbus in aircraft manufacturing.

Some of the major characteristics of industries exhibiting intensive rivalry are summarized below.

Many or Balanced Competitors. The fast-food, automobile, and soft drink industries each have several large, well-endowed competitors.

Slow Growth. Again, fast food, autos, and soft drinks qualify. In mature markets, growth can come only from another competitor.

High Fixed Costs. In such industries, there is extreme pressure to operate at full capacity to keep average unit costs down. For this reason, capital-intensive industries such as paper and chemicals are highly competitive.

Lack of Product Differentiation. Basic commodities, such as aluminum, cattle, and chemicals, suffer from this problem, as do consumer products such as air travel. In fact, any industry where the basic competitive weapon is price suffers from a lack of differentiation and its concomitant extensive rivalry.

Pressure from Substitutes

Substitutes are mainly generic or, to a lesser extent, budget competitors (see Chapter 2). Industries making products or delivering services for which there are a large number of substitutes are less attractive than those delivering a relatively proprietary service. Almost all industries suffer from the availability of substitutes. However, some of the highest rates of return are earned by industries in which the range of substitutes is low. For example, as mentioned earlier, the drug industry, in which few legal substitutes are available, earns a high profit margin.

Capacity Utilization

Chronic overcapacity is not a positive sign for long-term profitability. When an industry is operating at capacity, its costs stay low and its bargaining power with buyers is normally high. Thus, often a key indicator about the health of an industry is whether there is a consistent tendency toward operating at or under capacity.

Related to capacity utilization is the ease or difficulty of either adding new capacity or retiring unused capacity. This is typically assessed in terms of the financial resources and time required. The trend toward outsourcing, using suppliers rather than producing parts inside the firm, is a way to gain more capacity flexibility. Hence many firms' capacity depends heavily on their network of suppliers' capabilities.

FIGURE 3–2 **Attractiveness to Entrants**

	Attractiveness	
	High	*Low*
Market Factors		
Size	Large	Small
Growth	High	Slow
Stage in life cycle	Early	Late
Cyclicity	Low	High
Seasonality	Low	High
Marketing spending	Low	High
Profits	High	Low
Financial ratios	High	Low
Competitive Factors		
Concentration	Low	High
Power of buyers	Low	High
Power of suppliers	Low	High
Rivalry	Low	High
Pressure from substitutes	Low	High
Capacity utilization	High	Low
Threat of entry	Low	High

Threat of Entries and Exits

As mentioned earlier, the same industry may be attractive for one company and unattractive for another. Nonetheless, there is a general pattern of characteristics that tends to make them attractive. Basically an industry tends to be attractive when it is large, growing, profitable, and noncompetitive, as Figure 3–2 indicates. It is important to analyze the likelihood of entrants and exits from a market and, if possible, their identity.

A high threat of new entrants diminishes the attractiveness of an industry. Except for the early stages of market development when new entrants can help a market expand, these companies bring additional capacity and resources that usually heighten the competitiveness of a market and diminish margins. Even at early stages of market growth, the enthusiasm with which additional firms are greeted is tempered by who the competitor is. For example, while Apple publicly welcomed IBM's entry into the personal computer market, it is unlikely that there was genuine private elation in Cupertino, California.

Key to the likelihood of new competitors entering a market are the barriers to entry erected by the competition. Often these barriers are legal, such as those based on legislated monopolies (e.g., utilities) or patents. It is important to note that these barriers can change over time. When Xerox's patent on its basic copying process expired, the number of competitors in the copier market expanded dramatically. Besides formal barriers to entry or exit, other influences on entry/exit decisions include the following.

Economies of Scale

An important barrier to entry into the automobile industry is the large plant size needed to operate efficiently, obtain quantity discounts on raw materials, and so on. Small manufacturers such as Ferrari must be content with serving the high-priced market segment. Areas other than manufacturing can obtain economies of scale. For example, hospital supply margins are better on large orders when many products are distributed simultaneously since order-taking costs are largely fixed. Similarly advertising is sold with quantity discounts.

Product Differentiation

Well-established brand names and/or company reputations can make it difficult for new competitors to enter a market. In the ready-to-eat breakfast cereal industry, the big four—Kellogg Co., General Foods (Post), General Mills, and Quaker Oats—have such long-established reputations that a new competitor would find it difficult to establish a brand franchise.

Capital Requirements

These requirements could be related to both manufacturing facilities and marketing. For example, a major use of capital in the fast-food industry is for advertising and sales promotion. Most of the capital expenditure required to enter the farm equipment industry is for manufacturing facilities.

Switching Costs

These are costs to buyers of switching from one supplier to another. If switching costs are high, such as they are in the mainframe computer business, it is difficult to convert a competitor's existing customers to you. For example, in 1974, American Hospital Supply (AHS) installed order-taking terminals in the stockrooms of large hospitals. This created a barrier to potential new entrants, as hospitals routinely ordered AHS supplies through its proprietary system. Similarly Nintendo and SONY video games only accept their own games so the game inventory deters switching.

Distribution

Shelf space can be difficult for new products to obtain. The splitting of Coke into Classic and New Coke, Coca-Cola's introduction of Diet Coke and Cherry Coke, and similar brand extensions by major competitor Pepsi increased the pressure on competitors such as Seven-Up, since this barrier to entry was raised even higher. The practice of supermarkets charging "slotting allowances," a fee to manufacturers for placing goods on shelves, is a related barrier to entry, particularly for small firms. Similarly, some have argued that United's and American's airline reservation services provide an unfair advantage to those airlines.

The industry's willingness to vigorously retaliate against newcomers can also act as a barrier. When small Minnetonka Inc. introduced a pump for hand soap, both Colgate and Procter & Gamble immediately copied the package and outspent Minnetonka in promotion. That story has been replayed in numerous other industries.

Environmental Factors

The environment includes those factors outside the control of both the firm and its industry. High susceptibility to changes in the environment is generally undesirable. As mentioned earlier in this chapter, if an industry's sales are tied to the domestic economic situation, cyclicity can result. On the other hand, industries that are well positioned to take advantage of environmental changes may prosper.

Environmental factors to be examined can be put into five groups: technological, social, political, economic, and regulatory. These factors should be examined not only to assess industry attractiveness but also to determine if any forecasted changes in these areas dictate changes of strategy.

Technological

Technology refers to the procedures used for developing, making, and distributing a product or service to customers (Capon and Glazer, 1987). In the narrowest sense, technology refers to the state of the art for *product design* (e.g., memory chips based on silicon) as well as the *production process* (i.e., hand versus automated assembly). A key issue, therefore, is whether technologies are emerging that can affect or replace current industry technology.

Technological obsolescence is a major factor in many industries. Gradual obsolescence occurs as capabilities are upgraded (as in microprocessors, which went from 8086 to 286 to 386 to 486 to Pentium, each successive generation providing more speed and power). More discrete changes periodically occur in fabrics (e.g., nylon, Dacron, Gore-Tex) and in document production (mechanical to electromechanical to electronic typewriters to PC-based word processing). Monitoring both continuous improvements and possible discrete changes is extremely important.

Major changes continue to occur in the energy, materials, transportation, information, and genetic (bioengineering) areas. With respect to information, for example, scanning systems installed at the cash registers in supermarkets enable retailers to monitor sales of different items for both inventory and shelf-space allocation decisions. Bioengineering research is being used (controversially) both to improve crop yields and to find cures for various diseases, including cancer.

Less technologically strong industries are particularly vulnerable to competition from new industries and foreign competitors that have invested in technology. In the 1980s, most major U.S. steel firms still used the blast furnace technology developed in the 1800s. Foreign steel firms and those domestic companies that invested in modern manufacturing technology have been highly successful in the past decade.

There is, however, a point beyond which technology can create a backlash, particularly among consumers. Naisbitt (1984) refers to this as "high-tech versus high touch." For example, automatic teller machines have depersonalized banking to the point where some consumers yearn for the human contact afforded by tellers. Several years ago, Citibank in New York proposed to allow only its wealthiest customers to have personal contact for most transactions while others were forced to use machines. Consumers protested so vehemently that Citibank scrapped the idea.

Economic

Almost all capital goods industries (machine tools, computers) are sensitive to *interest rate fluctuations* since their high costs to buyers are often financed at short-term rates. Consumer durables such as homes, cars, and stereos, are also sensitive to interest rates, although consumer credit rates do not react as much to changes in the prime lending rate as do commercial rates. *Inflation rates* are tied in with interest rate fluctuations and have a similar impact. Again, the impact of having foreign markets or producing in other countries can vary widely over time depending on *currency exchange rates*.

Since service businesses often hire relatively unskilled labor at low wage rates, they are highly dependent on *employment conditions*. When employment rates are high, for example, fast-food employees are hard to find, as higher-paying jobs are available. The conditions of demand and supply of labor for each industry must be considered as well. The supply of engineers is cyclical. When supply is down, many firms in technical businesses suffer from a shortage of skilled labor.

Industries that have broad customer bases (machine tools, copiers) are often sensitive to *fluctuations in GDP growth*. When the country is in a recession, so are these industries.

Social

Trends in demographics, lifestyles, attitudes, and personal values among the general population are of particular concern for consumer products manufacturers for several reasons. In the United States, changes in the birth rate, aging, shifting ethnic and geographic composition, and the increased availability of home technology are all significant factors. New products have been developed to fit today's lifestyles. Frozen entrees and prepared meals at supermarkets, for example, were developed to suit dual-career households with a need for convenience and easy preparation at dinnertime. Second, new features have been added to existing products. More upper-income households have ice water dispensers in refrigerators, global positioning systems (GPS) in cars, and telephones with built-in calculators, a memory for frequently called numbers, and Web access. Finally, promotion has changed as well. How often do we see the aging "yuppie" or baby boomer on television ads?

Understanding lifestyle trends is also important for industrial product industries. Since the demand for industrial products is often derived demand (i.e., generated ultimately by consumers), changes in consumer product sales in turn affect demand for the product. For example, when car sales slump, so does the demand for steel, plastic, aluminum, and other industries heavily dependent on the auto industry.

For industrial companies, the key question to ask is whether the customers of the industry being considered are in the right industries. Clearly, firms supplying the "hot" industries will do well, while those that are heavily tied to declining consumer products will not.

For consumer businesses, a key question to ask is whether the industry is positioned to take advantage of current trends. Some product areas that are "hot" because they appeal to baby boomers are furniture and electronic appliances, upscale fast-food chains, clothing, financial and travel services, and upscale baby accessories. Other products have been developed for consumers on the older edge of the baby boom generation. For example, a large part of the market for the Mazda Miata and Porsche Boxster are people over 40 who wish to reduce their psychological age. Industries in trouble include colleges, coffee, cigarettes, and brown alcohol because they are being buffeted by either demographic or taste trends.

Because of the rise of the Internet globally, many pundits forecast that the twenty-first century will be the age of the customer. The shift of power from seller to customer is facilitated by both the increase in information that customers have available to them and the lowering of shopping costs, which makes it easier for customers to compare options in terms of features and price. It has been said that today, customers can pretty much have what they want when they want it and at the price they wish to pay.

At least in the early part of the twenty-first century, the major demographic changes in the United States that will underlie consumer demand are the following (Miller, 1999):

- The aging of the baby-boom generation (those born between 1945 and 1964); Figure 3–3 shows the projected change in the U.S. population for the years 1995–2000. Witness the growth in the 40–59 age bracket. Clearly, this has tremendous implications for products and services targeting more mature consumers.

FIGURE 3–3

Projected change in U.S. population 1995–2005

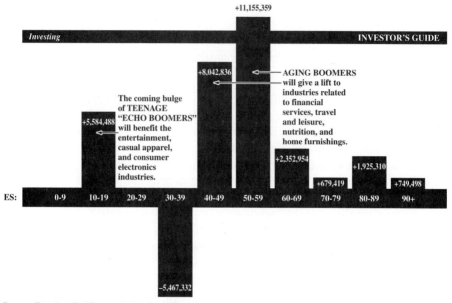

- The increasing importance of children as consumers; see Figure 3–4 for one writer's conceptualization of how today's children or N-Geners (for the net generation) can be characterized. It is undoubtedly the case that children growing up in today's technology-charged society will be different consumers when they reach their prime spending years than their parents.
- A growing gap between society's haves and have-nots. Despite overall increased prosperity, the differences between the wealthier U.S. households and the poorer is increasing.
- An increasingly diverse population; by 2025, non-Hispanic whites will comprise 62.4 percent of the U.S. population, down from 72.5 percent in 1998.

Given this backdrop, some key forces driving the era of the consumer are the following:

1. The shrinking day. More time spent working and committing to family-related activities means less time doing things they do not want to do like housework and cooking. This latter phenomenon is manifested in the growth of the share of food purchases in restaurants versus supermarkets. The share of purchases in restaurants passed the supermarket share in 1992 and the gap is widening.

FIGURE 3–4   **The 10 Themes of N-Gen Culture**

The Net Generation: Youth between 4–20 who are computer and Internet literate.

1. Fierce independence: A strong sense of independence and autonomy.
2. Emotional and intellectual openness: When N-Geners go online, they expose themselves.
3. Inclusion: A global orientation in their search for information, activity, and communication.
4. Free expression and strong views: The Internet has exposed them to a much greater range of ideas, opinions, and arguments than they would have experienced without it.
5. Innovation: A constant search for ways to do things better.
6. Preoccupation with maturity: N-Geners insist that they are more mature than adults expect.
7. Investigation: A strong ethos of curiosity, investigation, and the empowerments to change things.
8. Immediacy: The children of the digital age expect things to happen fast, because in their world, things *do* happen fast.
9. Sensitivy to corporate interest: They believe that too many perspectives are being left out of the broadcast images and they believe corporate agendas play a role in this shortfall.
10. Authentication and trust: Because of the anonymity, accessibility, diversity, and ubiquity of the Internet, N-Geners must continually authenticate what they see or hear on the Web.

Source: Don Tapscott, *Growing Up Digital,* 1998.

What consumers increasingly value in terms of products and services is time and convenience. Dual career (or job) households in particular are likely to "outsource" activities formally done in person including lawn care, cleaning, and child care.

2. Connectedness. It is predicted that the Web will be where people turn for a sense of community—between buyers and sellers, information suppliers and consumers, friends and family. While it is perhaps premature to say that all of this exists today (2001), clearly the trends point in that direction. It is common for students to get on America Online and chat for hours with their friends using AOL's Instant Messenger service.

3. Body versus soul. Some forecast that the new consumers will increasingly stay home to shop, meditate, and pamper their bodies and that they will also expect more in terms of entertainment. An example of this is what has been termed the "entertainmentization" of retailing where stores stage events, show videos on big screens, and attempt to add entertainment to everyday shopping experiences. The shrinking day also leads to consumers placing higher value on the spiritual. Witness Campbell Soup's motto: "M'm! M'm! Good for the Body. Good for the Soul." Investments in personal fitness will remain strong as well as expenditures on expensive junk food (e.g., super-premium ice cream).

4. Individualism. Consistent with the trend toward individualism is an increase in products and services tailored to small groups, called *mass customization.* From Levi's custom fit jeans to Dell's made-to-order personal computers, customers want products built for them (or at

least to be given the impression that they are). This trend toward the individual has also led to a dramatic growth in the small office, home office (SOHO) market to about 4 million workers now claiming their main offices in their homes. Accompanying mass customized products are marketing programs tailored to individuals or *one-to-one marketing*.

Any attempt to draw these kinds of trends is fraught with difficulties, of course; the landscape is littered with forecasts that have gone awry (see, for example, Schnaars's 1989 book describing a number of such erroneous forecasts). In addition, many books continue to be produced that attempt such forecasts (books by Popcorn and Marigold, 1998, and Wacker et al., 2000, are examples). However, the fundamental demographic and socioeconomic factors that underlie the forecasts provide incontrovertible evidence that change will occur. It is essential the product managers think about the impact of these changes on their businesses.

Political

An important environmental consideration is the industry's sensitivity to political factors. These are particularly relevant for products that have substantial foreign markets. Figure 3–5 describes the sources of political risk, the groups through which political risk can be generated, and the political problem's effect on the operation of the business.

For example, consider businesses operating in China, India, Thailand, and other Pacific Rim countries as well as in Eastern Europe. Here the political systems are very different, and in many cases at some risk of turning away from being open markets or even erupting in open warfare as in the Balkans.

Domestic U.S. political risk is generally not so great, but it is still important. It is usually related to which political party is in power. Republicans tend to favor free market economies. Therefore, industries hard-pressed by foreign competition (e.g., shoes, textiles) would probably not receive any relief through quotas or tariffs. Democrats, tending to support some market intervention, might favor not only some of the above programs but also an industrial policy that would benefit certain industries. Defense spending and, hence, the fortunes of defense-related industries also have this type of political risk, as was quite apparent in the early 1990s.

Regulatory

Government and other agencies affect industry attractiveness through regulations. Some industries have become less attractive over time because laws have restricted their abilities to market or raise the overall cost of doing business. For example, government has restricted which media the cigarette industry can use for advertising. The mining, steel, and auto industries have all been affected by environmental and safety laws. Pharmaceuticals and foods have extensive testing and labeling requirements, and these seem

FIGURE 3–5 **Conceptualizing Political Risks**

Sources of Political Risk	Groups through Which Political Risk Can Be Generated	Effects on International Business Operations
Competing political philosophies (nationalism, socialism, communism) Social unrest and disorder Vested interests of local business groups Recent and impending political independence Armed conflicts and internal rebellions for political power New international alliances	Government in power and its operating agencies Parliamentary opposition groups Nonparliamentary opposition groups (Algerian "FLN," guerrilla movements working within or outside country) Nonorganized common interest groups: students, workers, peasants, minorities, and so on Foreign governments or intergovernmental agencies such as the EEC Foreign governments willing to enter into armed conflict or to support internal rebellion	Confiscation: loss of assets without compensation Expropriation with compensation: loss of freedom to operate Operational restrictions: market shares, product characteristics, employment policies, locally shared ownership, and so on Loss of transfer freedom: financial (dividends, interest payments, goods, personnel, or ownership rights, for example) Breaches or unilateral revisions in contracts and agreements Discrimination such as taxes or compulsory subcontractings Damage to property or personnel from riots, insurrections, revolutions, and wars

Source: Stefan H. Robock, "Political Risk: Identification and Assessment." *Columbia Journal of World Business,* July–August 1971, p. 7. Copyright 1971. Reprinted with permission.

more likely to be tightened than loosened. (Notice the backlash against bio-engineered food in the U.S. and Europe.)

Environmental Factors Summary

In this section, we identified major factors in the environment related to an industry and its attractiveness. While each major factor is too complex to conveniently summarize here, it is clear that important influences on the long-term prospects for an industry lie outside its control.

While we have emphasized using environmental data to assess an industry's future health, it also can and should be used to plan new products and product improvements and select market segments to target.

Examples

Super-Premium Ice Cream

Figure 3–6 summarizes a category attractiveness analysis for Super-Premium Ice Cream. Sources of information for this and the PDA illustration are listed in Figures 3–7 and 3–8. The aggregate market factors overall are fairly positive. The total market size for super-premium ice creams is not large but it is

FIGURE 3–6   Category Attractiveness: Super-Premium Ice Cream

Factor		Attractiveness
Aggregate market factors:		
Market size	$348 million	+/0
Market growth	10–20% in dollars	+
Product life cycle	Late growth	+
Profits	High	+
Sales cyclicity	Low	+
Seasonality	Moderate	0/–
Category factors:		
Threat of new entrants	Low; while manufacturing process is easy, strong distribution barriers (shelf space, logistics for perishable product) are very high	+
Bargaining power of buyers	High for consumers, high for channel members	–
Bargaining power of suppliers	Low; milk-based products are commodities	+
Company rivalry	Small number of key players but not large or aggressive	+
Pressure from substitutes	High; many snacks, etc. (see Chapter 3)	–
Category capacity	Not a problem	+
Environmental factors		
Technological	Not applicable	+
Political	Not applicable	+
Economic	Positive; more disposable income→higher spending on luxury goods	+
Social	Possible health/diet issue	0/–
Regulatory	Low; some labeling/ingredient issues	+/0

FIGURE 3–7   Reference Source for the Super-Premium Ice-Cream
             Category

A.C. Nielson
Brandweek
Consumer Reports
Dairy Field
Information Resources Incorporation
International Ice Cream Association/USDA publications
The Latest Scoop, annual published by the International Dairy Foods Association
Mediamark Research Inc.
Refrigerated & Frozen Foods

Various newspapers including:
The Arizona Republic
The Boston Herald
The Financial Times
The Houston Chronicle
The Milwaukee Journal Sentinel
Newsweek
The New York Times
The Ottawa Citizen
The San Diego Union-Tribune

FIGURE 3–8   Reference Sources for the PDA Category

Brandweek
Business Week
CNET News.com
CNN.com
Computer Reseller News
Electronic News
Forbes
Forrester Research reports
Fortune
Frost & Sullivan reports
Gartner Group reports
Handspring: www.handspring.com
The Industry Standard
International Data Corporation reports
OneSource Information Services
Pen Computing
San Francisco *Chronicle*

the fastest growing ice cream category (a respectable 10–20 percent) and profit margins are very high. While there is some seasonality for ice cream generally, increased distribution and a proliferation of products and flavors make this a minimal problem. In terms of the category factors, significant barriers to entry, particularly distribution (shelf space and logistics), make this a category that is relatively safe from new entrants. The main problem in this set of factors is the pressure from substitutes. The economic factors are also largely favorable. Particularly important is the fact that with incomes generally rising, more people are able to indulge in this category.

These are, of course, those factors with minus signs next to them. In the super-premium ice cream category, the most notable negatives are bargaining power of buyers and pressure from substitutes. Buyer power can be reduced by limiting competition (clearly illegal) or by building strong brand names that increase "pull" demand (i.e., customers demanding specific brands due to their brand equities). Since the analysis in the previous chapter showed that there are many generic competitors to super-premium ice cream, an important focus of product managers in this category is to create primary demand for the product. That is, advertising and other communications should focus not only on the specific brand but also on the category itself, indicating why a consumer should choose to purchase ice cream over other snacks.

Personal Digital Assistants

Figure 3–9 shows a category attractiveness analysis for PDAs in 2000. The aggregate market factors show a market that is in the growth stage of the product life cycle. The factors here are all positive. The Palm Pilot has created a market out of one thought dead by many observers. The market size, growth, and profitability of this category are all very positive factors that

FIGURE 3–9   **Category Attractiveness Analysis: Personal Digital Assistants**

Factor		Attractiveness
Aggregate market factors:		
Market size	$2.3 billion	+
Market growth	30–40%	+
Product life cycle	Growth	+
Profits	Good	+/0
Sales cyclicity	None	+
Sales seasonality	None	+
Category factors:		
Threat of new entrants	Moderate; R&D required, distribution	0
Bargaining power of buyers	Low; high switching costs	+
Bargaining power of suppliers	Moderate; PC's use similar components	0
Category rivalry	Intense	−
Pressure from substitutes	High	−
Category capacity	Not a problem for now	+
Environmental factors:		
Technological	Very sensitive	−
Political/regulatory	Telecommunications deregulation	+
Economic	Relatively inexpensive	+
Social	More work done on the road	+

have led to increased competition. With little cyclicity or seasonality, it is easy to see why. The category factors are mixed. On the plus side, the bargaining power of buyers is low due to strong brand names (Palm, Casio) and switching costs exist in changing brands due to different interfaces, file formats, etc. Supplier components are relatively standard, although on occasion, semiconductor supplies become tight. On the downside, the rivalry between brands is intense and there is increasing price competition. Perhaps more important, there are significant substitutes on the horizon in the form of wireless cellular phones that can perform many functions. Of course, the old standard, Day-Timers, are still very popular. The environmental factors are mixed. Further deregulation of the telecommunications industry will help the high-end PDAs due to their extensive communications capabilities. The main plus for the product category from this set of factors is that it is in line with the way work is changing: more work out of the office and on the road increases the need for quick convenient ways to take notes and keep records of phone numbers and appointments. The main negative factor is technology. Continued miniaturizing of components and product innovation could make the PDA category obsolete if the functions were transferred to phones, watches, or "wearable" computers such as those that have come out of MIT's Media Lab. While the basic customer benefits provided will not change, the form certainly could.

Summary

This chapter has presented a framework for analyzing an industry. The three major sets of factors to consider are market factors such as market size and growth, competitive factors such as power of buyers and suppliers, and environmental factors such as demographic and regulatory trends. Data on this can be assembled from a variety of sources. The most useful include trade associations, government publications, general business publications (*Forbes, Fortune, Business Week*) and company sources such as annual reports.

References

Bellotti, Fabio, Olivier Girard, and Omar Tellez (1995) "Snapple 1996 Marketing Plan," Master's thesis, Haas School of Business, University of California at Berkeley.

Capon, Noel, and Rashi Glazer (1987) "Marketing and Technology: A Strategic Coalignment," *Journal of Marketing,* 51, July, 1–14.

Etzel, Doug, Paul Musembwa, Henri Udhara, and Kenichiro Yamada (1995) "U.S. Marketing Plan for the Sharp 'Wiz' Personal Digital Assistant," Master's thesis, Haas School of Business, University of California at Berkeley.

Harrigan, Kathryn Rudie (1980) *Strategies for Declining Businesses.* Lexington, MA: Lexington Books.

Kerin, Roger A., Vijay Mahajan, and P. Rajan Varadarajan (1990) *Strategic Market Planning.* Boston: Allyn and Bacon.

Miller, Annetta (1999) "The Millennial Mind-Set," *American Demographics,* January, 60–65.

Naisbitt, John (1984) *Megatrends: Ten New Directions for Transforming Our Lives.* New York: Warner Books.

Popcorn, Faith, and Lys Marigold (1998) *Clicking: 17 Trends That Drive Your Business—And Your Life.* New York: Harperbusiness.

Porter, Michael E. (1980) *Competitive Strategy.* New York: The Free Press.

Robock, Stefan H. (1971) "Political Risk: Identification and Assessment." *Columbia Journal of World Business,* July–August, 7.

Standard & Poor's (1986) *Analyst Handbook.* New York: Standard & Poor's Corporation.

Schnaars, Steven P. (1989) *Megamistakes.* New York: The Free Press.

Thomas, Philip S. (1974) "Environmental Analysis for Corporate Planning," *Business Horizons,* 17, October, 27.

Wacker, Watts, Jim Taylor, and Howard B. Means (2000) *The Visionary's Handbook: Nine Paradoxes That Will Shape the Future of Your Business.* New York: Harperbusiness.

4 Competitor Analysis

Overview

As Porter (1979) has said, "The essence of strategy formulation is coping with competition." Competitor analysis, which involves study of individual competitors in an industry (as opposed to the overall characteristics of an industry), has received more attention in the last few years for several reasons. First, many product categories are mature businesses, with slow or zero growth rates. In such markets, competitive pressures are intense as volume gains are derived from the other firms; that is, the market can be described as a zero-sum, or in a recession even a negative-sum, game. As a result, firms that understand their competitors' possible future strategies have an advantage over inward-oriented firms.

A second impetus to competitor analysis comes from the belief that product life cycles are shortening. Accordingly, there is more pressure on product managers to recoup investments made in a shorter period, which makes errors of judgment about competition difficult to overcome.

Finally, the last decade has been perhaps the most turbulent period ever faced by marketing managers because of increased foreign competition, dramatic changes in technology and rates of innovation, large shifts in interest rates and inflation, changing customer tastes, and major political shifts (e.g., new governments in Eastern Europe and Russia, the return of Hong Kong to Chinese control). When the environment contains so much uncertainty, it is important to keep abreast of the competition.

Many companies have discovered the importance of competitor analysis. For example, Marriott developed its low-priced Fairfield Inn chain only after spending six months studying competitors in the economy hotel business. Several companies have extensive operations devoted to studying and simulating competitors, as the following examples show (Gomes, 1999; Gruner, 1998; McCartney, 1999; Wasserman, 2000):

- Microsoft deployed a team of engineers and marketers specifically to track Linux, the fast-growing, free operating system that is becoming more popular. The team has attempted to convince potential corporate users that Linux is not a real competitor to Windows.
- Frontier Airlines competes head-to-head with United on many routes in the western United States. To try to anticipate United's moves, Frontier hired a former United planning executive as its planning director whose job it is to get "inside" its corporate head. For example, instead of swamping a market with flights, Frontier learned that if it flew only twice a day to a city, United was not likely to increase its capacity there.
- Every week, Tom Sternburg, founder and CEO of Staples, the office supply superstore, drops by one of his stores and a competitor's. He focuses mainly on what the competitor is doing well rather than simply criticizing the competitor for its weaknesses. He looks at customer service, store visibility, displays, and how easy the prices are to read.
- Palm Computing has a chief competitive officer whose job is to predict competitors' likely future strategies. His main job is to follow Microsoft and its Windows CE operating system. His methods include talking with customers, sales staff, and suppliers.

An annual survey of the Best American Players in the intelligence game found the following rank ordering (Green, 1998):

1. Microsoft.
2. Motorola.
3. IBM.
4. Procter & Gamble.
5. General Electric, Hewlett-Packard (tied).
7. Coca-Cola, Intel (tied).

It would be a mistake, however, to assume that competitor intelligence gathering is only for large companies. One example (from *The Wall Street Journal,* April 1989) illustrates that small companies also can profit from such activity. The CEO of a small company turned a discussion with a customer into a problem for a competitor. The company, an importer of lamps and office furniture, had recently faced increased competition. The CEO learned from a retailer that one of the company's competitors had just raised the prices of some expensive lamps. The executive quickly relayed the information to the firm's field salespeople who used the information to win new business.

Why don't all firms have a formal reporting system designed to collect and analyze information about competitors? First, overconfidence about a product's continued success can reduce the willingness to collect competitor information. There is an impressive list of manufacturers (General Motors,

Coca-Cola, McDonald's, IBM) who succumbed to this overconfidence at one time, along with an equally impressive list of competitors who were ignored until they made significant inroads into their markets (Toyota, Pepsi, Burger King, Compaq). A second reason for insensitivity to competition is uncertainty about where to collect the necessary information and how to analyze it. This excuse grows weaker all the time as consultants specializing in competitive intelligence gathering, articles containing tips on where to collect information, and computerized databases containing articles about companies proliferate, and the Web increases its reach.

A final reason for not collecting competitive intelligence is an ethical consideration—the fear that either illegal methods or otherwise dirty tricks have to be used to obtain such information. Many examples of such behavior exist. "Reverse" engineering (copying) is a popular method for shortening lead times in introducing "me-too" products. Running phony help wanted ads to lure and question competitors' employees is another frequently used ploy. However, the information obtained in such a manner can almost always be ethically obtained also.

At the minimum, firms should view methods for collecting information about competitors from a defensive perspective; that is, how they can prevent information about themselves from landing in the laps of important competitors. One company that takes this perspective seriously is Apple Computer. John Sculley, then CEO of Apple, became so alarmed at the number of leaks that he had a six-minute video shown to new employees warning them about the implications of "loose lips" (Zachary, 1989). Improved technology for "eavesdropping" and decreased employee loyalty because of corporate downsizings increase competitors' ability to obtain corporate secrets. A 1995 survey of Fortune 1000 companies showed that about 75 percent believe theft or attempted theft by computer of customer information, trade secrets, and new-product plans increased over the previous five years (Geyelin, 1995).

Analyzing competitors requires a commitment to expend resources collecting data. However, collecting the data is usually not the major problem facing marketing planners. There are many sources of competitor intelligence. What is often lacking is a structure to guide the collection and analysis of the data and a clear idea of what questions the data should address.

This chapter proposes a structure for collecting, organizing, and analyzing competitor information that includes four areas of interest:

- What are the competitors' objectives?
- What are the current strategies being employed to achieve the objectives, and how successful have they been?
- What are the capabilities of the competitors to implement their strategies?
- What are their likely future strategies?

The first three parts of the analysis are background data needed to predict competitors' future strategies. The fourth aspect of competitor analysis could be called the bottom line since the purpose of examining competitors is to forecast what they are likely to do over the next planning cycle.

Many analysts treat their own company separately and perform an "internal capabilities" or other similar analysis and consider only outside competitors in the competitive analysis. We intentionally include the company itself in the competitor analysis for two reasons. First, considering your own company as "special" creates a tendency toward an inward rather than an outward orientation. Second, it is not absolute strengths and weaknesses but relative ones that determine success, so it is important to get a comparative picture on as many important aspects as possible.

In performing a competitive analysis, some data may be hard or even impossible to obtain, thus leading to either blanks in certain portions of the analysis or very qualitative information (e.g., product quality is "high"). This is inevitable and should both be expected and serve as a guide to possible directions for future information gathering.

Sources of Information

Secondary Sources of Information

As with marketing research in general, product managers should always begin competitor analysis with a search of secondary sources of information. Secondary sources are generally less expensive and easier to obtain than primary data and often cover most of the important topics. Figure 4–1 identifies popular secondary sources used by companies. An exhaustive listing of

FIGURE 4–1

Secondary sources of competitor information

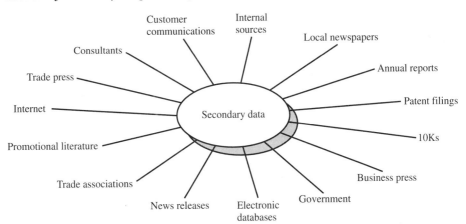

secondary sources of information is beyond the scope of this book; however, many good listings of these sources exist (see, for example, Lehmann, Gupta, and Steckel, 1998; Patzer, 1995). Fortunately, with the explosive growth of the Internet, many of these sources are available from your desktop, rendering obsolete the former term for secondary sources of information, *library sources.*

Internal Sources
Data can be found in past marketing plans, special studies commissioned by strategic planning groups, or simply in someone's office. As noted at the beginning of the chapter, some companies establish competitor hot lines or databases that can be accessed easily.

Local Newspapers
An excellent inexpensive source of information about competitors is local newspapers. For example, if a key competitor's product is manufactured in a small town or a foreign country, subscribing to the local newspaper is an excellent way to keep tabs on hirings and other changes. A U.S. medical supply manufacturer was shocked when a Japanese competitor significantly increased output at a new plant in Kentucky. The U.S. company had to reduce prices to maintain market share. What is interesting is that many details about the new plant—cost, number of employees, the products to be produced—were reported in the *Lexington Herald-Leader* in 1987, three years before the plant opened (Teitelbaum, 1992).

Annual Reports
Much of the information in an annual report is for public relations value, and the discussion is at the corporate, not product, level. However, careful analysis of annual reports can produce some interesting insights even at the product level, particularly by examining the product areas the report does *not* mention. Often one can get useful information about areas of corporate emphasis from the message from the chairman or the text. Annual reports sometimes mention locations of manufacturing facilities and the names of key corporate decision makers. Although the financial information is aggregate, some data on cost of goods sold can be useful. These reports are, of course, available only for publicly held companies. For private companies, Dun & Bradstreet publishes its famous D&B reports, which estimate the financial performance of those firms.

10K Statements
Another reporting requirement for publicly held corporations is the 10K statement. Often this is more useful than the annual report because it is broken down by line of business and does not have the "gloss" of the annual report.

One clear implication of these two sources of information is that a cheap way to keep up with the corporate parent of a competitor is to become a shareholder (preferably a small one!). Shareholders receive the annual reports and 10Ks as well as admission to the annual shareholder meetings, which can be another useful resource.

Financial documents, including annual reports and 10Ks, are also available at most business libraries and stockbrokerage offices, where other useful financial documents such as new business prospectuses can be found.

Patent/Trademark Filings
Within the last decade, commercially available data networks such as CompuServe have made patent filings available. Obviously, patents give some notion of the manufacturing process and technology underlying the product. However, companies have been known to apply for patents on mistakes or on products that they have no intention to market. MicroPatent (*www.micropatent.com*) permits the downloading of patents and technical diagrams via its Web-based service.

General Business Publications
Excellent sources of information about products and companies are general business publications such as *Business Week, Fortune, Forbes,* and *The Wall Street Journal.* One might wonder why companies are often willing to disclose what should be proprietary information concerning, for example, future marketing strategies. Some potential audiences are investors, employees, and perhaps even competitors who might be the target for strategic warnings. To get information from these publications, product managers can subscribe to clipping services and electronic databases or clip appropriate articles themselves.

News Releases.   Companies usually retain public relations firms to release information to the press concerning new products, senior management appointments, and the like. These releases often show up in newspapers and trade publications, but it is possible to get on a direct distribution list.

Promotional Literature.   Sales brochures (often referred to as *collateral material*) or other promotional literature focusing on a competing product or product line are extraordinarily valuable. Sales literature is a rich source of information concerning the product's strategy, since it usually has details about how the product is being positioned and differentiated versus those of competitors (including your product) and product attribute and performance data.

Trade Press.   These periodicals focus on a particular industry or product category. Representing this class of literature is *Women's Wear Daily* for the retail clothing trade, *Billboard* for the record and video industry, *Rubber Age* and *Chemical Week* for their respective industries, and *Test and Measurement World* for semiconductor testing equipment. This class of publications is obviously a rich source of information concerning new-product announcements, personnel shifts, advertisements for products, and industry or category data on sales and market shares. Somewhat broader are "new economy" magazines such as *Industry Standard, Business 2.0,* and *Red Herring.* These publications follow the Internet economy on a biweekly basis. Some "e"-zines such as *ICONOCAST* deliver information about e-commerce companies on a weekly basis to your e-mail address. Virtually every product category has its own set of publications.

Consultants
Many consulting firms sell industry reports to different companies. They usually develop these reports from secondary sources and thus sell a service that substitutes for the firm's own efforts. One type of company services all industries. For example, New York–based Market Research.com distributes a quarterly catalog of available reports. The fourth quarter 2000 issue offered a 180-page report on the "U.S. Candy & Gum Market" profiling the major marketers, consumer behavior, and social trends affecting the market at a price of $2,750.

Employee Communications
Companies often publish internal newsletters targeted toward employees. These newsletters may report on new vendors, new employees, and so forth.

Trade Associations
Most companies are members of trade associations (a listing of such associations is available in business libraries). These associations are usually formed for public relations or lobbying purposes, but they also often perform market research for the member firms. While usually focused on customers, this research may also provide some information about market shares, price levels, and so on.

Government Sources
The U.S. government collects a considerable amount of information about industries. However, the data are usually at the SIC level and therefore are not very useful for understanding specific product competitors. More useful information is collected by agencies such as the Federal Communications Commission, the Food and Drug Administration, and state agencies. For example, if Pacific Bell submits a request for a rate increase, competitors such as Sprint and MCI can obtain cost information from the filing since the request is public information.

Electronic Data Services
Much of the information just described can be found on electronic databases or networks accessible via the Internet or compact disks. Most good business libraries provide access to the latter, and most companies subscribe to the computer-based services. An example of such a database is DIALOG Infor-

FIGURE 4–2

Primary sources of competitor information

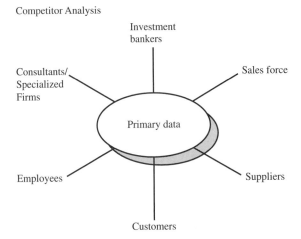

mation Services (*www.dialog.com*). DIALOG offers access to information about companies around the world using sources such as the following:

> *American Business Directory.*
> *Asia–Pacific Directory.*
> *D&B* (Europe, United States, Canada, Asia–Pacific).
> *ICC British Company Directory.*
> *Standard & Poor's* (Global).
> *Thomas Register* (United States, Canada).
> *Who Supplies What?* (Germany, Austria).

The Internet

As the reader can doubtless tell by now, today much information is available through the World Wide Web. A convenient way to search through the Web is with a search engine such as Yahoo!, Google, Excite, or Lycos. The user can type a company name, such as "Sony," and (eventually) reach Sony's home page and other pages linked to Sony. At Hewlett-Packard's page (*www.hp.com*), a browser can find product information and news about HP. Information seekers can determine HP's resellers, extent of technical support, and a large amount of other data.

Primary Sources of Information

Figure 4–2 lists the most important primary sources of information about competitors. Many of these are also sources of secondary information, depending on when the information was originally collected.

Sales Force/Customers

One of the most underutilized sources of information in companies is the sales force. Since they interact with customers on a regular basis, salespeople are in an excellent position to find out about recent competitor sales pitches, pricing, and many other dimensions. Xerox salespeople, for example, are trained to note competitor copiers. With notebook computers, salespeople can make their calls, fill out call reports electronically, and send information back to the local office or headquarters via modem. For competitor tracking, the call report should have a section related to noting anything new or different picked up during the call.

Of course, the salespeople must get the information from customers. Every attempt by suppliers and vendors to cultivate a potential customer involves the transmission of information. Unfortunately, customers may be reluctant to give away such information, believing it means playing "dirty tricks" on the competition. To aid in overcoming this reluctance, the data collection can be presented as giving the vendor an opportunity to provide better service or products to the customer, that is, by clearly showing that the customer will benefit by passing along the information. Usually the data can be obtained from public sources anyway; it is just quicker for the vendor to obtain it from the customer (Yovovich, 1995).

Employees

Generalizing from the use of salespeople to collect competitor intelligence, much can be learned about competition from observation in the marketplace by any company employee. If the product category in question is sold in the supermarket, an employee can easily observe changes in price, packaging, and shelf display.

Suppliers

Often competitors' suppliers are willing to give information about shipments to impress potential buyers. Imprints on packaging cartons can provide useful information because they often disclose the name and address of the carton's maker. Following up with the carton manufacturer may lead to estimates of sales volume.

Consultants/Specialized Firms

Consultants can often be used to develop special-purpose reports, as opposed to the off-the-shelf variety referred to under secondary sources. For example, Adscope, Inc., tracks advertising spending, campaigns, and media placement for the high-tech industry. One of the largest consulting/accounting firms in the United States, Deloitte & Touche, markets a service called *PeerScape* that conducts detailed financial and benchmarking analyses of competitors for its clients. An innovative service marketed by Competitive Media Reporting delivers a warning signal through a personal computer when a competitor ran a TV ad during the previous 36 to 48 hours. Besides downloading the text of the copy, the customer receives information about the markets in which the ad ran, the stations that carried it, and the times it ran.

Some interesting Web-based services for tracking competitor's moves have been developed in recent years:

- NetMind's (*www.netmind.com*) technology lets you track any Web page at any level of detail—including images, forms, links, and key-words—then alerts you via mobile access (cell phone, PDA, or pager), e-mail or My Page when a change has been made.
- AdRelevance (*www.adrelevance.com*) performs an analysis similar to Adscope's but for online advertising. The company tracks ad spending, impressions, and placement, and it is updated weekly.
- Vividence (*www.vividence.com*) conducts primary marketing research by sending target customers to your own and competitors' Web sites and measuring their "experience" at the sites. The company maintains a panel of about 100,000 consumers who provide the company with feedback about the site in question.

Investment Bankers

Investment bank reports are excellent sources of both secondary and primary data on competitors, particularly if a bank wishes to gain the firm as a new client. Analysts employed by the investment banks develop detailed analyses of the prospects of different firms and products in an industry. While their perspective is financial performance, much of the information is useful to marketing managers.

Other Sources

Help-Wanted Advertisements

Often help-wanted ads contain valuable information, such as job requirements and salary levels. Other information is available as well; sometimes the purpose of the ad is to fill positions opened by an expansion of business or a new plant opening. Although many ads disclose only a box number for a reply, many provide information about the organization paying for the ad. This can be done online as well, through searches of help-wanted ads from Monster Board (*www.monsterboard.com*), the Online Career Center (*www.occ.com*), and other similar sources.

Trade Shows

Company representatives often attempt to obtain information at the booths of competitors. This is becoming more difficult, however, as companies increasingly try to screen the people to whom they provide information to keep it away from competitors. In addition, spying is now so common at trade shows that hot new products are usually displayed only in hotel suites open to major customers, joint venture partners, and industry reporters who agree not to disclose information until product release dates. This is particularly true at large trade shows such as Comdex, the computer industry trade show, where industry players like Michael Dell, founder of Dell Computer Corporation, roam through the aisles trying to pick up information quickly before they are recognized. Even if some information is gained, however, about as much is lost from your own company, so usually the net gain is small.

Plant Tours

This is a rapidly disappearing phenomenon, largely because companies are becoming skittish about giving away valuable information (Upton and Macadam, 1997). The most popular tourist destination in Battle Creek, Michigan, was Kellogg's cereal plant until the company stopped giving tours several years ago, citing competitor information gathering as the reason. Gerber stopped its Fremont, Michigan, plant tours in 1990 after spotting sales representatives from competitor firms taking the tour. Although there are some exceptions, most tours today are like the amusement park–like tour at Hershey Foods' facility in Hershey, Pennsylvania, which offer little to be learned about how the products are really made.

Reverse Engineering

A common way to analyze a competitor's product is to purchase it and take it apart. This is referred to as *reverse engineering* in high-technology industries and sometimes as *benchmarking* in service markets.[1] It is wise to become a customer of a competitor by, for example, purchasing a computer or software, opening a small bank account, and so forth. One important reason to do so is to estimate the competitor's costs of manufacturing or assembly. Another objective is to assess the product's strengths and weaknesses. Companies such as Emerson Electric, General Motors, and Xerox perform this kind of analysis routinely. For example, in the late 1970s, Xerox benchmarked Canon's copiers and tried to beat each component of the latter's machines on cost and quality. In designing the Lexus, Toyota bought competitors' cars, including four Mercedes, a Jaguar XJ6, and two BMWs, put them through performance tests, and then took them apart (Main, 1992).

Monitoring Test Markets

Some companies test market products in limited areas of the country or the world to better understand decisions about pricing, advertising, and distribution. While this is often useful, test markets can be fertile grounds for competitors to get an early view of the product and how it will eventually be marketed after rollout to the larger market.

---

[1]The term *benchmarking* is also used more generally to refer to the tracking and analysis or any process such as manufacturing, billing, customer service, and so on, in both competing and noncompeting organizations.

Hiring Key Employees
This practice obviously provides a considerable amount of information. However, new employees may not legally transmit what are considered to be trade secrets to new employers. Trade secrets can have a narrow interpretation, however, that does not cover marketing strategies or complete plans. Some companies attempt to hinder employees, particularly senior managers, from jumping to a competitor by including a special noncompete clause in the employment contract. At Hewlett-Packard, new employees are asked to sign nondisclosure agreements and attend a training program, complete with video, that defines how HP interprets "trade secrets" (Guthrie, 1993).

Some Sources with Ethical Considerations

Our purpose in describing some of the unethical approaches to collecting competitor information is not to encourage readers to use them but to point out that such activities do occur. As mentioned earlier in the chapter, a key reason to learn about the various approaches to collecting information about competitors is to become more defensive minded. Of course, it is virtually impossible to completely defend against lying and cheating. However, on a hopeful note, these approaches rarely uncover something an ethical approach cannot.

Aerial Reconnaissance
It is illegal in the United States for a company to hire an airplane or a helicopter to take aerial photographs of a competitor's facilities as they are being constructed because this action is interpreted as trespassing. Procter & Gamble won a lawsuit against Keebler for spying on a new soft-cookie-making facility being constructed in Tennessee in 1984. Companies can, apparently legally, purchase photographs taken from satellites: Sweden and France are partners in a satellite joint venture that sets aside a limited percentage of the transponder time for commercial purposes (usually mapmaking and municipal planning). In 1994, Lockheed Missiles & Space Company, a subsidiary of Lockheed Corporation, received the first license from the U.S. government to sell spy-quality satellite pictures for commercial use. Lockheed has the technology to photograph a car from 400 miles in space.

Buying/Stealing Trash
It is not illegal to take a company's trash after it leaves the firm's facility. However, companies have been known to either bribe employees or otherwise obtain access to discarded documents. Avon admitted it had hired private detectives to run through rival Mary Kay's trash to attempt to defend against a takeover attempt by the latter. The maneuver was not illegal because Mary Kay's dumpster was in a public parking lot (Zellner and Hager 1991). In a highly publicized 2000 incident, Oracle hired a firm to sift through the trash of the Independent Institute, a think tank Oracle accused

of having a tie to Microsoft after it ran a high-profile ad criticizing the U.S. government's antitrust case against the software company. Simple defensive mechanisms include shredders and incinerators. Unfortunately, in today's online world, "trash" also means electronic mail thought to be discarded that was not.

Printers
Some companies attempt to obtain predistribution copies of catalogs and other collateral material.

Phony Want Ads
Not all help-wanted ads are for actual positions. Some companies run ads in an attempt to get disgruntled employees from competitors to apply. These applicants then can be probed for information.

Snooping on Airplanes
Two trends—squeezing more seats into airplanes and the proliferation of laptops—provide ample opportunity for business travelers to collect information from screens. Some flights are notoriously packed with executives from particular industries; for example, the flights from San Jose to Austin are generally filled with computer industry people. One executive was creative in deterring such snooping. On a flight from San Francisco, he detected a pair of eyes intently looking at his computer screen. Having experienced this before, with a few keystrokes, he opened a file called READTHIS.doc, which produced a single sentence on the screen: "If you can read this, you ought to be ashamed of yourself." The passenger in the next seat retreated (de Lisser, 1999).

The ethics of various data collection methods is a continuum from methods that are clearly illegal (stealing a competitor's marketing plans) to obviously legal (reading an article in a trade magazine). Today there is more pressure than ever to uncover information about competitors. The Society of Competitive Intelligence Professionals, now numbering nearly 3,000 members, has established an ethical code that requires members to comply with the law, identify themselves when seeking information about competitors, and respect requests for confidentiality. However, those bent on violating legal and ethical standards do not tend to join such societies. It is therefore incumbent on companies to develop policy statements that clearly define the standards expected from employees in this area of competitor intelligence gathering and strongly enforce them (Rangan and Porter, 1992).

Assessing Competitors' Current Objectives

The first step in competitor analysis is to assess the current objectives for the major competitor brands. An assessment of current objectives provides valuable information concerning the intended aggressiveness of the competitors. It also provides a context within which to assess the capabilities of the competitors; that is, whether the firm marketing Brand A has the resources to successfully pursue an objective.

When discussing objectives, it is important to define the term precisely, for there are many different types of objectives. In the context of marketing planning, three basic brand or product objectives can be identified. The *growth objective* usually implies growing the brand in terms of either units or market share with profit conditions being secondary. The *hold objective* could also be termed a consolidation objective. A hold scenario might be logical for a brand that is losing market share, in that a reasonable first step in reversing its fortunes is to put a brake on the slide. Finally, the *harvest scenario* could also be termed a *milking* objective. Here, profit is of paramount importance.

At the product level, objectives are typically stated in terms of either market share or profits. At the corporate level, return on investment or other more aggregate statistics become more relevant.

While objectives determine to a great extent what strategies will be pursued and, hence, what actions will be taken in the marketplace, it usually does not take a substantial amount of research to uncover them. What is required is sensitivity to competitors' actions through observation, salesperson call reports, and so on.

Let us consider the two major options outlined above—the growth versus harvest choice. If a competitor's product is being pushed to improve its market position at the expense of short-term profits, then some of the following are likely to occur: product upgrades, a cut in price, increased advertising expenditures, increased promotional activity both to consumer and trade, or increased distribution expenses.

In other words, a firm that is trying to expand a brand's market share will be actively spending money on market-related activities and/or reducing price. Such actions can be easily monitored by brand managers, advertising account representatives, and other parties with access to information about the rival brand's actions.

Brands being harvested would be marketed in the opposite way. An increase in a competitor's price, decreases in marketing budgets, and so on can be interpreted as a retreat (perhaps only temporary) from active competition in the market. While exact estimates of the size of the share loss expected cannot be obtained, it is not difficult to establish the direction of the objective.

Two other factors are relevant to the assessment of competitors' objectives. First, the objectives of a foreign brand or a product marketed by a firm with a foreign parent are often affected by the country of origin. In many cases, such firms have financial backing from a government or major banks and are not as concerned with short-term losses as they are with establishing a viable market position or obtaining foreign currency. Thus, depending on the competitor, clues concerning the competitor brand's objectives can be obtained from the geographical home of the parent firm.

A second relevant factor is whether the ownership of the competitor firm is private or public. Since private firms do not have to account to financial analysts, long-term profits may be more important than showing positive quarterly returns. On the other hand, if a family depends on the firm for current income, profits may be more important than market share. In these cases, knowledge of the ownership situation provides vital cues concerning the likely objectives. For example, government controlled firms often have objectives such as maintaining employment, providing service, or obtaining foreign currency.

An interesting variant of the impact of private ownership on objectives occurs if the privatization resulted from a leveraged buyout (LBO). In these cases, even though the company is private, it is often more interested in profits and cash flow to pay down debt than it is in plowing money into market share gains. An excellent example is the well-publicized LBO by Kohlberg Kravis Roberts & Company (KKR) of RJR Nabisco in 1988. Because of the large load of debt the firm took on, many of RJR's brands became vulnerable to competitors that took advantage of the opportunity to go for market share gains. These included Philip Morris in tobacco products because RJR was reluctant to enter the low-price cigarette category, and competitors in snack foods, which took advantage of cuts in advertising and promotion expenditures for Ritz crackers and Planters products. A similar result often occurs as a result of mergers (Lorge, 1999).

A less apparent level of objectives can be deduced from a firm's operating philosophy and procedures. For example, a firm that seeks to minimize capital investment will be slow to respond to a competitor that makes a heavy capital outlay (e.g., as Emery Air Freight was when Federal Express bought its own planes in the mid-1970s). Similarly, firms that compensate their sales staff based on a percent of sales commission indicate that volume (rather than profitability) is a key objective. In fact, the key performance measure (e.g., return on fixed assets) often has a distinct influence on a firm's behavior.

In sum, estimates of the objectives pursued by competitors provide important information for the development of strategy. A product that is being aggressive in its pursuit of market share must be viewed as a different type of competitor than one that is primarily attempting to maximize profits. The latter product would clearly be vulnerable to an attack against its customers, while a confrontation with the former product might be avoided.

This type of analysis has been profitably applied. During the late 1970s, Coca-Cola was primarily concerned with holding market share and improving profits. Pepsi, on the other hand, viewed Coke's relative passivity as an opportunity and became more aggressive, gaining share points and improving its position versus Coke in store sales. Miller's successful attack on Budweiser during the 1970s was prompted by a similar observation.

Assessing Competitors' Current Strategies

The second stage in competitor analysis is to determine how competitors are attempting to achieve their objectives. This question is addressed by examining their past and current strategies.

Marketing Strategy

Many authors have attempted to define the concept of strategy. A marketing strategy can be thought of in terms of three major components: target market selection, core strategy (e.g., differential advantage), and implementation (e.g., supporting marketing mix).

The first major component is the description of the market segment(s) to which the competing brands are being targeted. Customer market segments can be described in various ways. (See Chapter 5.) Since few products are truly mass marketed (i.e., marketed to all potential customers), the key is to determine which group(s) each has targeted. This is important to (1) avoid segments where there may be intense competition, and (2) determine under-targeted segments, which may represent opportunities.

Typically, market targets are fairly easy to determine. First, customers self-select as targets based on the product or service. Second, companies often reveal the target. Sometimes they do this explicitly in annual reports, 10Ks, speeches, and other public pronouncements. Other times the target can be deduced from marketing mix decisions. Distribution choices disproportionately serve different types of customers, as do different pricing strategies. Media advertising helps define the target both by demographics of the media and the copy appeal used. When combined with sales data, a competitor's marketing mix decisions can lead to a clear description of market targets by competitors, and hence identification of particularly close competitors.

The second strategy component is what is called the core strategy. This is the basis on which the rival competes; that is, its key claimed differential advantage(s). This critical component of strategy usually forms the basic selling proposition around which the brand's promotion is formed and is often called the brand's *positioning* or value proposition.

Product managers essentially have a choice between two types of differential advantages: price/cost–based and product–feature based. In other words, products are usually positioned by price or quality. Concentration on price follows the classic approach developed by the Boston Consulting Group (Henderson, 1980), which advocates taking advantage of the experience curve that drives down unit costs and provides the ability to cut prices and maintain margins over time. The quality differential advantage is a claim to be superior on some other product dimension, such as service, packaging, or delivery. For such a core strategy to be successful, customers must value the characteristics claimed as advantages, and the differential must be maintained for a significant period of time without being copied.

Quality differential advantages can often be *perceived* rather than *actual* differences. For example, IBM's core strategy since its inception has been service based. This advantage can be supported by hard data (e.g., number of field service representatives or mean response time). On the other hand, Reebok's "UBU" campaign related to individuality and not product. Such positioning is clearly outside the domain of physical product differences but can nonetheless be effective in differentiating. Physical product differences are often stressed in industrial, durable, or new, frequently purchased product strategies. Mature, frequently purchased products that are physically similar or commodities often emphasize perceptual differences.

The final strategy component of competitors that must be assessed is the supporting marketing mix. The mix provides insight into the basic strategy of the competitor as well as specific tactical decisions. The areas to consider and some questions to consider follow. It is also important to assess how successful the strategy has been. A strategy that has been associated with achieving objectives and good results is likely to be repeated; one that leads to poor performance is likely to change.

Pricing

Pricing is a highly visible element of a competitor's marketing mix; therefore several questions can be addressed. For example, if a brand's differential advantage is price based, is the list price uniform in all markets? If the strategy is quality based, what is the price differential? Are discounts offered? How is price changing over time? In general, any price-related information pertaining to the implementation of strategy is relevant.

Promotion

With respect to sales management, what kinds of selling approaches and salespeople are being employed? Are the salespeople being aggressive in obtaining new accounts? In terms of advertising, what media are used? What creative strategies? What timing pattern? Sales promotion questions are also important; for example, which types and how often?

Distribution

Have the channels of distribution shifted? Is the brand being emphasized in certain channels? Is the manufacturer of the competing product changing the system, for example, by opening its own retail outlets or using more direct marketing? More generally, how is the value chain (Figure 4–3), which includes everything from component suppliers through to the final customer, organized?

Product/Service Capabilities

A major determinant of a company's capabilities, at least in the short run, is the "physical" makeup of its product/service offering that is, in general, less easily changed than, say, price or advertising. Products filled with expensive

FIGURE 4–3

Value chain

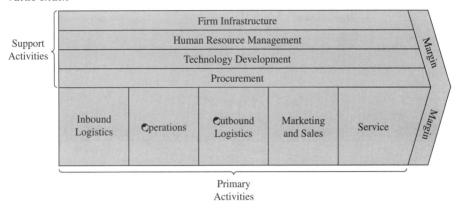

Source: Michael Porter (1980), *Competitive Advantage* (New York: Free Press), p. 37.

parts are unlikely to be positioned as low-end products. Similarly, physical properties (e.g., stability under high temperatures, moldability, corrosion resistance, durability of packaging) go a long way toward dictating target uses and hence strategy. Many engineering plastics markets segment themselves on the basis of physical properties (e.g., DuPont's Delrin versus Celanese's Celcon), with different applications dominated by different companies' offerings. Hence at a minimum, the competitive product offerings (that is, the actual product or service plus how it is presented and sold) should be compared.

Although product features do not translate into benefits sought by customers, a very useful graphic is a chart of the differences between the main products or services offered in the category. The basic structure of the matrix is shown in Figure 4–4. A useful complement to the features matrix is a set of importance weights or at least some indicator of the relative importance of the different features. Taking the basic feature information together with the relative importance weights gives you a good idea of the strengths and weaknesses of your product relative to competition.

Perhaps equally important is the image associated with companies. This image (or brand equity) enables some companies to compete, for example, at the high end of the market even though their product is at best equivalent in quality. By the same token, unknown brands are often assumed to be of inferior quality even when they are not. Of course quality is usually eventually observable, so perceptions tend toward objective quality in most markets. The convergence, however, may be slow (as in the slow acceptance of Japanese cars in the United States and the current difficulty American manufacturers have convincing customers of their improved quality). Still, the gap between objective and perceived quality provides a predictor of likely future movement and strategy. Thus, any competitive analysis should include information on perceived quality and satisfaction among current users.

FIGURE 4–4   Product Features Matrix

Features	Competitor A Brand $1 \dots K_A$	Competitor B Brand $1 \dots K_B$	....
F_1			
F_2			
.			
.			
.			
F_n			

How to Assess Competitors' Strategies

The two key elements of a strategy are the segments appealed to and the core strategy. For industrial products, both can be easily determined by examining three sources of information: company sales literature, your own sales force, and trade advertising. The former provides information about the core strategy; brochures usually go into detail concerning points of difference between the firm's product and those of competitors. Even if the sales literature provides no direct comparison between brands, it should indicate the brand's major strengths. A firm's own sales force can provide some data concerning targeted companies or industries. Much of this is of an informal nature resulting from contacts, trade show discussions, and the like. Finally, trade advertising is useful for discovering both the segments being targeted and the differential advantage touted. The latter can be determined directly from the copy while the former can be at least partially determined by the publication in which the ad appears.

For consumer goods, simply tracking competitors' ads provides most of the necessary information. Television ads can be examined in terms of message (differential advantage) and program (target segment). TV advertising is quite useful for determining the core strategy. Similarly, print advertising can provide equivalent information but with more elaboration.

For example, consider the print ad in *Forbes* for eGain, shown in Figure 4–5. eGain offers licensed and hosted applications for e-mail management, interactive Web and voice collaboration, intelligent self-help agents, and proactive online marketing. At least part of eGain's marketing strategy can be determined by the fact that the ad appeared in that particular magazine and from the copy itself. From data obtained from Mediamark Research's magazine *Total Audiences Report,* Spring 1998, we know that 73.8 percent of the readers are 18–49, 38.8 percent have household income over $75,000, and 83.3 percent either attended or graduated from college (among many other variables measured by Mediamark Research). It is probably not a surprise that readers are businesspeople with high incomes. Looking at the copy itself, the ad is a classic "fear appeal" in that it warns companies that poor

FIGURE 4–5

Detecting a competitor's strategy

Source: *Forbes* Magazine, June 12, 2000, p. 221.

operations and customer communications can lead to deteriorating customer relationships and lower sales. Note that there is no explicit mention of the competition. However, it is clear that eGain is trying to position itself as a company that is ready to help "immediately," has existing customers (not necessarily commonplace for e-commerce companies) and whose product has broad applications ("sales, service, and marketing"). The cost of the ad is obtainable from publications such as *Marketer's Guide to Media*.

Information concerning implementation of the current strategies is also easily found. Pricing information can be obtained from basic market observation: distributors, salespeople, customers, advertising agencies, or even a firm's own employees acting as consumers. Promotion, distribution, and product-related facts can be obtained from similar sources. In other words, as in the case of objective determination, it takes market sensitivity to assess much of the competitive activity rather than sophisticated management information systems.

One apparent but often overlooked source of information is being a customer and/or stockholder of the competitors. Both customers and stockholders get special mailings and information that makes strategy assessment easier. Furthermore, personal use of competitors' products often gives one a feeling for them that does not come through even the best prepared research. Thus, policies that forbid or discourage the use of competitive products are usually foolish.

Technological Strategy

Another important task is to assess the technological strategies of the major competitors; that is, how they approach market conditions. This can be done using the framework of Maidique and Patch (1978) who suggest that six decisions need to be made.

1. Technology selection or specialization.
2. Level of competence.
3. Sources of capability: internal versus external.
4. R&D investment level.
5. Competitive timing: initiate versus respond.
6. R&D organization and policies.

These decisions generally lead to four basic strategies, each of which has different requirements for success (see Figure 4–6). For example, consider the blank audio cassette market in the early 1970s. This was the early stage of the product life cycle, with no major competitors. Gillette's Safety Razor Division was considering entering this market as was Memorex, a manufacturer of computer tape and related products. While Gillette had slight competitive advantages over Memorex in marketing and finance, it was at a disadvantage in terms of R&D and manufacturing as well as perceived competence to produce high quality audio tape. The end result was success for Memorex and a

FIGURE 4–6 Typical Functional Requirements of Alternative Technological Strategies

	R&D	Manufacturing	Marketing	Finance	Organization	Timing
First to market	State-of-the-art R&D	Pilot and medium scale manufacturing	Stimulating primary demand	Access to risk capital	Flexibility over efficiency; encourage risk taking	Early-entry inaugurates the product life cycle
Second to market	Flexible, responsive, and advanced R&D capability	Agility in setting up manufacturing medium scale	Differentiating the product; stimulating secondary demand	Rapid commitment of medium to large quantities of capital	Flexibility and efficiency	Entry early in growth stage
Late to market or cost minimization	Skill in process development and cost-effective production	Efficiency and automation for large-scale production	Minimizing selling and distribution costs	Access to capital in large amounts	Efficiency and hierarchical control; procedures rigidly enforced	Entry during late growth or early maturity
Market segmentation	Ability in applications, custom engineering, and advanced product design	Flexibility on short to medium runs	Identifying and reaching favorable segments	Access to capital in medium or large amounts	Flexibility and control required in serving different customers' requirements	Entry during growth stage

FIGURE 4–7   Format for Competitive Product Analysis

	Competitor A Brand 1...K_A	Competitor B Brand 1...K_B
Product:		
Quality		
Value Chain		
Benefits		
Target segment:		
Who		
Where		
When		
Why		
Place:		
Distribution method		
Distribution coverage		
Promotion:		
Total effort ($)		
Methods		
Advertising:		
Strategy/copy		
Media		
Timing		
Total effort ($)		
Price:		
Retail		
To trade		
Technological strategy		

Gillette failure in test markets (see the Harvard Business School case, "Gillette Safety Razor Division: The Blank Cassette Project" for more details).

At this point in the analysis it is often useful to summarize the products of the major competitors. Figure 4–7 provides a general format that is useful both for summarizing the results and for communicating them.

Assessing Competitors' Capabilities

It is assumed that evidence has been accumulated thus far concerning competitors' current objectives and strategies. Recall that the ultimate goal of this analysis is to predict the competitors' likely future strategies. While past actions are often a good predictor, so are current capabilities.

Several frameworks have been proposed to indicate which information to collect about competitors (Ansoff, 1979; Hussey, 1971). One that has been used extensively was developed by Rothschild (1979). He divides the necessary information into five mutually exclusive categories concerned with the competitors' "abilities" to conceive and design, to produce, to market, to finance, and to manage (Figure 4–8).

FIGURE 4–8 **Competitor Capabilities**

A. Ability to conceive and design
  1. Technical resources
    a. Concepts
    b. Patents and copyrights
    c. Technological sophistication
    d. Technical integration
  2. Human resources
    a. Key people and skills
    b. Use of external technical groups
  3. R&D funding
    a. Total
    b. Percentage of sales
    c. Consistency over time
    d. Internally generated
    e. Government supplied
  4. Technological strategy
    a. Specialization
    b. Competence
    c. Source of capability
    d. Timing: initiate vs. imitate
  5. Management processes
    a. TQM/Six Sigma
    b. House of Quality

B. Ability to produce
  1. Physical resources
    a. Capacity
    b. Plant
      (1) Size
      (2) Location
      (3) Age
    c. Equipment
      (1) Automation
      (2) Maintenance
      (3) Flexibility
    d. Processes
      (1) Uniqueness
      (2) Flexibility
    e. Degree of integration
  2. Human resources
    a. Key people and skills
    b. Work force
      (1) Skills mix
      (2) Unions
  3. Suppliers
    a. Quality
    b. Capacity
    c. Commitment

C. Ability to market
  1. Sales force
    a. Skills
    b. Size
    c. Type
    d. Location
  2. Distribution network
    a. Skills
    b. Type
  3. Service and sales policies

  4. Advertising
    a. Skills
    b. Type
  5. Human resources
    a. Key people and skills
    b. Turnover
  6. Funding
    a. Total
    b. Consistency over time
    c. Percentage of sales
    d. Reward systems

D. Ability to finance
  1. Long term
    a. Debt/equity ratio
    b. Cost of debt
  2. Short term
    a. Cash or equivalent
    b. Line of credit
    c. Type of debt
    d. Cost of debt
  3. Liquidity
  4. Returns from operations
    a. Margin
    b. Profits
    c. Cash flow
    d. Return on sales, assets,
       marketing expenditures
    e. Inventory, receivables turnover
  5. Human resources
    a. Key people and skills
    b. Turnover
  6. System
    a. Budgeting
    b. Forecasting
    c. Controlling

E. Ability to manage
  1. Key people
    a. Objectives and priorities
    b. Values
    c. Reward systems
  2. Decision making
    a. Location
    b. Type
    c. Speed
  3. Planning
    a. Type
    b. Emphasis
    c. Time span
  4. Staffing
    a. Longevity and turnover
    b. Experience
    c. Replacement policies
  5. Organization
    a. Centralization
    b. Functions
    c. Use of staff

Ability to Conceive and Design

This category relates to the quality of the firms' new product development efforts. Clearly, a firm with a high ability to develop new products is a more serious long-term threat than a firm that has not been innovative. The use of procedures such as TQM (Total Quality Management) and the House of Quality generally improves product design capabilities.

Ability to Produce

In this category, we attempt to determine the production capabilities of the firms. For a service business, this category might be termed *ability to deliver the service*. A firm that is operating at capacity for a product is not as much a threat to expand in the short run as is a firm that has slack capacity, assuming a substantial period of time is required to bring new capacity on line. One aspect of ability to produce involves the quality, productive capacity, and commitment of suppliers of crucial parts and services. Programs such as Six Sigma improve product quality.

Ability to Market

How aggressive or inventive are the firms in marketing their products? Do they have a strong presence in key distribution channels? A competitor could have strong product development capabilities and slack capacity but be ineffective at marketing.

Ability to Finance

The lack of available financial resources clearly acts as a constraint to being an effective competitor. Divisions up for sale or recent LBOs generally have limited financial reserves. While firm level financial ratios are key pieces of information, how the competitor firm shifts its resources between products is also critical.

Ability to Manage

In the mid 1980s, Procter & Gamble replaced the manager of its U.S. coffee business with the coffee general manager from the United Kingdom. The new manager had a reputation for developing new products: In 15 months, for example, he oversaw the launch of four new brands, which was above average for the company. The message to competitors such as General Foods was clear. In general, the characteristics of key managers provide signals to competitors concerning likely strategies.

What to Do with the Information

This is the stage at which many competitor analysis efforts fall flat. What do we do with all the information that is collected? A useful format for synthesizing the large quantity of information is needed.

FIGURE 4–9   **Competitive Capability Assessment**

	Competing Firm				Own Company
	A	B	C	D	
Conceive and design:					
• Technical resources					
• Human resources					
• Funding					
•					
•					
•					
•					
Produce:					
• Physical resources					
• Human resources					
•					
•					
•					
•					
•					
Finance:					
• Debt					
• Liquidity					
• Cash flow					
• Budget system					
•					
•					
•					
Market:					
• Sales force					
• Distribution					
• Service and sales policies					
• Advertising					
• Human resources					
• Funding					
•					
Manage:					
• Key people					
• Decision process					
• Planning					
• Staffing					
• Organization structure					
•					
•					

A first step toward making some sense out of all the data is to construct a table patterned after Figure 4–9. This forces the manager to boil down the information to its essential parts and provides a quick summary of a large amount of data. Note that one column of the table is labeled "Own Company." This forces what is termed *an internal assessment;* the firm performing the analysis ultimately must see how its resources compare with those of its competitors.

Figure 4–10 presents an example of a competitor analysis in the wine industry. Figure 4–11 illustrates a further simplification. This entails

FIGURE 4–10   Competitor Capabilities Matrix for Wine (c. 1989)

	Gallo	Heublein	Vintners	Canandaigua	Seagram
Commitment to wine market	Deeply committed	Questionable	Deeply committed	Committed	Somewhat committed
Major brands	Gallo, Bartles & James, Carlo Rossi, Andre, Thunderbird	Inglenook, Almaden, Lancer	Paul Masson, Taylor (California and New York), Great Western, Partager	Richards Wild Irish Rose, Sun Country Cooler	Seagram's Wine Cooler, Perrier-Jouet Champagne, Mondavi & Sons
Ability to develop new products	Excellent in low end	Very good	Poor	Good	Excellent
Brand recognition	Excellent in low end	Very good	Very good	Good	Very good
Ability to market: Advertising	Industry leader willingness to invest heavily	Parent is talented marketer	Unproven	Questionable	Talented
Philosophy	Out-muscle the competition	Undetermined	Return to basics	Undetermined	Become premium beverage leader
Adaptability to changing markets	Good but becoming more risk averse	Undetermined	Poor	Poor	Very good
Ability to finance: Cash position	Unknown but believed excellent	Excellent	Poor	Poor	Excellent
Debt levels/debt potential	Undetermined	Undetermined	Highly leveraged; perhaps at limit	Can borrow on assets	Acceptable debt levels/large debt potential
Ability to produce	Large production ability, low acreage	Undetermined	Good production ability	Good production ability	Undetermined
Leadership	Talented	Undetermined	Talented	Undetermined	Talented

FIGURE 4–11   **Simplified Competitive Analysis: Wine**

Criteria	Gallo	Heublein	Vintners	Canandaigua	Seagram
Commitment to wine	1	5	2	3	4
Financial strength	2	1	4	5	3
Brand awareness	1	2	3	5	4
Management ability	1	4	2	3	5

Highest = 1.
Lowest = 5.

(1) determining key factors for success in the business in question, and
(2) based on the data from Figure 4–10, rating the competitors along those
key factors or dimensions. This simplification produces clearly identifiable
conclusions. Gallo has a significant competitive advantage on almost every
key dimension, while Canandaigua is clearly in an inferior position in the
market. Thus, a two-step data reduction approach often results in a clarified
picture of the competitive situation and relatively clear directions for strategy development.

Assessing a Competitor's Will

Even the strongest competitor can be overcome if it is not committed to the
market. Similarly, even a weak competitor can cause massive damage if it is
fanatically committed. At some point, it is crucial to assess the competitors'
strength of will or commitment. This requires going beyond objectives (What
do they want?) to assess the intensity with which they approach the task
(How badly do they want it?). Most competitions involve several key times at
which each competitor has the choice of backing down or continuing the
fight. In assessing the likelihood of a competitor continuing the fight (an act
that sometimes is not "rational" in a profit sense), one should assess the following questions:

1. How crucial is this product to the firm? The more crucial in terms of
   sales and profits, number of employees, or strategic thrust, the more
   committed most companies will be to it. This helps explain why efforts
   to unseat a market leader by attacking the heart of its market pro-
   voke violent reactions (If those . . . think they can take our market
   without a fight . . .), whereas a strategy that nibbles away at secondary markets is more likely to go unmatched (Well, it only represents
   2 percent of our sales, so we shouldn't be too concerned about it).
2. How visible is the commitment to the market? It may be difficult to
   admit you are wrong. A good example of this is Exxon's Office Systems
   Division, which was clearly in trouble for a long time before it was sold
   in 1985.

3. Are the best employees and managers involved, or is the second or third team in charge? How aggressive are the managers? Some people are more combative than others. The most combative opponents react with a fervor that makes reaching a business détente almost impossible.

Only by knowing how badly a competitor "wants it" can we successfully approach the next task, predicting future strategies.

Predicting Future Strategies

The manager is now armed with three sets of information about major competitors. First, we have assessed what their likely objectives are; that is, for what reward they are currently playing the game. Second, we have a view on their current strategy. Finally, we have some idea about their resources, abilities, and will to compete. The final step is to put it all together and answer the question we started with: What are they likely to do in the future? In particular, we are interested in their likely strategies over the subsequent planning horizon, often a year.

Sometimes, the competitors disclose their likely future strategies through sources previously listed. For example, Warner-Lambert (Giges and Jervey, 1982) indicated that for its over-the-counter health care products, including Myadec vitamins and Benylin cough syrup, it was going to redirect promotion from health care professionals alone to include consumers as well. This indicated a clear shift in strategy—a change in market segments to which it was appealing.

Similarly, in an article in a major newspaper, MCI gave six-months' notice to the regional Bell operating companies (RBOCs) by naming the 10 U.S. cities where it was going to begin offering local phone service to businesses. While a major target of the article was the investment analyst community, we are sure the RBOCs were also quite interested in the announcement (*San Francisco Chronicle*, 1995). Of course, the product manager must be aware that such signals could be of the "cheap talk" variety.

Often, however, the competition does not come right out and indicate what strategies they will pursue. In that case, subjective estimates are based on the information previously collected and analyzed. One way to approach the problem is to emulate what forecasters do with historical data. With historical observations of both a dependent variable to predict (in our context, a competitor's strategy), and independent variables useful to predict the dependent variable (in our context, the resource variables), the forecaster might do one of two things. First, she or he might simply assume the trend will continue; that is, suppose that the only relevant information is the historical pattern of past strategies. For example, if a firm had a track record of selling brands with a premium image and high price, one could extrapolate into the future and assume this will continue. Similarly, if a brand has been appealing to increasingly mature consumers, a manager might assume that the trend will continue. This implicitly assumes there is no information in the independent variables.

An alternative way for the forecaster to proceed is to try to establish a cause-and-effect relationship between the resource variables and strategy. In other words, the forecaster could try to link changes in resources or abilities to the strategies to be pursued.

Several examples help clarify this approach. Several years ago, Merrill Lynch spent heavily to bring in managers with packaged goods experience to develop the markets for its financial services. Competitors (E. F. Hutton, Dean Witter) could forecast that this would result in an emphasis on market segmentation (pursuing high-potential customers) and increased spending on marketing-related activities such as advertising. Similarly Bethlehem Steel invested billions of dollars to upgrade its flat-rolled-steel facilities. Competitors could forecast that this investment in highly efficient capacity would improve Bethlehem's ability to simultaneously cut price and protect margins. RCA tried for years to sell its Hertz subsidiary (it finally sold it in the mid-1980s to UAL, subsequently Allegis Corporation). This resulted in RCA diverting marketing funds from Hertz to "fatten up" its bottom line and make it look more attractive to a potential buyer. Competitors of Hertz were, of course, delighted since this decreased Hertz's ability to market and therefore limited its strategic options. Finally, both Bell Labs and DuPont spent considerable resources training employees in the marketing concept, suggesting a change in direction (e.g., Lucent Technologies).

A third approach to strategy forecasting makes use of historical data in a different way. Corning Glass's highly profitable Corning Ware line was coming off patent. At the same time, it was well known that several companies (Libby-Owens-Ford, Anchor Hocking) were looking at that business. Corning was interested in how a competitor would enter so it could preempt the entry strategy, and asked senior managers to role-play (i.e., simulate) a competitor to determine how they might attack Corning Ware. This forecasting exercise provided useful defensive information to Corning.

Thus, a third approach to forecasting competitors' possible actions is to simulate them. One can take the existing data already collected, play the role of the competitor, and develop competitor action scenarios. SmithKline did exactly that when Tagamet, at that time the largest-selling prescription drug in the world and the source of one-third of SmithKline's profits, was coming off patent. In this case, it knew the competitor was going to be Glaxo Holdings. SmithKline prepared its sales force for how it expected Glaxo to promote its drug, Zantac, in terms of differential advantage (fewer doses needed per day) and how to counteract arguments against Tagamet. The simulation helped dampen the impact on Tagamet. Other companies who follow this approach include Intel, Charles Schwab (versus Merrill Lynch), and GE.

FIGURE 4–12

Game theory illustration

Payoff matrix

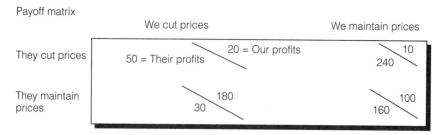

When there are few competitors, it is possible to use a combination of game theory and decision trees to predict competitive behavior. To use these, we assume the objective of both firms is known, such as annual profits. Then, for a particular decision, such as whether to cut versus maintain current prices, we can calculate the profitability to both parties as shown in Figure 4–12, which represents a "game" between the two competitors. Here we see that total profits are maximized if both maintain prices. Notice, however, that both parties are better off cutting prices if their competitor maintains them. This makes the situation inherently unstable and also makes predicting competitor strategy crucial to maximizing profits.

In response to this situation, it is apparently in the best interest of both parties to collude to maintain prices and, if they are sophisticated, to divide the extra profits they gain proportionally to their respective gains. Assuming such a cartel is illegal or unstable, the key to understanding behavior is often to assume that one competitor moves first and the other responds. For example, the decision tree in Figure 4–13 depicts a situation where we move first and the competitor responds. Given the estimated response probabilities (which should be based on the competitor analysis), we can compute the results of the two decisions:

$$\text{We cut price: } .9 (20) + .1 (180) = 36$$

$$\text{We maintain price: } .3 (10) + .7 (100) = 73$$

Therefore, allowing for competitive response leads to the conclusion that, on average, we would be better off maintaining price.

While building decision trees is clearly one way to proceed, it can be unwieldy given multiple competitors and the many possible strategies that could be employed. Moreover, the probabilities needed are at best estimates. Consequently, as a first cut, it is often useful to simply predict the basic strategy of competitors. This can be done as suggested in Figure 4–14. Then, assuming we are contemplating an unexpected strategy, we can simply indi-

FIGURE 4–13

Conditional strategy probabilities

cate the likely reactions of the competitors to various strategic alternatives as in Figure 4–15. While Figures 4–14 and 4–15 are much less elegant than either game theory or decision tree analysis, they are both easier to use and a more appropriate reflection of the typical level of information available for competitor analysis.

In general, there has been little systematic study of how to predict competitor moves. Using the airline industry as a case history, research examined

FIGURE 4–14   Expected Competitor Behavior

	Product Form Competitors		Product Category Competitors	
	Diet Coke	*"Price"—Diet Colas (Vintage, C&C, ...)*	*Coke*	*7UP*
Objective				
Strategy				
Mix elements:				
Product				
Price				
Advertising				
Promotion				
Distribution				

FIGURE 4–15   **Expected Competitive Response**

	Product Form Competitors		Product Category Competitors	
	Diet Coke	"Price"— Diet Colas	Coke	7UP
Environmental change:				
Overall demand				
Regulatory				
Competitive strategy change:				
1. (e.g., new product)				
2. (e.g., price cut)				

how competitors react to a competitive move (Chen, Smith, and Grimm, 1992). The main empirical findings were:

- The greater the competitive impact, the greater the number of responses made.
- The greater the intensity of the move, the greater the number of counteractions.
- The greater the implementation requirement, the smaller the number of responses.
- The more tactical the move, the greater the competitive response.

Illustrations

Super-Premium Ice Cream (ca. 1999)

The major competing brands to Dreyer's Dreamery are Ben & Jerry's, Häagen-Dazs, Starbucks, and Godiva. A product feature matrix is shown in Figure 4–16. A summary of the strategies, capabilities analysis, and expected future strategies, abbreviated to conserve space, is shown in Figure 4–17.

Objectives
All four brands appear to be pursuing market share strategies but for different reasons. Häagen-Dazs and Ben & Jerry's, as the category leaders with 42 percent and 38 percent shares respectively, are seeking to increase their category dominance with the latter attempting to overtake the former. Starbucks and Godiva, on the other hand, are attempting to gain enough share for a permanent foothold in the category.

FIGURE 4–16   Premium Ice Cream Product Features Matrix

	Dreamery	Ben & Jerry's	Häagen-Dazs	Starbucks	Godiva
Product Specifications					
Package size	16 oz. (pint)	16 oz. (pint)	16 oz. (pint)	16 oz. or 32 oz. (pint or quart)	12.5 oz.
Price per 1/2 cup serving*	0.82	0.82	0.80	0.82	1.05
Calories per 1/2 cup serving	220 to 310	250 to 280	230 to 310	250 to 280	250 to 340
Grams of fat per 1/2 cup serving	11 to 18	14 to 25	13 to 20	14 to 17	12 to 22
Packaging theme	Dreamy, colorful	Fun, goofy	Nonpictorial burgundy	Nonpictorial, green	Elegant, gold-colored
Texture					
Smooth	5	3	16	7	5
Chunky	13	17	7	4	1
Variety					
Total number of flavors	18	20	23	11	6
Chocolate	3	3	3	2	5
Vanilla	1	2	5	1	1
Strawberry	4	4	3	0	0
Exotic	9	10	9	1	0
Coffee	1	1	3	7	0
Reach					
Product-line extensions Distribution channels/ Strongest market	Supermarkets	Supermarkets, outlets	Supermarkets, outlets	Supermarkets,	Supermarkets

Source: *Dryer's Marketing Plans,* Haas School of Business, undated, p. 9.

Strategies

Ben & Jerry's: They are taking a very tactical view of the market with heavy expenditures on promotions.

Häagen-Dazs: The managers of this brand are focusing on the positioning of "indulgence." They are also targeting ethnic groups such as Hispanics.

Starbucks: Leveraging the Starbucks brand name from coffee is a primary strategy as well as targeting coffee-lovers. They are using a low price (within the category) to gain share.

Godiva: As might be expected, they are leveraging name strength in chocolates. Going upscale in the category by positioning as an "ultra"-

FIGURE 4-17 Super-Premium Ice Cream Competitor Analysis Summary

	Ben & Jerry's	Häagen-Dazs	Starbucks	Godiva
Strategies:	Heavy targeted promotions	Promotions focus on indulgence every day—contest to select the U.S.'s most indulgent cities "Passport to Indulgence"	Leverage the strength of the Starbuck's coffee brand name	Leverage the strength of the 75-year-old Godiva brand name in hand-crafted chocolates
	Elicit customer participation through contests, free cone days, mail-in offers		Target niche markets among coffee-lovers, where they have credibility, and those who have a "passion for chocolate"	Form successful ventures such as that with Dreyer's for quicker market penetration
	In addition to radio, which began two years ago, testing full-scale TV efforts in Phoenix and Sacramento on Memorial Day targets; hand-held cameras and footage of real-life fans of the folksy brand	Unveiled new flavors developed in direct response to demand for more ethnically diverse products. After Dulce de Leche, introduced Pineapple Coconut due to the many Hispanic consumers that have become loyal H-D users	Offer a lower price than the dominant players' in order to gain market share	Position itself as "America's first ultra-premium ice cream" by leveraging its reputation as ultra-premium confections
			Enter quickly by forming partnership with an industry powerhouse (Dreyer's)	Price their product higher, sell it in slightly smaller, elegant packaging to enhance its ultra-premium brand image
				Enhance reputation of decadence and luxury through product names
Differential Advantages/ Resources:	Socially responsible company = great PR	Worldwide brand: "We are the only brand in the world that uses the same brand name for all of its package forms, whether it's a packaged pint or quart or stick bar or whether we sell it to a food-service customer or in our dipping shops." Advantage when it comes to reinforcing brand with consumers	An established brand name; the largest coffee bar chain in the Western U.S.	Godiva's brand equity, which provides immediately credibility and name recognition in their target market
	1. Eco-Pint is an unbleached paperboard cup with printable clay coating (took three years to design); B&J is happy to share the recipe with anyone who takes them up		Specialty coffee flavors	Affordable luxury product. The ultimate in premium ice cream
	2. 7.5% of pretax profits donated to charity	Joint venture with Nestlé: complementary products in fragmented market—unites HD's powerful brand name with Nestlé's technology skills and broad distribution channels		
	Use of small "mom & pop" vendors			
	On a first-name basis with anyone that has tried their brand—very approachable brand image			
	Brand awareness generated by scoop shops (has 5% of retail ice cream sales in the US.)			
	Multiple product lines			

| Expected Future Strategies: | Increase advertising

Innovation—new flavors, look at consumer fad (new category: B&J's smoothies can be eaten out of the carton or as a blender drink).

Continue to develop "Healthy" line—a little bit older or consumers that need lower cholesterol or no dairy. Need to stock those products since consumer purchases won't be transferring over to full-fat—might lose purchase altogether

Channels—convenience stores, movies, etc.; 85% of sales are through grocery stores

Expansion to international arena | Innovation—new flavors, continue to try to capture various ethnic groups

Expand distribution through Nestlé's existing channels | Continue their expansion into nonchocolate market | Expand market share of their very niche market

Continue to focus on niche market of fine confection lovers and image-conscious individuals with limited resources who desire luxury |

Source: *Dryer's Marketing Plans*, Haas School of Business, undated, pp. 10–11.

premium is an attempt to further segment the category. General luxury positioning again is consistent with brand.

Capabilities Analysis

Ben & Jerry's: This company has been very successful at differentiating itself through a social responsibility theme as well as the personalities of its owners.

Häagen-Dazs: Main point of difference is a global brand name. This is aided by its joint venture with Nestlé.

Starbucks: The success of this brand is totally dependent upon its ability to extend the brand name from coffee to ice cream. The main strength is its huge retail coffee presence in the United States. The company has also developed a number of specialty coffee flavors that no one else offers.

Godiva: Like the other brands, the main point of difference is the name. None of the three main competitors can match the Godiva name for its symbolism of luxury.

Expected Future Strategies

Ben & Jerry's: The company was recently (2000) purchased by Unilever. With added financial strength, it will spend heavily on advertising and product development and expand distribution.

Häagen-Dazs: H-D will also look to develop new flavors and use its Nestlé connections to improve distribution.

Starbucks: The company has the most difficult job in the category as the brand name is perhaps too closely related to coffee. They will probably continue to expand their flavors (outside of the chocolate that they have been emphasizing) and their positioning.

Godiva: They will probably continue to do what they have been doing: emphasizing the luxury name and segment.

Personal Digital Assistants

In this category, there are many competitors and product features. A sampling of the features matrix is shown in Figure 4–18. The analysis focuses on the offerings from Handspring's two major competitors representing different operating system platforms, Palm (Palm OS) and Casio (Windows CE).

Brand Objectives

Since the PDA is in the growth stage of the life cycle, all of the products are trying to gain volume to bring down costs and establish market positions. This has resulted in a recent price drop of the major competitors (e.g., Palm) following the usual early skimming approach to grab those who need to be the first with the latest technology (at the highest price).

Figure 4-18 PDA Product Features Matrix

	Visor	Visor Deluxe	Palm III	Palm IIIe	Palm Pilot PE	PV-100	PV-200	Cassiopoeia E-100	Cassiopoeia E-11
Price (suggested retail price)	$179 ($149++)	$249	$162	$205	$235	$123	$100	$499	$276
Physical Properties									
Form factor	Pad	Pad	Pad	Pad	Pad	Pad	Pad	Pad	Pad
Size	4.8×3.0×0.7	4.8×3.0×0.7	4.7×3.6×0.7	4.7×3.2×0.7	4.7×3.2×0.7	4.9×3.2×0.6	4.9×3.2×0.6	5.1×3.3×0.8	4.9×3.3×0.8
Weight, oz.	5.4	5.4	6.4	5.8, 6.0 with battery	5.1		4.8	9	6.7
Memory and Processor Speed									
RAM, Processor speed	2 MB	8 MB	2 MB,16 MHz	2 MB	1 MB, 16 MHz	1 MB	2 MB	16 MB, 131 MHz	8 MB, 100 MHz
Expandable RAM	No	No	No	No	No	No	No	Yes	No
Display									
Diagonal screen size	3 in	3 in	4.1	4.1 in	4.1 in	4 in	4 in	3.9 in	3.9 in
Resolution			160 × 160		160 × 160	128 × 128	128 × 128	240 × 320	240 × 320
Color (If no, gray shades)	No, 16 shades	No, 16 shades	No, 4 shades	No	No, 4 shades	No, 4 shades	No, 4 shades	Yes	No, 4 shades
Touch screen	Yes	Yes	Yes	Yes	Yes	Yes	Yes	Yes	Yes
Backlight	Yes	Yes	Yes	Yes	Yes	Yes	Yes	Yes	Yes
Other									
Interfaces									
Total # of serial ports	0	0	1	1	1	1	1	1	1
Number of type II PC cards	0	0	0	0	0	0	0	0	1
IR port	Yes	Yes	Yes	Yes		0	0	Yes	Yes
Other ports		USB, Spring-board Slot							

101

Brand Strategies

Palm: This company has been decreasing price on the low-end models (Palm III) and introducing higher-end models (Palm V) with advanced features and color screens. The strategy is clear: offer different product options for different target segments. Of particular interest to Palm is the nonbusiness user, that is, an expansion into the "average" or home user segment.

Casio: Differentiating on the basis of the operating system is not working as, despite Microsoft's feelings to the contrary, users do not see the advantages of Windows CE over Palm's operating system. Therefore, Casio is attempting to differentiate on the basis of product features and not price.

Capabilities Analysis

Figure 4–19 shows a competitive capabilities matrix. The main implications follow.

Palm

Strengths: Market leader, cash availability, large number of software developers, large and strong community of users, strong brand equity.

Weaknesses: Lost key managers to Handspring, uncertainty from the spin-off from 3Com.

Casio:

Strengths: Economies of scale in production, creativity, good brand name (though weaker than Palm in this category).

Weaknesses: Dilution of resources into 61 different businesses run by the corporation.

Expected Future Strategies

Palm: Continued licensing of its operating system and establishing the Palm OS as the industry standard. If the Palm III does not work with the low-end, nonbusiness market, they will probably develop a new product just for this market. Possible venture into non-PDA products and applications that use the Palm OS (e.g., home Web appliances).

Casio: Continue to develop its head-to-head rivalry with Palm and build a brand around advanced and creative product innovation. Unlike Palm, Casio is already a known brand with the consumer market. Thus, like Palm, they will probably introduce a product into this segment soon.

FIGURE 4–19 Comparison of Competitive Resources: PDAs

Company's Ability to	Palm Pilot	Casio (Windows CE Platform)	Handspring
1. Conceive & Design (Technical and human resources, funding, etc.)	Loss of talent (many original Palm founders have left) may negatively impact its ability to create new products.	Casio is a Japanese company and given the way Japanese companies normally operate, we assume it has plenty of resources, both human and capital.	• Handspring has a great ability to conceive and design products since its founders created the Palm Pilot. They have a lot of experience, vision, and creativity. • Due to the founders' success, they have a lot of funding available to them since investors are confident with their ability to succeed. • Again, due to the founders' prior success and high-profile careers, Handspring has attracted the best talent to work here.
2. Produce (Physical and human resources)	Palm relies on contract manufacturers to produce its products. Given the volume produced by Palm, its leadership position, and the abundance of electronic contract manufacturers, Palm probably has no problems with production.	Great economies of scale. Plants worldwide.	• We depend on contract manufacturers to make the PDAs. Upside: many contract manufacturers so there is flexibility and we make what we need. Downside: we depend on someone else so we cannot entirely control quality and also in times when demand is great, we may not get what we want. We also have lower bargaining power relative to Palm due to smaller production volumes. • Handspring has good contacts with manufacturers since founders previously transacted with them. • Handspring depends on the module producers to make the modules. But again, we believe that, due to the abundance of consumer electronic manufacturers, the production of modules will not be difficult or too risky.
3. Market (Sales force, distribution, service/ sales policies, advertising, human resources, funding)	Palm is the leader and has been in the industry for several years. As such, it will have very good and strong relations with retailers. Retailers know that Palm sells and they will give Palm a relatively higher portion of the shelf space.	Strong marketing experience of electronics products to the channels.	• Because of start-up status, Handspring has limited, overworked resources. We are limited in how many PDAs we can sell and distribute over year 2000. • Need to market the most strategically attractive segments since we are resource (human and financial) constrained. • Limited sales force. • New and not very strong relationships with distribution channels, so may be harder to get Handspring in the door. • Internet is a good resource.
4. Finance (Debt, liquidity, cash flow, budget system, etc.)	Hard to separate from 3Com. Presumed to have growing sales with a 70+% market share.	Decreasing growth in sales and losses in the FY99.	Financially, we are limited to how much we can spend, so we can't be as aggressive as we would like. For example, we cannot target every segment in full force. We must focus on the most strategically attractive segment and will not be able to target all over the next year.

Summary

The analysis of competitors is a crucial element in preparing a sensible marketing strategy. Only by knowing what the competitors are likely to do can a firm hope to choose an optimal strategy. Essentially, competitor analysis involves: (1) assessing their objectives, (2) determining their current strategies, (3) evaluating their capabilities, and (4) forecasting their future strategies. This is the marketing equivalent of scouting and studying films in sports. Given the effort put into scouting in such diverse sports as high school football and America's Cup racing, where the financial gain is limited, it seems only reasonable that a company dealing with a multimillion-dollar product would want to be at least as well prepared.

References

Ansoff, H. Igor (1979) *Corporate Strategy.* Hammondsworth, Eng.: Penguin Books.

"At Apple Computer Proper Office Attire Includes a Muzzle." (1989) *The Wall Street Journal,* October 6.

Booz Allen & Hamilton Inc. (1982) *New Products Management for the 1980s.*

Chen, Ming-Jer, Ken G. Smith, and Curtis M. Grimm (1992) "Action Characteristics as Predictors of Competitive Responses," *Management Science,* 38:3, March, 439–55.

" 'Competitor Intelligence': A New Grapevine." (1989) *The Wall Street Journal,* April 12.

De Lisser, Eleena (1999) "Hearing and Seeing Business Travel Blab and Laptop Lapses," *The Wall Street Journal,* November, 8, A-1.

Fuld, Leonard M. (1988) *Monitoring the Competition.* New York: John Wiley & Sons.

Geyelin, Milo (1995) "Why Many Businesses Can't Keep Their Secrets," *The Wall Street Journal,* November 20, B-1.

Giges, Nancy, and Gay Jervey (1982) "W-L Plans Major Outlays," *Advertising Age,* May 3, 3.

Gilad, Benjamin, and Tamar Gilad (1989) "The Intelligence Audit." In *Advances in Competitive Intelligence,* ed. John Prescott. Vienna, Va.: Society of Competitive Intelligence Professionals, pp. 167–73.

Gomes, Lee (1999) "Upstart Linux Draws a Microsoft Attack Team," *The Wall Street Journal,* May 21, B-1.

Green, William (1998) "I Spy," *Forbes,* April 20, 90–96.

Gruner, Stephanie (1998) "Spies Like Us," *Inc.*

Guthrie, Julian (1993) "Brain Drain," *San Francisco Focus,* October, 24.

Hauser, John, and Donald Clausing (1988) "The House of Quality," *Harvard Business Review,* 66, May–June, 63–73.

Henderson, Bruce D. (1980) "The Experience Curve Revisited." *Perspectives,* no. 220. Boston: Boston Consulting Group.

Hussey, D. E. (1971) *Introducing Corporate Planning.* Oxford, Eng.: Pergamon Press.

Kahle, Lynn (1980) "Alternative Measurement Approaches to Consumer Values: The List of Values (LOV) and Values and Life Styles (VALS)," *Journal of Consumer Research,* 13, December, 405–9.

Lehmann, Donald R., Sunil Gupta, and Joel H. Steckel (1998) *Marketing Research.* Reading, MA: Addison-Wesley.

Lorge, Sarah (1999) "Attacking at a Moment of Weakness," *Sales and Marketing Management,* April, 13.

Maidique, Modesto A., and Peter Patch (1978) "Corporate Strategy and Technological Policy," working paper, Harvard Business School.

Main, Jeremy (1992) "How to Steal the Best Ideas Around," *Fortune,* October 19, 102–6.

McCartney, Scott (1999) "Upstart's Tactics Allow it to Fly in Friendly Skies of a Big Rival," *The Wall Street Journal,* June 29, B-1.

Mitchell, Arndt (1983) *The Nine American Life Styles.* New York: Warner Books.

Patzer, Gordon L. (1995) *Using Secondary Data in Marketing Research: United States and Worldwide.* Westport, CT: Quorum Books.

Porter, Michael E. (1979) "The Structure within Industries and Companies' Performance," *Review of Economics and Statistics,* 61, May, 214–27.

Prescott, John E., ed. (1989) *Advances in Competitive Intelligence.* Vienna, VA: Society of Competitive Intelligence Professionals.

Rangan, U. Srinivasa and Michael E. Porter (1992) "Ethical Dimensions of Competitive Analysis," Harvard Business School case #9-792-088.

Riche, Martha Farnsworth (1989) "Psychographics for the 1990s," *American Demographics,* 25–31.

Rokeach, Milton (1973) *The Nature of Human Value.* New York: Free Press.

Rothschild, William E. (1979) *Putting It All Together.* New York: AMACOM.

San Francisco *Chronicle* (1995) "MCI Details Assaults on the Baby Bells," March 7, D-2.

Teitelbaum, Richard S. (1992) "The New Race for Intelligence," *Fortune,* November 2, 104–7.

Upton, David M. and Stephen E. Macadam (1997) "Why (and How) to Take a Plant Tour," *Harvard Business Review,* May–June, 97–106.

Yovovich, B. G. (1989) "Customers Can Offer Competitive Insights," *Business Marketing,* March, 13.

Wasserman, Todd (2000) "Spy or Spinmeister?" *Marketing Computers,* 53–58.

Zachary, G. Pascal (1989) "At Apple Computer Proper Office Attire Includes a Muzzle," *The Wall Street Journal,* October 6, A–1.

Zellner, Wendy and Bruce Hager (1991) "Dumpster Raids? That's Not Very Ladylike, Avon," *Business Week,* April 1, 32.

5 Customer Analysis

Overview

Without customers, a business cannot survive. Although this may seem obvious, and despite the widespread adoption of the "marketing concept," many managers have regretted not obtaining sufficient information about their customers to develop products or strategies that meet customer needs. For example, despite spending millions of dollars on marketing research, automobile manufacturers missed the female market for years because they failed to adapt products and the sales environment to the fact that women were both influencing and making more automobile purchases.

In this chapter the term *customer* refers not only to current customers of a given product but also to both customers of competitors and current noncustomers of the product category (i.e., potential customers). It also refers to both immediate customers[1] (i.e., supermarkets and discount stores for consumer product companies such as P&G and manufacturers for component manufacturers such as Intel) and final customers (i.e., individuals and businesses).

Each customer is unique to some degree. As a consequence, mass marketing (one marketing program for all customers) is typically inefficient. Since it is time consuming and not very profitable to develop a separate strategy for each customer, some grouping of customers into segments is often useful.[2] Segmentation is a compromise between treating each cus-

---

[1]Customers, of course, include channel members. While we focus on end customers for the product or service, most of the analyses discussed apply equally to channel members.

[2]Some categories have so few customers that each can be treated as a separate segment and analyzed separately. Examples are passenger aircraft, military products (e.g., battle tanks), and nuclear generators. In addition, there is a trend toward *mass customization,* or one-to-one marketing, which focuses on marketing products and services to individuals rather than to segments. Examples are Levis custom-tailored jeans for women and Internet-based services that the user can customize (Pine, Victor, and Boynton, 1993).

tomer as unique and assuming all customers are equal. Segmentation programs provide insights about different kinds of customer behavior and make marketing programs more efficient. Of course the ultimate segmentation is at the individual level. As information technology has advanced, so-called one-to-one marketing has become a more viable approach, but segmentation is still the norm.

In this chapter, we do three things. First, we suggest an approach to systematically analyzing customers (Figure 5–1). Marketers need to answer eight questions. Who are the customers for this product or service? What are customers buying and how do they use it? (Customers buy benefits rather than simply product features or characteristics.) Where do customers buy products? When are purchase decisions made? How do customers make purchase decisions? Why do customers choose a particular product? In other words, how do they value one option over another? How do they respond to marketing programs such as advertising and promotions? And finally, will they buy it again? Second, we introduce the concept of long-term value of a customer. Finally, we discuss market segmentation. Both general criteria and specific analytical methods are presented.

What We Need to Know About Customers
Who Buys and Uses the Product

Buyers versus Users
For most industrial goods and many consumer products, the *who* must be broken into several different entities within the organization or household, including the following:

1. Initiator (who identifies the need for product).
2. Influencer (who has informational or preference input to the decision).
3. Decider (who makes the final decision through budget authorization).
4. Purchaser (who makes the actual purchase).
5. User.

The identities of the above customers can differ widely, particularly the user and the buyer. For example, in an industrial market, the end user may be an engineer who is concerned mainly with technical features, whereas the purchasing agent emphasizes cost and reliability of delivery. One reason for the success of Federal Express was its ability to take the decision on how to send overnight packages away from the shipping clerk by making the user the purchaser. Similarly, adults often purchase cereal, toys, or fast-food meals even though the user of the product is a child. McDonald's ads clearly recognize this and attempt to target both teenagers (who have money of

FIGURE 5-1   **What We Need to Know About Current And Potential Customers**

Who buys and uses the product
What customers buy and how they use it
Where customers buy
When customers buy
How customers choose
Why they prefer a product
How they respond to marketing programs
Will they buy it (again)?

their own) and the family meal segment, in which the child is likely to influence where the family goes to eat. Products targeted toward gift givers (e.g., silverware as a wedding gift) also highlight the difference between the buyer and the user.

This distinction among buyer, user, and other purchase influencers is particularly important for industrial products. The mark of a top salesperson is the ability to identify the different people involved in making a decision, understand the relative power over the purchase each person holds, and learn what they value. For example, in selling word processing software to a law firm, the needs of the secretaries (ease of use, mouse support, readable screen) differ from those of the office manager (high productivity, no bugs in the software, good service) and from the person approving the purchase (low cost, reliable delivery). Figure 5–2 provides a template for this kind of analysis.

Descriptive Variables: Consumer Products

The most obvious and popular basis for describing consumers is their general characteristics (Figure 5–3). The key categories are these:

1. *Demographic.* The most commonly used demographics are age, sex, geographic location, and stage in the family life cycle. These characteristics have the advantage of being relatively easy to ascertain. Unfortunately in many cases, segments based on demographics are not clearly differentiated in their behavior toward the product.
2. *Socioeconomic.* Socioeconomic variables include income and such related variables as education, occupation, and social class, with income and education generally being more useful. As in the case of demographics, the relationship between these variables and purchase behavior can be weak.
3. *Personality.* Given the relatively limited predictive power of demographic and socioeconomic variables, the fact that many marketing people are trained in psychology and the natural desire to find a general basis for dividing up consumers that will be useful across many

FIGURE 5–2   **Buying Roles and Needs / Benefits Sought**

Needs/Benefits Sought	Buying Roles				
	Initiator(s)	*Influencer(s)*	*Decider(s)*	*Purchaser(s)*	*User(s)*
A					
B					
C					
D					

situations, it is not surprising that marketers have attempted to use personality traits as a basis for segmentation. Unfortunately, personality variables have proven even less useful than demographic or socioeconomic variables in predicting purchasing behavior.

4. *Psychographics and values.* Psychographics basically represent an evolution from general personality variables to attitudes and behaviors more closely related to consumption of goods and services. Also known as lifestyle variables, psychographics generally fall into three categories: activities (cooking, sports, traveling, etc.), interests (e.g., art, music), and opinions. They are thus, not surprisingly, often referred to as AIO variables. These have been widely used as bases for segmentation and for the creation of advertising themes. Many researchers have used the VALS (Values and Lifestyles) typology and its updated version, VALS2 (see Figure 5–4), developed by SRI International as a basis for defining segments.[3] Figure 5–4 also shows a lifestyle typology, GLOBALSCAN, which was developed by the advertising agency Backer Spielvogel Bates Worldwide. GLOBALSCAN was based on a survey of 15,000 adults in 14 countries.

Another typology, the List of Values (LOV) Scale (Kahle, Beatty, and Homer, 1986), delineates nine basic values:

1. Self-respect.
2. Security.
3. Warm relationship with others.
4. Sense of accomplishment.
5. Self-fulfillment.

---

[3]Readers interested in categorizing themselves on the VALS2 scale can do this through the World Wide Web site *http://future.sri.com/vals/survey.html.*

FIGURE 5–3   Major Segmentation Variables for Consumer Markets

Variable	Typical Breakdown
Geographic	
Region	Pacific, Mountain, West North Central, West South Central, East North Central, East South Central, South Atlantic, Middle Atlantic, New England
City or metro size	Under 5,000; 5,000–20,000; 20,000–50,000; 50,000–100,000; 100,000–250,000; 250,000–500,000; 500,000–1,000,000; 1,000,000–4,000,000; 4,000,000 or over
Density	Urban, suburban, rural
Climate	Northern, southern
Demographic	
Age	Under 6, 6–11, 12–19, 20–34, 35–49, 50–64, 65+
Gender	Male, female
Family size	1–2, 3–4, 5+
Family life cycle	Young, single; young, married, no children; young, married, youngest child under 6; young, married, youngest child 6 or over; older, married, with children; older, married, no children under 18; older, single; other
Income	Under $10,000; $10,000–$15,000; $15,000–$20,000; $20,000–$30,000; $30,000–$50,000; $50,000–$100,000; $100,000 and over
Occupation	Professional and technical; managers, officials, and proprietors; clerical, sales; craftspeople, foremen; operatives; farmers; retired; students; homemakers; unemployed
Education	Grade school or less; some high school; high school graduate; some college; college graduate
Religion	Catholic, Protestant, Jewish, Muslim, Hindu, other
Race	White, black, Asian
Nationality	American, British, French, German, Italian, Japanese
Psychographic	
Social class	Lower lowers, upper lowers, working class, middle class, upper middles, lower uppers, upper uppers
Lifestyle	Straights, swingers, longhairs
Personality	Compulsive, gregarious, authoritarian, ambitious
Behavioral	
Occasions	Regular occasion, special occasion
Benefits	Quality, service, economy, speed
User status	Nonuser, ex-user, potential user, first-time user, regular user
Usage rate	Light user, medium user, heavy user
Loyalty status	None, medium, strong, absolute
Readiness stage	Unaware, aware, informed, interested, desirous, intending to buy
Attitude toward product	Enthusiastic, positive, indifferent, negative, hostile

Source: Philip Kotler, Marketing Management, 8th ed. (Upper Saddle River, N.J.: Prentice Hall, 1994), p. 271. Adapted with permission.

FIGURE 5–4   **Lifestyle Typologies**

VALS	VALS2	GLOBALSCAN
Inner-directed consumers	Principle-oriented consumers	Strivers
Societally conscious	Fulfilleds	
Experientials	Believers	Achievers
I-am-me consumers		
Outer-directed consumers	Status-oriented consumers	Pressured
Achievers	Achievers	
Emulators	Strivers	Adapters
Belongers		
Need-driven consumers	Action-oriented consumers	Traditionals
Sustainers	Experiencers	
Survivors	Makers	
	Strugglers	

6. Sense of belonging.
7. Respect from others.
8. Fun and enjoyment.
9. Excitement.

These typologies are often related to purchasing patterns and afford the product manager the opportunity to match potential buyers with the appropriate media and message to communicate with them (Corfman, Lehmann, and Narayanan, 1991).

Descriptive Variables: Industrial Products

The same type of variables used to describe consumers can also be used to describe organizations (see Figure 5–5 for a list of some of the most popular variables used). For industrial product customers, the traditional focus has been on firm characteristics such as size of the company, industry, and location, that is, the demographic variables appropriate for describing companies. However, a variety of other kinds of variables can be used, such as operating variables (e.g., customer technology), purchasing approaches (e.g., centralized versus decentralized purchasing operations), situational factors (e.g., order size), and "personal" characteristics (e.g., attitude toward risk).

Concepts of personality and psychographics can also be applied in the context of organizations. Although it may be unusual to think of a firm as having a personality, one important segmentation variable in technologically oriented industries is innovativeness. The innovators, organizations that adopt new technologies earlier than others in their industry, are often referred to as "lead users." Lead users have two characteristics: (1) They face general needs months or years before the bulk of the industry does, and (2) they can benefit significantly by obtaining an early solution to those

FIGURE 5–5   Major Segmentation Variables for Business Markets

Demographic
- *Industry:* Which industries should we focus on?
- *Company size:* What size companies should we focus on?
- *Location:* What geographical areas should we focus on?

Operating Variables
- *Technology:* What customer technologies should we focus on?
- *User/nonuser status:* Should we focus on heavy, medium, light users, or nonusers?
- *Customer capabilities:* Should we focus on customers needing many or few services?

Purchasing Approaches
- *Purchasing-function organization:* Should we focus on companies with highly centralized or decentralized purchasing organizations?
- *Power structure:* Should we focus on companies that are engineering dominated, financially dominated, etc.?
- *Nature of existing relationships:* Should we focus on companies with which we have strong relationships or simply go after the most desirable companies?
- *General purchase policies:* Should we focus on companies that prefer leasing? Service contracts? Systems purchases? Sealed bidding?
- *Purchasing criteria:* Should we focus on companies that are seeking quality? Service? Price?

Situational Factors
- *Urgency:* Should we focus on companies that need quick and sudden delivery or service?
- *Specific application:* Should we focus on certain applications of our product rather than all applications?
- *Size of order:* Should we focus on large or small orders?

Personal Characteristics
- *Buyer–seller similarity:* Should we focus on companies whose people and values are similar to ours?
- *Attitudes toward risk:* Should we focus on risk-taking or risk-avoiding customers?
- *Loyalty:* Should we focus on companies that show high loyalty to their suppliers?

Source: Philip Kotler, *Marketing Management,* 8th ed. (Upper Saddle River, N.J.: Prentice Hall, 1994), p. 278. Adapted with permission.

needs (Urban and von Hippel, 1988). These are obviously valuable customers, as they not only provide early sales and spread (hopefully) favorable word of mouth information but also help the company make necessary product modifications and improvements.

Many of the same variables used to segment markets for consumer and industrial goods are used to segment markets internationally. Figure 5–6 lists key segmentation variables used in direct marketing campaigns in Europe.

What Customers Buy and How They Use It

The most obvious answer to the "what" question revolves around the identity of the items or services purchased (including market shares, purchase

FIGURE 5–6 Key Segmentation Variables Used in Direct Marketing Campaigns in Europe

	Belgium	Denmark	France	Germany	Greece	Ireland	Italy	Netherlands	Portugal	Spain	UK
Most commonly used consumer segmentation criteria	Social class Nielsen zones Geographic Database	Demographic from census Database	Sociodemographic Database	Age Profession Income Family status Lifestyle	Urban/rural Profession Database	Age Income Profession Family status Database	Age Sex Profession Housing types	Age Sex Geographic Lifestyle Database	Income Urban/rural Education Political bias Database	Age Sex Education Urban/rural Geographic proximity	Age Sex Profession Lifestyle Database
Most commonly used business segmentation criteria	SIC* Size VAT	SIC Size Turnover Decision	SIC Size Turnover	SIC Turnover Size	Size Turnover SIC	Size Turnover Location Liquidity	SIC Size Turnover Number of telephone lines	Size/SIC Turnover Branches Credit rating Decision makers	Size SIC	Database Size Turnover	SIC Size

*SIC: Standard Industrial Classification.
Source: *Marketing Director International*, 1991.

113

amounts, and features chosen). Any product manager who doesn't have such basic data is generally not long employed.

Benefits

Though many product managers do not seem to realize it, customers do not purchase products and services for the features of the product; rather, customers purchase the *benefits* the product provides. In other words, the firm produces features but customers purchase benefits. Recognizing this distinction is a particular problem in technology-driven companies that tend to focus on the development of new technologies and fancy products without adequate concern about whether the benefits the technology provides solve the customers' problems better than the old products do.

Focusing on benefits is also important in understanding the competitive set. The old story about the drill manufacturer that recognized it was selling holes, not drills, not only indicates that benefits are more important than the physical product but also helps to define the competition based on the benefit (referred to in Chapter 2 as *generic competition*). As Figure 5–2 shows, the needs or benefits sought can vary with the buying role in the decision-making unit (as well as by customer segment).

For example, consider a Cadillac Seville. The following distinction can be drawn between features and benefits:

Feature	Benefit
300 horsepower engine	The ability to pull away quickly from potentially dangerous situations. With the increased traffic, you'll feel much safer in this car.
Northstar engine	Engine will not need a tuneup for the first 100,000 miles. You'll enjoy a smooth-running engine with fewer trips to the dealer for service.
Adjustable seats	Controls allow you to make easy adjustments to your seating position so you'll stay fit, alert, and comfortable throughout your trip.
ABS brakes	Even if you step hard on these brakes, your wheels won't lock up and skid. This means you'll have an extra margin of safety.

This kind of description, which can be used in a print ad or as part of a sales pitch, appeals both to the features-hungry customer and to the customer who needs the features translated into terms he or she can understand.

One key trend is the increased use of customer databases for target marketing and customer retention programs. Database marketers often use three criteria for evaluating and segmenting customers in their databases:

1. Recency: How recently has the customer bought from you?
2. Frequency: How many different products does the customer buy, and what are the time intervals?
3. Monetary value: What is the value of the customer's purchases in terms of profits?

The RFM approach is used to rate each customer in the database on a scale, perhaps by multiplying the three criteria and then rank ordering customers in terms of attractiveness. When prospecting for new customers, top-ranked customers can be profiled using the descriptors noted earlier, and then potential customers can be matched against these descriptors.

Product Assortment
Another useful piece of information related to the "what" question involves the number of different brands purchased by customers in the segments. For many frequently purchased consumer goods, panel or similar data are available that provide purchase histories for individual consumers (e.g., brands purchased were A, A, A, B, A, A, C, A, A, A). For industrial products, it is useful to understand how many different vendors a customer employs and the assortment of models, quality levels, and the like from which the customer chooses. For example, a new plastic may be useful for replacing zinc, aluminum, brass, and so on. For Federal Express, segments might consist of customers of Emery, DHL, UPS, the U.S. Postal Service, fax, and e-mail.

Product Use
Arm & Hammer found out about putting a box in the refrigerator and using baking soda to deodorize drains from customer suggestions. Often customers find uses for a product that the company never dreamed of. Interestingly, the way a product is used may or may not be related to why customers originally bought it.

In addition, defining the exact situation in which the product or service is used is crucial to understanding customers. This includes both where they use it (e.g., at home or in the office) and on what occasions (e.g., for entertaining or everyday use).

Where Customers Buy

Where customers make purchase decisions is a critical input into decisions about the channels of distribution. Many product managers think of channels as being fixed and traditional, but customers migrate to other channels as their information needs and other market conditions change.

Take, for example, the home stereo market. During the 1960s, consumers started replacing consoles (the turntable, tuner, and amplifier housed in what looks like a piece of furniture) with stereo components. The locus of purchase was mainly small stereo stores and some mail-order firms. In the 1990s most of these purchases occurred in electronics superstores such as Circuit City. Recently the Internet has emerged as an important source.

Why did this happen? Several important changes occurred. First, consumers' need for information diminished over time. The component system is no longer a novelty; most people today are not buying their first system but upgrading an old one. Media such as *Consumer Reports* provide excellent information on features and quality. Thus, whereas customers relied on salespeople for technical information and product comparisons in the 1960s, the Circuit City salesperson merely indicates what is on sale and whether it is in stock. In addition, more products are available, which has brought down margins. Large-volume retailers typically dominate in such an environment.

A similar picture emerged in personal computers. The small computer retailers gave way to large hardware and software superstores such as CompUSA, specialized software discounters such as Egghead, mail-order firms such as Dell and Gateway 2000, and eventually Internet sites.

Therefore, tracking where customers are making purchases is very important. The phenomenon of moving from specialty retailer to discounter is often repeated and predictable.

When Customers Buy

A relevant dimension to understanding customers is the timing issue. When they buy encompasses time of year, time of month, and even time of day. Fast-food operators, for example, are known to segment by "daypart," that is, breakfast, lunch, dinner, and snacking times. *When* also includes when customers buy in terms of sales or price breaks and rebates, on the assumption that those who buy because of a special deal (i.e., deal-prone consumers) may be different than those who pay full price.

Some sales variation is predictable due to the nature of the product. Snowblower sales to end users are most likely to be highest during winter or in late fall; sales to channels occur earlier. Capital equipment sales are often made near the end of a fiscal year to spend money that may not be there next year. However, highly seasonal categories are less attractive due to the pressures placed on manufacturing, personnel, and cash flow. Thus, competitors in such categories look for ways to even out demand as much as possible. For example, cold remedies are marketed well before the major cold seasons to get households to stock up and lock out competing brands.

How Customers Choose

One major focus is on how customers collect (or are exposed to) information about products (e.g., advertisements, in-store personnel, brochures, magazines, or, increasingly, the Internet). In addition to defining information sources, the process used to make decisions is relevant. Often the decision process is emotional, holistic, automatic, and/or spontaneous. (Responses to the question "How did you choose it?" include "I just wanted it," "It was in stock," "The old one broke/ran out," or "I just grabbed something.") Knowing the manner in which choice is made is relevant to strategy decisions even when the decision process is not very deliberate. Frequently, however, the process is, or can be described as, "rational." For this type of decision, customers compare alternatives on features via a multiattribute model.

The Multiattribute Model

The process of how customers make decisions has been extensively studied (Wilkie, 1990). In addition, comprehensive models have been developed that focus on consumer decision processes (Howard, 1989), information processing (Bettman, 1979), and organizational buying behavior (Johnston and Lewin, 1996). It is thus impossible to provide a comprehensive discussion here of how customers make choices. However, the multiattribute model offers a concise and practical conceptualization of customer decision making that is useful in both consumer and industrial product contexts.

The multiattribute model of decision making is composed of four parts. First, the products or alternatives in a product category are assumed to be collections of attributes. Attributes can be defined in terms of physical characteristics or, as described earlier, as benefits sought. In addition, each customer is assumed to have a perception about how much of each attribute the alternatives in a product category contain. Third, each customer is assumed to place an importance value or weight on obtaining each attribute when making a choice in the category. Finally, customers are assumed to combine the attribute and importance weight information using some process, or *rule,* to develop their most preferred option in the product category. We therefore address four questions:

1. Which attributes do customers use to define a product?
2. How do customers determine how much of each attribute a brand possesses?
3. How are the importance weights determined?
4. What decision rule is used to combine the information?

Attributes.   To apply the multiattribute model, one must first identify the set of relevant attributes. This is not easy; using managerial judgment alone can seriously misestimate the number and types of attributes used in making decisions.

One way to collect such information is through focus group research. Participants in the focus group are first selected from the relevant segment(s). The moderator of the focus group then elicits from the set of respondents what characteristics or benefits the customers want to see in a product.

A second approach is through survey-based methods. Determining the set of attributes can be accomplished through open-ended and/or fixed-response questions. For example, to determine the set of attributes for a notebook computer, the product manager could ask the respondent to list (open-ended) or check off (closed-ended) those used in making a decision.

Perceptions. Once the attributes have been identified, the next step is to determine customers' perceptions of the amount of each attribute possessed by each brand or product option in the category. This is often done by direct questioning. Suppose that weight is a key attribute of a notebook computer. Then the following question could be asked: "On a 1 to 7 scale where 1 is the lightest and 7 is the heaviest, how heavy is the _____ brand of laptop computer?" This question would be asked for all the brands or models of interest to the product manager (often restricted to those the customer was familiar with). Similar questions would be used for other attributes.

An indirect approach to determining perceptions uses a marketing research methodology called *multidimensional scaling* (also referred to as *perceptual mapping*). This method provides a spatial representation of the brands in a product category based on customers' perceptions of similarity (or dissimilarity, depending on the exact method used). The characteristics used to differentiate customers' perceptions of the brands are inferred from their relative locations in the product space. The perceptions of the characteristics are inferred from their positions along the axes in the space.

Suppose a bank manager is interested in understanding customers' perceptions of the five retail (consumer) banks in a city. The manager could first enlist a sample of respondents, perhaps 100. The task could take several forms. One approach is to take all the possible pairs of the five banks (10) and ask each respondent to rate on some scale—say, 1 to 10, with 10 being the most similar—how similar each pair is. A computer program (e.g., SAS) would then be used to locate the banks in a multidimensional space such that the number of dimensions was as small as possible but that also replicated the implied perceptual distances between the banks. Figure 5–7 shows a representative output of such a program.

Each bank is represented by a point in the two-dimensional space. The distances between the points closely replicate the information given by the respondents. For example, banks B and E are the farthest apart in the space. This means that those two banks were perceived to be the most dissimilar. The labels on the two axes (the attributes) can be determined by two methods: judgmentally based on the manager's knowledge of the market, or estimated based on other information collected from the respondents. The map leads to two major implications. First, the two key characteristics used by bank customers in this city are the courtesy of the personnel and the convenience of the locations of the automated teller machines (ATMs). Second, the perceived performance of the banks on those attributes differs. Bank E

FIGURE 5–7

Bank perceptual map

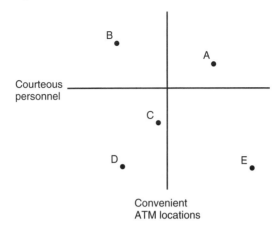

is perceived to have the surliest personnel, and bank D has the most convenient ATM locations.

   Thus, perceptual mapping can give useful information about both the characteristics being used in assessing perceived similarities and dissimilarities among products and perceptions of the products on those characteristics. While not generally thought of as a substitute for direct questioning, it can provide useful supplemental information.

Importance Weights.   Like product attribute ratings, attribute importance weights can be assessed through direct questioning. Returning to the notebook computer example, a sample question could be the following: "On a 1 to 7 scale with 7 being very important, how important is weight in your purchase decision?" The same question would then be asked on the other attributes, such as speed of the microprocessor, screen viewing characteristics, and so on. The respondent could also be asked to rank order the attributes in terms of importance.

   An alternative approach uses *conjoint analysis* (Green and Wind, 1975). This method permits the product manager to infer the importance of different product attributes from customer rank orderings of alternative product bundles of attributes.

   As an example, assume there are three important attributes in a notebook/subnotebook computer purchase decision: weight, battery life, and brand. Assume also that each characteristic can have two different levels or values, as shown in Figure 5–8. The respondent's task is to rank order the eight combinations from the most preferred to the least preferred.

FIGURE 5–8   Conjoint Analysis: Notebook Computers

Assume 3 attributes of laptop computer choice:
  Weight (3 pounds or 5 pounds)
  Battery life (2 hours or 4 hours)
  Brand name (Gateway, Compaq)
Task: Rank order the following combinations of these characteristics from 1 = Most preferred to
  8 = Least preferred

Combination	Rank
3 pounds, 2 hours, Gateway	4
5 pounds, 4 hours, Compaq	5
5 pounds, 2 hours, Gateway	8
3 pounds, 4 hours, Gateway	3
3 pounds, 2 hours, Compaq	2
5 pounds, 4 hours, Gateway	7
5 pounds, 2 hours, Compaq	6
3 pounds, 4 hours, Compaq	1

In Figure 5–8, a hypothetical response to the rank ordering task gives a 1 to the most preferred combination and an 8 to the least preferred. One combination (three pounds, four hours, and a Compaq) clearly dominates, and another (five pounds, two hours, and a Gateway) is clearly the least preferred. However, tradeoffs must be made for the combinations of attributes between those two options. In this case, the average rank for the three-pound options is 2.5 ($[1 + 2 + 3 + 4]/4$), for the five-pound options, 6.5; for the four-hour options, 4.0, for the two-hour option, 5.0; for the Compaq, 3.5, and for Gateway, 5.5. Looking at the differences in the average ranks, the most important characteristic to this respondent is weight (difference = 4.0), followed by the brand name (2.0) and finally battery life (1.0). While the actual analysis and design of conjoint studies are more complicated than this, the basic ideas are the same.

An example of how importance weights can vary by market segment is shown in Figure 5–9 for the personal computer market. There is a dramatic difference in the rankings of the attributes when comparing the attributes/benefits among home users, information systems (IS) professionals, and managers. Note also how price, commonly thought to always be the most important attribute, is way down the list for IS professionals and not even on the lists for the home users and managers.

Combining the Information.   The most common way to combine attribute information is to use a *compensatory* rule, which simply multiplies each attribute importance weight by the attribute value and sums these terms for each person and product as in Figure 5–10. The product of impor-

FIGURE 5–9

Importance weight variation by segment

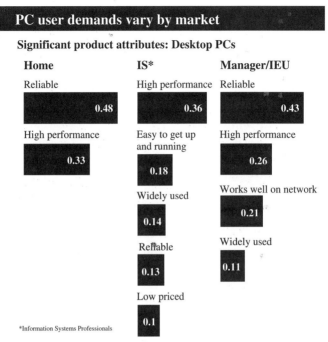

Source: *Brandweek,* December 5, 1994, p. 21. © 1994 ASM Communications, Inc. Used with permission.

FIGURE 5–10   Multiattribute Decision Making: Compensatory Rule

	Segment 1	Segment 2	Segment 3
Attribute A	Weight $\times$ Rating = Score$_{1a}$		
Attribute B	Score$_{1b}$		
Attribute C	Score$_{1c}$		
Attribute D	Score$_{1d}$		
Attribute E	Score$_{1e}$		
Segment Score	Score$_{1a}$ + ... + Score$_{1e}$		

tance weight times rating is simply summed down each column of the table to get a score for each segment. A separate score is constructed for each competing brand.

Although it is difficult to determine the combination rule, if the implied ranking of the brands from the algebraic combination of importance weights and attribute perceptions does not generally match the rank order of market shares, other rules may be in effect.[4] For example, a *lexicographic* rule first compares all products on the most important characteristic alone and eliminates those which are not at the top. A *conjunctive* rule assumes the customer sets minimum cutoffs on each dimension and rejects a product if it has any characteristic below the cutoff. A compensatory rule such as the multi-attribute model implies that all attributes are considered and that weakness in one can be compensated for (hence the name) by strength in another. However, since the conjunctive rule is not compensatory, weakness on one dimension (a "requirement") may rule out purchasing by many customers.

Customers as Problem Solvers

Customers can be described in terms of the difficulty of the problem they are attempting to solve (Howard, 1989). In extensive problem-solving (EPS) situations, customers are concerned mainly with understanding how the product works, what it competes with, and how they would use it. EPS is generally found among first-time purchasers and with products that are technologically new. Limited problem solving (LPS) occurs when the customer understands the basic functioning of the product and what it competes with, and is concerned with evaluating the brand on a small number of attributes, typically in comparison to alternatives. This is generally the approach to most large-ticket purchases when the customer has made purchases in the category before (e.g., consumer durables). The third basic type of purchase is routinized (RRB), where customers essentially follow a predetermined rule for making decisions. Most routine order purchases fall into this category, but so do many big-ticket items (e.g., some people always buy a Volvo). Since customers who follow this approach can be expected to ignore most information because they have already reached a decision, the implications for marketing strategy are dramatic. Product managers with a winning product that is bought routinely should make it easy for the customer to keep buying. If a product has little market share and the objective is to increase it, the product manager must "shock" the customer into considering the product to break him or her of the routine. Promotions, significant price breaks, and free samples are useful shock devices.

Why They Prefer a Product

The fourth, and in some ways the most critical, component of customer analysis examines why customers make purchase decisions. Central to this question is the concept of *customer value:* what the product is worth to the customer. Customer value thus depends on the benefits offered (from the

---

[4]Of course, there are other explanations, such as a dominated brand being a more effective marketer in terms of distribution. Many of the brands rated highly by *Consumer Reports* do not have the highest market shares in their categories.

customer's perspective) and the costs involved (price, maintenance, etc.). The concept of value is very different from cost: An item costing only pennies to produce may be worth thousands of dollars if it solves an important problem in a timely and efficient manner, and a product that is expensive to produce may have little value. Knowing the value customers place on a product makes it much easier to make key decisions such as setting price.

The customer value of a brand is composed of three basic elements:

1. Importance of the usage situation.
2. Effectiveness of the product category in the situation.
3. Relative effectiveness of the brand in the situation.

Thus, customer value involves two basic notions of value: *absolute* value, which essentially assumes no competing brand exists (points 1 and 2 above) and *relative* value, which involves comparison of a product with other products. Because new markets eventually attract competitors, it is the relative effectiveness of a brand that determines its eventual share and profitability. Put differently, customer value encompasses both product form and product category competitors. It is therefore important to determine not only the usage situations for which the product category has value but also how various competitive products compare (e.g., most chemical product categories in which formulations vary eventually are chosen based on physical properties such as rigidity and stability under different temperatures).

Sources of Customer Value

Sources of value (benefits) can be classified into three broad categories: economic, functional, and psychological.

Economic.   A fundamental source of value is the economic benefit a customer derives from using a product. This is a particularly relevant aspect in business-to-business situations and is often formalized as the economic value to the customer (see Appendix 5–A). Essentially it is the net financial benefit to the customer from using one product versus another.

Functional.   Functional value is defined by those aspects of a product that provide functional or utilitarian benefits to customers. In other words, value is provided by the performance features of a product (e.g., luggage capacity, fuel economy).

A particularly important category of functional characteristics involves service. Customers derive value from three kinds of service. Before-sales service involves providing information. Time-of-sales service facilitates purchase, such as reliable and fast delivery, installation and startup, and convenient financial terms. After-sales service involves providing both routine and emergency maintenance. Nothing is more likely to cement a long-term customer relationship than speedy and effective reaction to a problem or more apt to destroy one than a slow and bureaucratic response. Monitoring service quality has (appropriately) become a much more important activity.

Psychological: Brand Equity.   A third source of value is basically the image of the product. This includes how the product "feels" (e.g., sporty, luxurious, high-tech) and whether that feeling matches the image the customer wants to project. Price is clearly part of product image; some customers may prefer a high price (either because they view price as a signal of quality or engage in conspicuous consumption), whereas others prefer a low price. The importance of image (as opposed to functional attributes) was highlighted by adverse reaction to Coke's formula change (even though it was preferred in blind taste tests) and the strong positive reaction to the reintroduction of Classic Coca-Cola.

Recently, partly inspired by a wave of corporate takeovers, the value of the brand name per se has received much attention (Aaker, 1991, 1996). To a customer, *brand equity* is the value of a product *beyond* that explainable by economic and functional attributes. (Brand equity also represents value to the manufacturer, which is discussed in Chapter 7.) It can be represented by the premium a customer would pay for one product over another when the economic and functional attributes are identical.

A number of methods exist for measuring brand equity at the customer level including Y&R's Brand Asset Valuator, Research International's Equity Engine, and Millward-Brown's Brand Z. Basically they break down into four broad categories (see also Aaker, 1996; Keller, 1998):

1. *Awareness.* Being aware of a brand is usually a requirement for its purchase (at least for sober customers) and tends to lead to more favorable opinions by reducing the risk associated with a familiar option.
2. *Associations.* Images related to overall quality as well as specific product attributes and user characteristics (e.g., young, hip) impact the reaction to a brand.
3. *Attitude.* Overall favorability toward a brand is a critical part of brand equity. A special form of this is inclusion in the consideration set (that is, the willingness to consider buying the brand, similar to being on an approved supplier list in business-to-business marketing) or put differently, acceptability.
4. *Attachment.* Loyalty to a brand is the strongest type of equity (although in the extreme case of addiction it may have some undesirable consequences), and most beneficial for sellers. In the extreme (100 percent retention), it guarantees a nonending stream of income.

Manifestations of Customer Value

A variety of signs of the value of a product are evident even without special efforts to measure them:

Price. Price is the company's assessment of the product's value.

Price sensitivity. A product with constant sales when prices increase generally is of greater value than one for which demand slumps.

Satisfaction. Survey-based satisfaction measures are standard practice in our business (e.g., course evaluations).

Complaints and compliments. The number of complaints or compliments the company receives indicates the product's value.

Word-of-mouth. Although often difficult to track, spoken and written comments provide a useful subjective assessment of a product's value. (Monitoring chat rooms and bulletin boards on the Web is a useful way to track word-of-mouth.)

Margin / profit contribution. Generally, higher margins indicate partially monopolistic positions due to greater communicated value.

Dollar sales. Total dollar sales provide an aggregate measure of the value of a product as assessed by the market.

Competitive activity. Competitive activity such as new-product introductions indicates that the total gap between customer value and company costs is sufficiently large to allow for profits even when more companies divide the market.

Repeat purchase rate. High loyalty indicates high brand value.

Assessing the Value of the Product Category

Many ways can be devised to estimate the value of a product category. One particularly useful method focuses on the value of different uses or applications of a product.

1. Determine the uses of the product. Like the substitution in use approach discussed in Chapter 2 for generating generic competitors, a first step is to determine the present and potential uses to which a particular product category can be put.
2. Estimate the importance of the uses. This estimate could focus on individual customers or market segments and may simply be projected sales to the segment.
3. List competing products for the uses.
4. Determine the relative effectiveness of the product category in each usage situation.

An overall value of the product category can be estimated by summing over all uses of the importance of the use times the relative effectiveness of the

FIGURE 5–11   Personal Computer Product Category Value

Use	(IMP) Importance	Competitive Products	(REL) Relative Effectiveness	Category Value (IMP) × (REL)
Video games	Some 20	TV attachments, board games	Very good	High
Bookkeeping	None 1	Accountant, service bureau, "books"	Marginal	Low
Learning skills	Very low 4	Books, school	Inferior	Low
Data analysis	Large 65	Large-scale computer, time sharing, consultant, calculator	Good	High
Report preparation	A little 10 100	Typewriter, word processor, secretarial service	OK	Fairly low

product category. A hypothetical example of this approach, based on the personal computer category, appears in Figure 5–11. Rather than using numbers, this scale uses adjectives. Although it is fairly easy to structure a table like Figure 5–11, some of the entries will be hard to quantify. However, the main value of the exercise is to generate broad indicators toward which particular uses of the microcomputer should be targeted.

Assessing the Value of the Brand/Product/Service

Assessing the total value of a brand can be done indirectly. A high value brand has high share, high repeat purchase rate, low elasticity with respect to price, and limited competitive brand shopping. Using customer responses to estimate the value of a brand generally involves direct ratings. This includes several different approaches:

1. *Direct ratings* on a scale (e.g., "How good is X for use Y?") for competing products. Remember we are generally interested in relative and not absolute value. Therefore, an average of 4 on a 5-point scale indicates good value if the other products are getting 2s and 3s, but little value if the other products are getting averages of 4.5 and 4.8.
2. *Constant sum ratings across brands,* such as "Please rate the following brands by dividing 10 points among them":

   Brand A   _____
   Brand B   _____
   Brand C   _____
   Brand D   _____
   Total   10

3. *Graded paired comparisons,* which require customers to indicate which of a pair of products is preferred and by how much. This is often done in terms of dollar amounts (Pessemier, 1963), as shown in Figure 5–12.

Figure 5–12   Dollar Metric Example: Soft Drink Preference

Pair of Brands (more preferred brand circled)	Amount Extra Willing to Pay to Get a Six-Pack of the More Preferred Brand (cents)
Data	
(Coke) Pepsi	2
(Coke) 7UP	8
(Coke) Dr. Pepper	5
(Coke) Fresca	12
(Pepsi) 7UP	6
(Pepsi) Dr. Pepper	3
(Pepsi) Fresca	10
7UP, (Dr. Pepper)	3
(7UP) Fresca	4
(Dr. Pepper) Fresca	7

	Analysis		
Coke:	+ 2 (versus Pepsi) + 8 (versus 7UP + 5 (versus Dr. Pepper) + 12 (versus Fresca)	=	27
Pepsi	− 2 + 6 + 3 + 7	=	17
7UP	− 8 − 6 − 4 + 4	=	−13
Dr. Pepper	− 5 − 3 + 3 + 7	=	2
Fresca	− 12 − 10 − 4 − 7	=	−33

4. *Conjoint analysis* of customer ratings of products described in terms of attributes, including price and brand name. Through analysis (basically regression analysis), the relative importances of the attributes, as well as the values of different levels of these attributes, are determined.

How They Respond to Markting Programs

In addition to the product itself, sensitivity to and preference for prices (and means of payment), distribution and availability (including the effect of direct marketing), advertising, promotion, and service are fundamental aspects of a market. Moreover, sensitivity typically varies by customer and at least a segment-level analysis is usually called for. Methods for assessing sensitivity include:

1. *Expert judgment,* using the knowledge of managers, the salesforce, and the like.
2. *Customer survey–based methods,* including both direct questioning (e.g., "How important is . . . ?") and more subtle approaches such as conjoint analysis.
3. *Experiments,* in both controlled settings (e.g., in shopping malls or specially designed stores or labs) and actual markets.

4. *Analyses of past data,* comparing results across markets, or where individual customer record data are available (e.g., scanner data) at the individual level. Such analysis often uses techniques such as regression analysis to predict sales as a function of mix elements or logit analysis (basically a type of regression) to assess the impact of mix elements on market share or individual choice probabilities.

Assessing sensitivity to elements of the marketing mix is a large, ongoing task. The output of this assessment has implications primarily for the tactical/programmatic elements of marketing (e.g., how much to spend on advertising). Since this assessment requires specialized data not readily available outside the company, we do not discuss mix assessment in detail here.

Will They Buy It (Again)?

A critical issue involves whether customers will purchase the product in the future, which heavily depends on their satisfaction with the product.

Satisfaction

Perhaps the most obvious trend in business in the late 1980s and early 1990s was the religious zeal with which quality programs were promoted, especially in the United States. Providing quality in order to satisfy current customers and retain them in the future is a logical consequence of the basic principle of marketing, to create and maintain customers. So-called relationship marketing also stresses the long-term value of a customer where a single transaction (sale) is not the ultimate goal.

Quality is ultimately measured in terms of customer satisfaction. Further, satisfaction has a strong relative component to it. (Are customers of a certain product category more or less satisfied than those of a different but potentially substitutable one? Are customers of my company's product more or less satisfied than customers of a competitor's?)

The direct measurement of satisfaction has evolved to consider several aspects:

1. Expectations of performance/quality.
2. Perceived performance/quality.
3. The gap between expectations and performance.

Much of the early work on satisfaction focused on the gap between expectations and performance, and a widely used scale called SERVQUAL (Parasuraman, Zeithaml, and Berry, 1988) was developed based on it. Subsequently, however, emphasis has also been placed on the direct impact of expectations and performance on satisfaction as well as the effect of expectations on perceived performance (Anderson and Sullivan, 1993; Boulding, Staelin, Kalra, and Zeithaml, 1992). Thus satisfaction is now typically modeled as a function of (1) expectations, (2) performance, and (3) the difference between expectations and performance (with "negative disconfirmation," when performance falls short of expectations, having a much stronger impact than positive disconfirmation.) In assessing satisfaction it is important to compare satisfaction with one's own company with that of (1) other companies in the industry/category and (2) other companies in general, especially those in categories that are potential substitutes.

Of course indirect measures of satisfaction abound. These include word-of-mouth comments, complaints, and perhaps most importantly repeat purchase (or lack thereof). The basic reason for caring about satisfaction is that it leads to customer retention. Hence, measures of intended or actual repeat purchasing provide a useful way to simultaneously measure satisfaction and its impact. Note that it is possible for customers to be satisfied but not repurchase due to, among other things, poor product supply, variety seeking/multiple sourcing, and large promotional deals. Similarly they may be unsatisfied but continue to purchase, for example when dealing with a monopoly. Several authors have assembled satisfaction data across industries and demonstrated its link to retention (Fornell, 1992) and profitability (Anderson, Fornell, and Lehmann, 1994).

Intentions
Intentions are imprecise predictors of future purchase (as in he/she "had good intentions but . . ."). Still they provide early signs of future sales. In fact, surveys of customers (asking "Would you buy _____?" and/or "How much _____ will you buy?") are a staple input to sales forecasts, especially for industrial products, and we discuss them in greater detail in the Chapter 6.

The Long-Term Value of Customers

A fundamental issue in marketing strategy is the long-term value of a customer to the firm. Decisions about customer acquisition and retention (i.e., will they buy it again) as well as the level of effort to direct to each customer depend on the future net revenues expected from them. While measures such as size, wealth, and past purchases provide crude estimates of worth, the value of a customer is the discounted sum of future net revenue of the customer. The net revenue depends on the amount and type of transactions (i.e., volume and margin) as well as the cost to service (retain) the customer.

On a direct cost basis, not all customers are profitable. Often small accounts do not generate sufficient revenue to cover the cost of servicing them, although the cost of dealing with large accounts often makes them unprofitable as well. In fact, some companies estimate that 80 to 90 percent of their customers are nonprofitable, leading to such contested practices as "slamming" (transferring accounts to other companies without their consent). Credit card holders who pay off their balances on time, cable subscribers in remote areas, and "high service" customers who heavily use toll-free numbers are common examples of unprofitable customers.

On the other hand, customers that are unprofitable in the short run may be very profitable in the long run. While the cost of acquiring a customer (solicitation plus special deals) is typically greater than first year profits for life insurance, magazine subscriptions, and many other businesses, lower long-run maintenance costs (due to high repeat rates) lead to strong positive returns in subsequent years.

Calculating the value of a customer is straightforward, although heavily influenced by assumption. We discuss this concept in detail in Appendix 5–B.

Segmentation

Desirable Criteria for Segments

Given the tremendous number of potential bases for segmentation, a pertinent question is which one to use. Actually, several can be used in combination, so the question is really: What makes a good basis for segmentation? While there is no single way to say what is best (anyone suggesting there is probably doesn't understand the problem or is selling a particular segmentation method), the following six criteria provide a useful standard for evaluation:

1. *Sizeable.* Segments must be of sufficient size in terms of potential sales (but not in terms of number of customers; some customers may be large enough to consider on their own) to be worth worrying about. As a rule, billion-dollar companies don't care much about J.R. Smith at 1188 Maple Street, or all the people on Maple Street for that matter.

2. *Identifiable.* Segments should be identifiable so that when presenting results they can be referred to by more pleasing titles than segment A and segment B (e.g., the 35-to-50 segment, the sports-minded, companies in New York). More importantly, the identity of the segments provides an aid to strategic and tactical decisions.

3. *Reachable.* It may be sufficient for strategic purposes to identify a segment. For purposes of planning the marketing mix (e.g., advertising), however, it is useful to be able to target efforts on a segment. A sports-minded segment tends to be reachable through the media (e.g., *Sports Illustrated,* ESPN), whereas people who prefer the color blue, though identified, may be harder to reach efficiently (except by labels on blue towels, or by copy that employs the color blue).

4. *Respond Differently.* Ideally, segments should respond differently to at least some of the elements of the offering. If all segments respond the same, then no specialized programs can be used. For example, some customers may be sensitive to advertising but not price, whereas others are concerned about price but unaffected by advertising, and still others care about a single attribute such as downtime. The sensitivity to changes in market offering forms a useful basis for both describing the overall market and defining segments. It also makes the "why they buy" part of the analysis particularly crucial.

5. *Coherent.* When interpreting a segment, it is implicitly assumed that all members are homogeneous. This assumption is always violated to some extent. What is important is that the average member of a segment be reasonably close to the rest of the members. Hence, an important conceptual requirement of a segment is that the within-segment variation in behavior be (much) smaller than between-segment variation. (This desired condition is often operationalized as the basis for statistical tests for determining the number of segments.)

6. *Stable.* Since future plans are based on past data, segments (and hopefully but not necessarily the members of those segments) should be fairly stable over time.

Methods for Market Segmentation

Many of the methods developed for market segmentation, particularly by marketing academics, are highly technical and are not in widespread use among product managers. In this section, we focus on three methods that are simple to apply and for which there is easy-to-use computer software: (1) cluster analysis, (2) tabular analysis, and (3) regression analysis. We also briefly describe a fourth approach, latent class analysis.

A basic approach to segmentation analyses relates information about the two kinds of segmentation variables: descriptors and behavioral variables. Neither type by itself is very useful. We know that approximately 50 percent of the population is men and 50 percent women. This information alone is not helpful to the product manager because it does not indicate whether men or women have a greater propensity to buy our product. Alternatively, suppose we know that 20 percent of the population consists of heavy buyers, 40 percent of medium buyers, and 40 percent of light buyers. Again, this information is not very useful if we do not know who these buyers are (in terms of income, geography, and so forth); that is, we have no way to reach any of the groups. As a result, the methods on which we focus relate descriptor and behavioral data about customers in different ways to form market segments.

FIGURE 5–13

Cluster analysis illustration

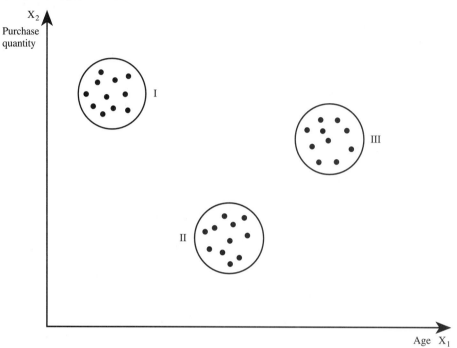

Cluster Analysis

One way to generate segments is to collect data about the descriptor and behavioral variables from a sample of customers and then form groups by means of cluster analysis. Cluster analysis examines the values of the variables for each respondent (from a sample of customers) and then groups respondents with similar values. Consider Figure 5–13. Each dot represents a combination of factors, say, age (X_1) and purchase quantity (X_2). In this case, three obvious clusters emerge. These clusters are appealing in that the members of each cluster are similar to one another and different from members of other clusters in terms of age and purchase quantity. A manager would conclude from this analysis that the youngest customers purchase the most, oldest customers the second most, and that the product does not appeal to middle-aged people. Cluster analysis programs are widely available in commercial computer software packages such as SAS and SPSS. (Unfortunately, such clear clusters rarely emerge.)

For example, a regional phone company employed cluster analysis to understand its residential customers. The company collected information on descriptors, attitudes, and behavior (usage was measured in dollars) and

FIGURE 5–14   Cluster Analysis: Phone Company Market Segmentation Scheme

	Fledglings	*Thrifties*	*Contenteds*	*Climbers*	*Techies*	*Executives*
Mean age	37	51	44	43	38	40
Mean income	$26k	$27k	$37k	$31k	$40k	$48k
Occupation	Blue collar	Retired/blue collar	Administrative/ professionals	Administrative/ sales	White collar	White collar
Education	14	12	14	16	18	18
Married	60%	72%	76%	65%	33%	72%
Children	44%	38%	51%	54%	75%	33%
Mobility	High	Low	Medium	Medium	High	Low
Home value	$70–85k	$60–80k	$70–85k	$60–80k	$80k+	$90k+
Dual income	Low	Medium	Medium	High	Highest	Medium
Number of phones	Low	Low	Medium	Medium	High	High
Type of phones	Basic/standard	Basic/standard	Medium mix	Medium mix	All types	All types
Monthly bill	Low	Low	Medium	Very high	Very high	Very high
Technology adoption	Late adopters	Laggards	Late adopter	Early adopter	Innovator	Early adopter
Purchase criteria	Value/money	Security	Convenience	Status	Environmental control	Quality
Application	Social interaction	Safety and protection	Social interaction	Social interaction	Personalized systems	Time saving

formed six segments based on clustering those households that "looked the same" based on the variables:

1. Low income/blue collar: "Fledglings."
2. Frugal/retired: "Thrifties."
3. Contented middle class: "Contenteds."
4. Aspiring middle-class status seekers: "Climbers."
5. Technology-driven strivers: "Techies."
6. Contented upper-middle class: "Executives."

A more detailed profile of the segments is shown in Figure 5–14.

Mobil also applied cluster analysis to gasoline buyers to tailor different stations to neighborhoods with different profiles and needs (Sullivan, 1995). The company identified five segments of gasoline buyers:

1. Road warriors: higher-income, middle-aged men who drive 25,000 to 50,000 miles per year, buy premium gas with a credit card, and buy sandwiches and drinks from the convenience store (16 percent of buyers).

2. True blues: men and women with moderate to high incomes who are loyal to a brand and sometimes to a particular station (16 percent).

3. Generation F3 (fuel, food, and fast): upwardly mobile men and women, half under 25 years old, who are constantly on the go; drive and snack a lot (27 percent).

4. Homebodies: usually homemakers who shuttle their kids around during the day and buy gas from whatever station is along the way (21 percent).

5. Price shoppers: not loyal to a brand or station; rarely buy premium (20 percent).

Most gas companies have targeted the last group. However, Mobil emphasized better service and amenities to customers in the first two segments and was able to charge 2 cents more per gallon than competitors in some markets.

A third example highlights the use of a geodemographic system called PRIZM (Potential Rating Index by Zip Market), marketed by Claritas Corporation. PRIZM's basic analysis is performed on U.S. ZIP codes. Based on the 1990 census, the PRIZM system examined the means of a set of demographic variables for all of the nearly 40,000 U.S. ZIP codes. Using the demographic variables, the ZIP codes are then clustered into 62 different groups. These 62 groups are given catchy names based on the mean levels of the variables, such as "Norma Rae–ville," "Cashmere & Country Clubs," and "American Dreams." The final crucial step, of course, is to relate membership in the geodemographic clusters to purchasing of various products and services (the behavior variable).

Figure 5–15 shows an application of PRIZM to the beer market (Martin, 1994). The graphs clearly indicate the different amounts of market potential for various kinds of beer in the various PRIZM segments. Families in the "Blue Blood Estates" and "Urban Gold Coast" clusters are particularly good targets for imported beer (they are about seven times more likely to drink imported beer than malt liquor), whereas "Southside City" families show the reverse behavior.[5]

Figure 5–16 provides another example of segmentation, this one from Strategic Mapping, Inc.'s ClusterPLUS 2000 for the disposable diaper market. This analysis developed 60 segments using data similar to that used by PRIZM. Figure 5–16 provides the number of households in each segment, the percentage of U.S. households in the segment (% Base), the

---

[5]There is a "chicken and egg" problem here: Do "Southside City" families have a naturally high propensity to drink malt liquor, or is it high due to intensive marketing efforts? Products developed for particular segments and heavily marketed to them will naturally have higher purchase incidence rates unless there is a total market/product mismatch. The reader should also note the ethical implications of target marketing by demographic/ethnicity variables for certain kinds of products, such as malt liquor.

FIGURE 5–15

Prizm Geodemographic Segmentation

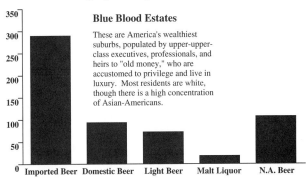

Blue Blood Estates

These are America's wealthiest suburbs, populated by upper-upper-class executives, professionals, and heirs to "old money," who are accustomed to privilege and live in luxury. Most residents are white, though there is a high concentration of Asian-Americans.

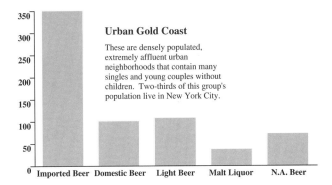

Urban Gold Coast

These are densely populated, extremely affluent urban neighborhoods that contain many singles and young couples without children. Two-thirds of this group's population live in New York City.

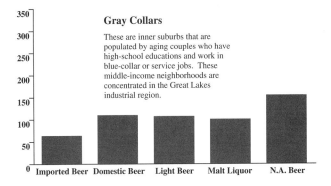

Gray Collars

These are inner suburbs that are populated by aging couples who have high-school educations and work in blue-collar or service jobs. These middle-income neighborhoods are concentrated in the Great Lakes industrial region.

FIGURE 5–16 ClusterPLUS 2000 Product Potential Report

Item: S1150: NUMBER OF DISPOSABLE DIAPERS USED IN HH ON AVG DAY
Market: U.S.
Demographic Base: Households
Group Set: Clusters

Description	Base Count	% Base	Usage	% Usage	Avg Use	Index
Totals: U.S.	96,976,894	100.00	44,435,425	100.00	0.46	100
C54:Young Blacks with Kids	796,378	0.82	656,588	1.48	0.82	180
S45:Low Income Younger Blacks	794,712	0.82	623,785	1.40	0.78	171
C40:Younger Mobile Singles	1,551,509	1.60	1,072,648	2.41	0.69	151
U10:New Families, New Homes	1,794,370	1.85	1,208,366	2.72	0.67	147
S22:Young Families, Dual Income	2,545,890	2.63	1,696,654	3.82	0.67	145
S07:High Inc, Young Families	1,582,765	1.63	1,026,304	2.31	0.65	142
T53:Low Income Ethnic Mix	2,408,568	2.48	1,532,643	3.45	0.64	139
U44:Young Black Families	1,097,859	1.13	694,500	1.56	0.63	138
U48:VYng BCollar Hispanic Fams	887,710	0.92	544,265	1.22	0.61	134
C57:Black Lowest Inc Fem Hd HH	1,102,997	1.14	670,655	1.51	0.61	133
S35:Avg Age/Inc, Blue Collars	3,111,554	3.21	1,831,753	4.12	0.59	128
C27:Yng Avg Inc Hispanics Apts	1,606,595	1.66	922,631	2.08	0.57	125
R26:Yngr Settld BCollar Fams	2,202,399	2.27	1,224,826	2.76	0.56	121
U30:Yngr Homeowners, Lval Home	1,777,653	1.83	946,531	2.13	0.53	116
R47:Below Avg Inc Work Couples	3,295,708	3.40	1,732,530	3.90	0.53	115
U18:Yngr Hisp/Asian Homeowners	1,336,855	1.38	696,558	1.57	0.52	114
U23:Yngr Families Lo Val Homes	2,342,629	2.42	1,195,549	2.69	0.51	111
C52:Mid-Age Old Apts	1,111,753	1.15	562,416	1.27	0.51	110
T37:Below Avg Inc Blue Collar	2,726,056	2.81	1,343,793	3.02	0.49	108
R28:Settld Couples Lo Val Homes	5,259,551	5.42	2,547,153	5.73	0.48	106
U46:Above Avg Age Low Inc/Rent	1,281,639	1.32	597,541	1.34	0.47	102
C55:Low Inc Mobile Hispanics	1,725,271	1.78	800,347	1.80	0.46	101
R43:Below Avg Inc Blue Collars	3,991,458	4.12	1,802,116	4.06	0.45	99
S03:Well Educated Professional	1,972,176	2.03	877,473	1.97	0.44	97
S50:Very Young Hispanics	560,158	0.58	243,992	0.55	0.44	95
S12:High Inc Settled Families	2,208,503	2.28	960,122	2.16	0.43	95
U08:Hi Inc Urban Professionals	1,390,450	1.43	593,088	1.33	0.43	93
U04:Upscale Urban Couples	1,635,493	1.69	671,429	1.51	0.41	90
C29:Avg Age & Inc Few Kids	1,731,043	1.79	700,570	1.58	0.40	88
C25:Young WCollar Singles Apts	2,472,066	2.55	954,393	2.15	0.39	84
U31:Very Young Apt Dwellers	3,196,517	3.30	1,202,506	2.71	0.38	82
S05:Younger Affluent w/Kids	1,812,746	1.87	676,769	1.52	0.37	81
T19:Above Avg Age White Collar	2,141,629	2.21	793,668	1.79	0.37	81
U24:Avg Inc Apts Fewer Kids	1,728,593	1.78	611,974	1.38	0.35	77
U36:Avg Income Hispanics	1,098,132	1.13	380,782	0.86	0.35	76
U14:High Inc WCollar Apt/Condo	2,741,736	2.83	945,426	2.13	0.34	75
C34:Younger, Hispanics/Asians	2,031,995	2.10	699,422	1.57	0.34	75
S13:WCollar High Value Homes	1,539,106	1.59	519,431	1.17	0.34	74
S21:Suburban Married Couples	1,989,228	2.05	619,096	1.39	0.31	68
S38:Retired Homeowners	1,187,663	1.22	368,475	0.83	0.31	68
R06:Rural Affluents, New Homes	919,158	0.95	281,294	0.63	0.31	67
C15:Single Prof High Rent Apts	2,159,119	2.23	634,909	1.43	0.29	64
S09:Mature Couples Profs	1,139,545	1.18	321,101	0.72	0.28	61
R16:Younger Couples with Kids	2,509,079	2.59	681,097	1.53	0.27	59
S02:Mid-Age Affluent w/Kids	718,314	0.74	194,525	0.44	0.27	59
S01:Established Wealthy	543,731	0.56	135,722	0.31	0.25	54
C17:Prof & Retirees Apt/Condo	1,266,237	1.31	274,325	0.62	0.22	47
C11:Ctr City Affluent Few Kids	968,301	1.00	185,212	0.42	0.19	42
*G59:GQtrs: Military	45,649	0.05	29,083	0.07	0.64	39

*Results should be viewed with caution—insufficient sample size.

Note: Calculations are based on Source Market Usage.

Source: Simmons Market Research Bureau. Copyright 1995 Strategic Mapping, Inc. All rights reserved.

136

estimated number of disposable diapers used in one day in the segment (Usage), the percentage of U.S. daily disposable diaper use (% Usage), the average number of diapers used per household in that segment (Avg. Use), and an index that is the ratio of % Usage/% Base and gives some idea about the usage rate of that segment relative to the size of the segment. The indexes are rank ordered for easy analysis by the product manager. While this index obviously is not the only criterion for choosing a target segment (e.g., no data by brand are shown), the information is a useful part of an overall picture of consumer behavior in the disposable diaper category.

Industrial customers can also be segmented on the basis of reactions to marketing mix variables (Rangan, Moriarty, and Swartz, 1992). For example, a large industrial product company segmented its national accounts based on the trade-offs made between price and service to form four segments:

Programmed buyers: small customers that do not consider the product important and make routine purchases.

Relationship buyers: small buyers, loyal to the supplier, that pay low prices and obtain high service levels.

Transaction buyers: large buyers that consider the product important and obtain price discounts, expect high service levels, and switch suppliers.

Bargain hunters: large buyers that get the lowest prices and the highest service.

Using electronic scanner data, product managers can segment by store. For example, Kraft can alter the mix of flavors of cream cheeses sold by supermarkets across different neighborhoods. Retailers also can use this analysis. Target's store on Phoenix's eastern edge sells prayer candles (the area is heavily populated by Catholic Hispanics) but no child-toting bicycle trailers. The Target 15 minutes away in affluent Scottsdale sells the trailers but no portable heaters. Heaters can be found 20 minutes south in Mesa, which has a cooler climate (Patterson, 1995).

Of course segmentation is not a new topic. In February 1949 critic Russell Lynes produced a segmentation of American consumers that was both insightful and led to a Broadway show (Figure 5–17).

Tabular Analysis

This analysis uses categorical variables constructed from customer membership in a category. For example, surveys usually ask respondents to identify the range in which their incomes fall, such as "$20,000–$29,999," "$30,000–$39,999," and so on, or what their favorite brand is. Sometimes surveys ask questions that are continuously "scaled," for example, "How many times did you go to the movies last month?" The answers can then either be analyzed as given or be placed in categories (e.g., 0–2 times, 3–5 times, 6 or more).

FIGURE 5-17

Taste segmentation

	CLOTHES	FURNITURE	USEFUL OBJECTS	ENTERTAINMENT	SALADS	DRINKS	READING	SCULPTURE	RECORDS	GAMES	CAUSES
HIGH-BROW	TOWN Fuzzy Harris tweed suit, no hat / COUNTRY Fuzzy Harris tweed suit, no hat	Eames chair, Kurt Versen lamp	Decanter and ash tray from chemical supply company	Ballet	Greens, olive oil, wine vinegar, ground salt, ground pepper, garlic, unwashed salad bowl	A glass of "adequate little" red wine	"Little magazines," criticism of criticism, avant garde literature	Calder	Bach and before, Ives and other	Go	Art
UPPER MIDDLE-BROW	TOWN Brooks suit, regimental tie, felt hat / COUNTRY Quiet tweed jacket, knitted tie	Empire chair, converted sculpture lamp	Silver cigaret box with wedding usher's signatures	Theater	Same as high-brow but with tomatoes, avocado, Roquefort cheese added	A very dry Martini with lemon peel	Solid nonfiction, the better novels, quality magazines	Maillol	Symphonies, concertos, operas	The Game	Planned parenthood
LOWER MIDDLE-BROW	TOWN Splashy necktie, double-breasted suit / COUNTRY Sport shirt, colored slacks	Grand Rapids Chippendale chair, bridge lamp	His and Hers towels	Musical extravaganza films	Quartered iceberg lettuce and store dressing	Bourbon and ginger ale	Book-club selections mass circulation magazines	Front yard sculpture	Light opera, popular favorites	Bridge	P.T.A.
LOW-BROW	TOWN Loafer jacket, woven shoes / COUNTRY Old Army clothes	Mail order overstuffed chair, fringed lamp	Balloon-stuffed pillow	Western movies	Coleslaw	Beer	Pulps, comic books	Parlor sculpture	Jukebox	Craps	The Lodge

FIGURE 5–18   **Raw Data: Cranberry Sauce Usage**

Cooking Attitude	Heavy Users	Medium Users	Light Users	Total (row marginal)
Convenience oriented	81	144	74	299
Enthusiastic cook	97	115	45	257
Disinterested	35	108	127	270
Decorator	45	96	37	178
Column total (marginal)	258	463	283	1004

As an illustration, consider the data in Figure 5–18. These data were taken from a survey of 1,004 users of cranberry sauce (DeBruicker, 1974). The descriptor variables, located in the leftmost column, are based on some prior analyses of data concerning attitudes toward cooking. These four categories are "convenience oriented," "enthusiastic cook," "disinterested," and "decorator." The descriptor variable is sometimes referred to as the *independent* variable. The behavioral categories, located across the top, are divided into three groups based on self-reported usage: heavy, medium, and light. This variable is referred to as the *dependent* variable. Entries in the table or cells indicate the number of consumers who simultaneously satisfy both a descriptor group and a behavioral group. In other words, 81 people were both heavy users of cranberry sauce and convenience oriented. The row sums and the column sums are called *marginals*.

The basic issue facing the manager, assuming she or he is interested in understanding how to segment the market based on the behavioral variable of usage quantity, is whether attitude toward cooking is a useful variable. Managers have many descriptor variables to choose from, not to mention several behavioral variables. An important task is to sift through the candidate descriptors to find some that are useful to describe the heavy, medium, and light buyers.

Before analyzing the results in great detail, it is useful to first determine if there is a *statistically significant* relationship between the independent variable, cooking attitude, and the dependent variable, usage quantity. The most common and simplest approach to this task is a *chi-square* test. In this test, each cell based on the survey results (e.g., Figure 5–18) is compared to an *expected* cell size or the number of people that would be expected in that cell if attitude toward cooking were independent of usage quantity. The expected cell size can be calculated by multiplying the marginal for the row in which the cell is located by the marginal for the column in which the cell is located and dividing by the total sample size. For example, the expected cell size for the convenience-oriented–heavy usage cell is $(299 \times 258)/1{,}004 = 77$. Then the chi-square value is determined by taking the sum over all

FIGURE 5–19 Cranberry Sauce Usage Percentages

Cooking Attitude	Heavy Users	Medium Users	Light Users
Convenience oriented			
Row %	27%	48%	25%
Column %	31	31	26
Enthusiastic cook			
Row %	38	45	18
Column %	38	25	16
Disinterested			
Row %	13	40	47
Column %	14	23	45
Decorator			
Row %	25	54	21
Column %	17	21	13

cells of the (observed − expected)^2/expected. For Figure 5–18, the chi-square value is 86. Combined with the number of degrees of freedom of the table (the number of rows minus 1 times the number of columns minus 1) and the significance level of the test, it is compared to a table of chi-square values found in any statistics book. In this example, the chi-square value of 86 with 6 degrees of freedom exceeds the table value of 12.6 at the 95 percent confidence level. Thus there is a significant relationship between consumers' attitudes toward cooking and their reported cranberry sauce usage levels.[6]

A second step in the analysis is to better understand the nature of the relationship between the two variables[7] by calculating percentages. The two most common ways to calculate percentages are to divide each cell by its row marginal to obtain row percentages or to divide each cell by its column marginal to obtain column percentages. Figure 5–19 shows the row and column percentages for the cranberry sauce data.

The row percentage indicates what percentage of the row category customers are in the column group. In the example, 27 percent of convenience-oriented consumers are heavy users. The column percentage indicates what percentage of the column category is in the row group. In the example,

---

[6]The chi-square tests from different descriptor variables can be compared to see which of these the product manager should consider further in the segmentation analysis. This is more complicated than it sounds, as the chi-square values of tables with different numbers of rows and/or columns (degrees of freedom) cannot be directly compared. One alternative is to standardize all the tables to the same size. A second alternative is to use a computer program such as SAS that prints out the exact level of significance of each chi-square result and rank orders the descriptors by this number.

[7]Cross-tabular analysis can easily be extended to tables with more than one independent variable. The same logic for the chi-square test holds.

31 percent of heavy users are convenience oriented. Of course the manager must interpret these two types of percentages differently.[8]

Assume the manager is interested in medium users because heavy users are saturated and light users probably cannot be convinced to consume more cranberry sauce. Which customers should the product manager pursue? One obvious group is convenience-oriented cooks, as this group has the largest number of medium buyers (31 percent) and is the second most "concentrated" (48 percent of them are medium users). Enthusiastic cooks might also be targeted, as they are the largest group of heavy users (38 percent).

Note that the cranberry sauce example illustrates the use of psychographics as potential segmenting variables. However, since media are not all measured by psychographics, an additional cross-tabular analysis matching demographic or socioeconomic variables with the lifestyle variable may be necessary for lifestyle segmentation. In other words, if the product manager wishes to target convenience-oriented customers, it is useful to know income, geographic, and other information about them to implement the segmentation strategy.

Regression Analysis

Like cross-tabular analysis, regression analysis is used when the product manager can specify an explicit relationship between a dependent (behavioral) variable and one or more descriptor (independent) variables.[9] However, unlike cross-tabular analysis, regression theoretically assumes a continuously measured dependent variable. Using the cranberry sauce illustration, if the dependent variable is reported usage in number of cans rather than categories of consumption, then regression will be more appropriate.

Suppose we believe that income and family size are key segmentation variables in addition to the four categories of cooking attitudes. Assume three categories of income (low, medium, and high) are reported on the survey as well as the actual number of people in the family. We can then specify a *model* of the following form:

$$\text{Usage} = f(\text{CO, EC, DI, DE, LOWY, MEDY, HIGHY, FAMSIZE}),$$

where the dependent variable is the reported usage rate of cranberry sauce and the independent variables are the descriptors: convenience oriented, enthusiastic cooks, disinterested, decorator, low income, medium income, high income, and family size, respectively.

---

[8]To see this more clearly, consider the descriptor "men" and the behavioral variable "reads *Playboy* magazine." In this case, a large percentage of *Playboy* readers are men, but a small percentage of men are *Playboy* readers.

[9]We assume in this section that the reader has some working knowledge of regression analysis.

FIGURE 5–20   Cranberry Usage Data by Person

| Person | Cranberry Sauce Usage (Number of cans) | Cooking Attitudes | | | | Income | | | Family Size |
		CO	EC	DIS	DEC	LO	MED	HI	
1	5	0	1	0	0	0	1	0	4
2	2	1	0	0	0	0	0	1	3
3	0	0	0	1	0	1	0	0	5
4	6	0	0	0	1	0	1	0	4
5	3	1	0	0	0	1	0	0	3

Generally, a person can be in only one category of cooking attitude and one category of income. In addition, assume these two variables cannot be represented by continuously measured numbers such as reported usage (number of cans) and family size (number of people). Therefore we need to create *dummy variables* to represent the cooking attitude and income variables. These variables are simply 0 or 1, indicating membership in one of the categories.

Figure 5–20 provides a hypothetical representation of the survey responses of five individuals. The first column contains values of the dependent variable, usage of cranberry sauce in number of cans. The next four columns represent cooking attitude. However, each respondent can have 1 in only one of the columns and must have a 1 in one of them because the categories are mutually exclusive and collectively exhaustive. The next three columns represent the income variable. Finally, family size is reported as the actual number.

Due to statistical (and logical) restrictions, if a dummy variable has n categories, only $n - 1$ are needed in the regression. Therefore, rewriting the regression model in equation form, we obtain

$$\text{Usage} = a + b\text{CO} + c\text{EC} + d\text{DI} + e\text{LOWY} + f\text{MEDY} + g\text{FAMSIZE},$$

where a to f are regression coefficients estimated using the data in Figure 5–20 and some computer software (e.g., Excel).

The interpretation of the coefficients differs between the continuously measured variable, FAMSIZE, and the dummy variables. The coefficient g is interpreted in the usual way: For a one-person change in family size, usage changes by g units. For example, if g is positive, a one-person increase (decrease) in family size is predicted to increase (decrease) usage by g units. The coefficients b, c, d, e, and f, however, are interpreted differently. Recall that these variables are measured either as 0 or 1 depending on membership in that category. For each set of dummies, a coefficient is interpreted as the *contrast* from the omitted category. For example, *b,* the coefficient of the dummy variable "convenience oriented," is interpreted as the estimated difference in cranberry sauce usage between a person who is convenience oriented versus one who is a decorator (the omitted category). Likewise, *f,* the coefficient on "medium income," is the estimated difference in usage between a person who reports having medium income versus one who has high income. (It is irrelevant which category is dropped, as the estimated differences would be the same even though the coefficients themselves would change.)

Suppose we obtained the following results in which all coefficients are statistically significant:

$$\text{Usage} = 10.3 + 2.1 \times \text{CO} - 1.9 \times \text{EC} - 3.5 \times \text{DI}$$
$$- 2.5 \times \text{LOWY} - 1.1 \times \text{MEDY} + 0.9 \times \text{FAMSIZE}$$

What would be the market segmentation implications? In this case, convenience-oriented cooks have the highest usage rate: 2.1 units more, on average, than the omitted category, decorators. Both of the other categories of cooking attitude use less than decorators, as the negative signs on their coefficients indicate. In terms of income, high-income consumers are estimated to have the highest usage rate (both signs on the other income variables are negative). Finally, for every one-person increase in family size, reported usage increases an estimated .9 units (i.e, cans). Thus, the profile of the largest cranberry sauce users is (hypothetically) high-income, convenience-oriented cooks with large families.

One statistic produced with regression equations is R^2, which measures the degree to which the equation "fits" the data on a 0 to 1 scale, with 1 being a perfect fit. Unfortunately, for frequently purchased products, these kinds of equations tend to have low R^2 values. However, despite the poor fits, these regressions often point to useful bases for segmentation. Figure 5–21 shows that large and significant differences in product consumption can exist even when the R^2 values are low.

Latent Class Analysis

The previous methods begin with individual customers and then aggregate them. Latent class methods, by contrast, begin with the market as a whole and then determine what segmentation pattern best trades off parsimony (few segments) and the ability to explain overall behavior based on derived segments in which all customers in a segment behave identically. This relatively recent approach (see Appendix 5–C) is intriguing but requires considerable sophistication, and so is not yet widely employed. (What this means is you can either (1) ignore it, (2) use it for competitive advantage, or (3) drop the term in conversation to either impress or mystify others.)

A simple kind of latent structure analysis focuses on brand switching data. However, rather than estimating share at the individual level and then

FIGURE 5-21 Light and Heavy Buyers by Mean Purchase Rates for Different Socioeconomic Cells

R²	Product	Description		Mean Consumption Rate Ranges		Ratio of Highest to Lowest Rate
		Light Buyers	Heavy Buyers	Light Buyers	Heavy Buyers	
.08	Catsup	Unmarried or married over age 50 without children	Under 50, three or more children	.74–1.82	2.73–5.79	7.8
.07	Frozen orange juice	Under 35 or over 65, income less than $10,000, not college grads, two or less children	College grads, income over $10,000, between 35 and 65	1.12–2.24	3.53–9.00	8.0
.04	Pancake mix	Some college, two or less children	Three or more children, high school or less education	.48–.52	1.10–1.51	3.3
.08	Candy bars	Under 35, no children	35 or over, three or more children	1.01–4.31	6.65–22.29	21.9
.08	Cake mix	Not married or under 35, no children, income under $10,000, TV less than 3½ hours	35 or over, three or more children, income over $10,000	.55–1.10	2.22–3.80	6.9
.09	Beer	Under 25 or over 50, college education, nonprofessional, TV less than 2 hours	Between 25 and 50, not college graduate, TV more than 3½ hours	0–12.33	17.26–40.30	—
.02	Cream shampoo	Income less than $8,000, at least some college, less than five children	Income $10,000 or over with high school or less education	.16–.35	.44–.87	5.5
.06	Hair spray	Over 65, under $8,000 income	Under 65, over $10,000 income, not college graduate	0–.41	.52–1.68	—
.09	Toothpaste	Over 50, less than three children, income less than $8,000	Under 50, three or more children, over $10,000 income	1.41–2.01	2.22–4.39	3.1
.03	Mouthwash	Under 35 or over 65, less than $8,000 income, some college	Between 35 and 65, income over $8,000, high school or less education	.45–.85	.98–1.17	2.5

Source: Frank Bass, Douglas Tigert, and Ronald Lonsdale, "Market Segmentation—Group versus Individual Behavior," Reprinted from *Journal of Marketing Research*, 5 (August 1968) p. 267, published by the American Marketing Association.

grouping similar individuals together (e.g., via cluster analysis), this method simply derives segment level probabilities and market shares. Grover and Srinivasan (1987) provide an example of such segmentation for the instant coffee market. Subjects who always bought the same brand were classified as loyals while the rest (switchers) were then broken into various segments. Figure 5–22 shows the four-segment solution, which appeared to be the best compromise between explanation and parsimony. The results suggest very small hard-core loyal segments (which in total account for 35 percent of the market) and four switching segments with tendencies to favor two or more brands.

Kamakura and Russell (1989) extend this approach to include price sensitivity. They analyze 78 weeks of purchases of a refrigerated (once opened) food product with a 10-week average purchase cycle. The four brands (A, B, C, P) were average priced at $4.29, $3.54, $3.38, and $3.09 and had choice shares of 35.8, 27.8, 23.8, and 12.6 percent respectively. The resulting segments appear in Figure 5–23. Interestingly, these results also suggest about one-third (31.4 percent) of the customers are hard-core loyal. In addition, the segments differ in terms of price sensitivity. Segments one and two (which account for 19 percent of the market) appear to be relatively insensitive to price and fairly brand loyal. By contrast, segments three and four (which account for 42.2 percent of the market) are quite price sensitive and tend to spread purchases across several brands. Segment five appears not to respond to price or be very brand loyal; perhaps this small (7.4 percent) segment represents customers for whom the product is low involvement and who simply pick a brand by reaching for the most readily available one.

Judgment-Based Segmentation

There is a strong tendency to derive segments by examining data. Still, some of the most useful segmentation schemes are simply descriptors of bases selected by managers such as customer usage rate (heavy users, light users, nonusers) or product preference. While these are not elegant and are unlikely to suggest a new approach, they are often more useful than so-called natural clusters because the segments are readily identifiable and reachable and obviously have responded differently to the product offering. In fact, it is always advisable to use such a segmentation strategy as at least a basis for comparison with the results of approaches that are more "data mining" oriented.

No simple way exists to tell how to get the best segmentation scheme. In that respect it's a lot like art—you can tell whether you like it or not but never prove it's the best. The problem when segmenting based on intuition, of course, is that given faulty memory and perceptions, it may produce segments for a market that exist only in the mind of a manager.

FIGURE 5-22 Four-Segment Solution for the Instant-Coffee Market

Brand[a,b]		Type[c]	Manufacturer[d]	Aggregate Market Share (MS)	Loyal Segment Size	Switching Segments			
						1	2	3	4
							Size (total = .65)		
						.19*	.22*	.18*	.06*
						Within-Segment Market Shares (p)[e]			
HP	D	R	PG	.13	.05*	.09*	.20*	.13*	.08
TC	C	FD	N	.10	.04*	.07	.03	.18*	.03
TC	D	FD	N	.07	.01	—[f]	—	.32*	.12*
FL	C	R	PG	.12	.04*	.20*	.16*	.04*	—
MH	C	R	GF	.21	.08*	.42*	.15*	.07*	.06
S	D	R	GF	.16	.07*	.04	.22*	.11*	.15*
S	D	FD	GF	.03	.01*	—	.05*	.03*	—
MX	C	FD	GF	.04	.01*	.04	.03*	.04*	—
N	C	R	N	.06	.01*	.14*	—	—	.27*
N	D	R	N	.03	.01	—	.07*	—	.27*
B	D	FD	GF	.05	.02*	—	.09*	.08*	.02
Total				1.00	.35	1.00	1.00	1.00	1.00

*Parameter estimate/standard error > 2.

[a]Brand names: HP = High Point; TC = Taster's Choice, FL = Folgers, MH = Maxwell House, S = Sanka, MX = Maxim, N = Nescafé, B = Brim.

[b]D = decaffeinated, C = caffeinated.

[c]FD = freeze dried, R = regular (spray dried).

[d]PG = Proctor & Gamble, GF = General Foods, N = Nestlé.

[e]Underlined numbers denote the two largest choice probabilities within the segment.

[f]Probabilities constrained to zero for model identification.

Source: Rajiv Grover and V. Srinivasan, "A Simultaneous Approach to Market Segmentatin and Market Structuring," *Journal of Marketing Research 24* (May 1987), p. 147.

146

FIGURE 5–23   **Preference Segmentation and Price Sensitivity**

	Loyal Segments				Switching Segments*			
A	B	C	P	1	2	3	4	5
Choice probabilities								
A 1				.790	.219	.152	.095	.192
B	1			.089	.646	.259	.238	.332
C		1		.069	.092	.520	.301	.133
P			1	.052	.043	.065	.367	.343
Segment size (% of all households)								
19.0	5.8	3.9	2.7	9.3	9.7	25.8	16.4	7.4
Price sensitivity								
β				−1.87	−1.44	−3.07	−5.42	.37†

*For switching segments 1 through 4, purchase probabilities greater than .10 are underlined.
†Price coefficient statistically *insignificant* at the .05 level.
Source: Wagner A. Kamakura and Gary J. Russell, "A Probabilistic Choice Model for Market Segmentation and Elasticity Structure," *Journal of Marketing Research 26* (November 1989), p. 385.

Summary

The approaches discussed here can be applied to any product, consumer or industrial, low-tech or high-tech, as long as the required data is available. Many other methods have been used for segmentation. Two methods discussed earlier in this chapter, conjoint analysis and multidimensional scaling, are good examples. In addition, other multivariate techniques (e.g., analysis of variance, logit/probit, Automatic Interaction Detector, and CHAID) can be applied to obtain information about existing market segments.

Illustrations

Super-Premium Ice Cream

Who the Customers Are

Ice cream use in general is widespread. Figure 5–24 presents data from Mediamark Research, Inc.'s 1997 report, and Figure 5–25 provides data based on A.C. Nielsen's home-based scanner panel. Consumption is driven largely by stage in life cycle and income: High income families with larger families consume more. There is also some evidence that, in the United States, whites and Hispanics consume more than African-Americans or Asians.

FIGURE 5-24 Ice Cream Consumption

| | | All | | | | Pints/Last 7 Days | | | | | | | | | | | |
| | | | | | | Heavy More Than 3 | | | | Medium 2–3 | | | | Light Less Than 2 | | | |
Base: Female Homemakers	Total US. '000	A '000	B % Down	C % Across	D Index	A '000	B % Down	C % Across	D Index	A '000	B % Down	C % Across	D Index	A '000	B % Down	C % Across	D Index
All Female Homemakers	89443	63633	100.0	71.1	100	14231	100.0	15.9	100	15422	100.0	17.2	100	33980	100.0	38.0	100
Men	—	—	—	—	—	—	—	—	—	—	—	—	—	—	—	—	—
Women	89443	63633	100.0	71.1	100	14231	100.0	15.9	100	15422	100.0	17.2	100	33980	100.0	38.0	100
Household Heads	38147	25144	39.5	65.9	93	4545	31.9	11.9	75	5790	37.5	15.2	88	14809	43.6	38.8	102
Homemakers	89443	63633	100.0	71.1	100	14231	100.0	15.9	100	15422	100.0	17.2	100	33980	100.0	38.0	100
Graduated College	17169	12670	19.9	73.8	104	2396	16.8	14.0	88	3268	21.2	19.0	110	7006	20.6	40.8	107
Attended College	23736	17064	26.8	71.9	101	3704	26.0	15.6	98	3585	23.2	15.1	88	9775	28.6	41.2	108
Graduated High School	31977	22813	35.9	71.3	100	5660	39.8	17.7	111	5866	38.0	18.3	106	11287	33.2	35.3	93
Did not Graduate High School	16562	11086	17.4	66.9	94	2470	17.4	14.9	94	2703	17.5	16.3	95	5913	17.4	35.7	94
18–24	7845	4956	7.8	63.2	89	662	4.7	8.4	53	1250	8.1	15.9	92	3044	9.0	38.8	102
25–34	19184	13863	21.8	72.3	102	2533	17.8	13.2	83	3215	20.8	16.8	97	8114	23.9	42.3	111
35–44	20154	15567	24.5	77.2	109	4080	28.7	20.2	127	3386	22.0	16.8	97	8101	23.8	40.2	106
45–54	14824	10377	16.3	70.0	98	2774	19.5	18.7	118	2792	18.1	18.8	109	4811	14.2	32.5	85
55–64	10381	7455	11.7	71.8	101	1677	11.8	16.2	102	2181	14.1	21.0	122	3597	10.6	34.7	91
65 or over	17055	11414	17.9	66.9	94	2505	17.6	14.7	92	2598	16.8	15.2	88	6312	18.6	37.0	97
18–34	27029	18819	29.6	69.6	98	3195	22.5	11.8	74	4465	29.0	16.5	96	11158	32.8	41.3	109
18–49	55545	40303	63.3	72.6	102	9012	63.3	16.2	102	9483	61.5	17.1	99	21807	64.2	39.3	103
25–54	54163	39807	62.6	73.5	103	9387	66.0	17.3	109	9393	60.9	17.3	101	21027	61.9	38.8	102
Employed Full Time	40050	28442	44.7	71.0	100	5795	40.7	14.5	91	6561	42.5	16.4	95	16085	47.3	40.2	106
Part-time	10670	8109	12.7	76.0	107	1721	12.1	16.1	101	2360	15.3	22.1	128	4029	11.9	37.8	99
Sole Wage Earner	13368	8761	13.8	65.5	92	1517	10.7	11.3	71	2074	13.4	15.5	90	5171	15.2	38.7	102
Not Employed	38723	27082	42.6	69.9	98	6714	47.2	17.3	109	6501	42.2	16.8	97	13866	40.8	35.8	94
Professional	9157	6490	10.2	70.9	100	1152	8.1	12.6	79	1578	10.2	17.2	100	3760	11.1	41.1	108
Executive/Admin./Managerial	6777	4981	7.8	73.5	103	1078	7.6	15.9	100	1153	7.5	17.0	99	2750	8.1	40.6	107
Clerical/Sales/Technical	20244	14644	23.0	72.3	102	2880	20.2	14.2	89	3583	23.2	17.7	103	8180	24.1	40.4	106
Precision/Crafts/Repair	1058	709	1.1	67.0	94	*103	0.7	9.7	61	*207	1.3	19.5	113	*400	1.2	37.8	99
Other Employed	13484	9727	15.3	72.1	101	2303	16.2	17.1	107	2400	15.6	17.8	103	5024	14.8	37.3	98
H/D Income $75,000 or More	13615	10069	15.8	73.9	104	2387	16.8	17.5	110	2326	15.1	17.1	99	5355	15.8	39.3	104
$60,000–74,999	8572	6519	1.2	76.0	107	1410	9.9	16.4	103	1409	9.1	16.4	95	3700	10.9	43.2	114
$50,000–59,999	7341	5447	8.6	74.2	104	990	7.0	13.5	85	1286	8.3	17.5	102	3171	9.3	43.2	114
$40,000–49,999	9283	6695	10.5	72.1	101	1358	9.5	14.6	92	1701	11.0	18.3	106	3636	10.7	39.2	103

	C1	C2	C3	C4	C5	C6	C7	C8	C9	C10	C11	C12	C13	C14	C15	C16	C17
$30,000–39,999	11776	8296	99	70.5	13.0	1801	12.7	15.3	96	2164	14.0	18.4	107	4331	12.7	36.8	97
$20,000–29,999	13159	9596	103	72.9	15.1	2635	18.5	20.0	126	2210	14.3	16.8	97	4751	14.0	36.1	95
$10,000–19,999	14645	9923	95	67.8	15.6	2326	16.3	15.9	100	2712	17.6	18.5	107	4886	14.4	33.4	88
Less than $10,000	11051	7088	90	64.1	11.1	1323	9.3	12.0	75	1613	10.5	14.6	85	4151	12.2	37.6	99
Census Region: North East	17920	13518	106	75.4	21.2	3020	21.2	16.9	106	3454	22.4	19.3	112	7044	20.7	39.3	103
North Central	20997	16295	109	77.6	25.6	3912	27.5	18.6	117	3945	25.6	18.8	109	8438	24.8	40.2	106
South	32866	20803	89	63.3	32.7	4555	32.0	13.9	87	5265	34.1	16.0	93	10982	32.3	33.4	88
West	17660	13017	104	73.7	20.5	2744	19.3	15.5	98	2758	17.9	15.6	91	7515	22.1	42.6	112
Marketing Reg.: New England	4683	3585	108	76.6	5.6	787	5.5	16.8	106	1013	6.6	21.6	125	1784	5.3	38.1	100
Middle Atlantic	15091	11018	103	73.0	17.3	2395	16.8	15.9	100	2694	17.5	17.9	104	5930	17.5	39.3	103
East Central	12106	9334	108	77.1	14.7	2225	15.6	18.4	115	2200	14.3	18.2	105	4910	14.4	40.6	107
West Central	13576	10326	107	76.1	16.2	2692	18.9	19.8	125	2296	14.9	16.9	98	5337	15.7	39.3	103
South East	18186	10686	83	58.8	16.8	1833	12.9	10.1	63	2909	18.9	16.0	93	5943	17.5	32.7	86
South West	10325	7291	99	70.6	11.5	1929	13.6	18.7	117	1791	11.6	17.3	101	3570	10.5	34.6	91
Pacific	15477	11393	103	73.6	17.9	2369	16.6	15.3	96	2518	16.3	16.3	94	6506	19.1	42.0	111
County Size A	35404	25404	102	72.2	39.9	5123	36.0	14.6	92	6278	40.7	17.8	103	14004	41.2	39.8	105
County Size B	27427	19062	98	69.5	30.0	4318	30.3	15.7	99	4637	30.1	16.9	98	10106	29.7	36.8	97
County Size C	12976	8818	96	68.0	13.9	1946	13.7	15.0	94	1945	12.6	15.0	87	4927	14.5	38.0	100
County Size D	13861	10348	105	74.7	16.3	2843	20.0	20.5	129	2562	16.6	18.5	107	4943	14.5	35.7	94
MSA Central City	30121	20703	97	68.7	32.5	4401	30.9	14.6	92	4657	30.2	15.5	90	11645	34.3	38.7	102
MSA Suburban	40932	29522	101	72.1	46.4	6315	44.4	15.4	97	7565	49.1	18.5	107	15641	46.0	38.2	101
Non-MSA	18391	13408	102	72.9	21.1	3514	24.7	19.1	120	3200	20.7	17.4	101	6694	19.7	36.4	96
Single	13825	8991	91	65.0	14.1	1536	10.8	11.1	70	1786	11.6	12.9	75	5668	16.7	41.0	108
Married	52777	39574	105	75.0	62.2	9875	69.4	13.7	118	9822	63.7	18.6	108	19877	58.5	37.7	99
Other	22842	15068	93	66.0	23.7	2820	19.8	12.3	78	3814	24.7	16.7	97	8434	24.8	36.9	97
Parents	36556	27963	108	76.5	43.9	6832	48.0	18.7	117	6935	45.0	19.0	110	14197	41.8	38.8	102
Working Parents	24493	18794	108	76.7	29.5	4346	30.5	17.7	112	4541	29.4	18.5	108	9908	29.2	40.5	106
Household Size: 1 Person	14703	8864	85	60.3	13.9	1342	9.4	9.1	57	1845	12.0	12.5	73	5677	16.7	38.6	102
2 Persons	28180	19810	99	70.3	31.1	4096	28.8	14.5	91	5028	32.6	17.8	103	10687	31.4	37.9	100
3 or More	46561	34958	106	75.1	54.9	8793	61.8	18.9	119	8549	55.4	18.4	106	17616	51.8	37.8	100
Any Child in Household	40040	30625	108	76.5	48.1	7459	52.4	18.6	117	7629	49.5	19.1	111	15537	45.7	38.8	102
Under 2 Years	7574	5936	110	78.4	9.3	920	6.5	12.1	76	1421	9.2	18.8	109	3595	10.6	47.5	125
2–5 Years	16305	12340	106	75.7	19.4	2728	19.2	16.7	105	2968	19.2	18.2	106	6644	19.6	40.7	107
6–11 Years	18883	14756	110	78.1	23.2	4080	28.7	21.6	136	3581	23.2	19.0	110	7096	20.9	37.6	99
12–17 Years	16883	13418	112	79.5	21.1	3912	27.5	23.2	146	3298	21.4	19.5	113	6208	18.3	36.8	97
White	76161	55072	102	72.3	86.5	12339	86.7	16.2	102	13372	86.7	17.6	102	29362	86.4	38.6	101
Black	10317	6164	84	59.7	9.7	1338	9.4	13.0	81	1590	10.3	15.4	89	3236	9.5	31.4	83
Spanish Speaking	7447	5355	101	71.9	8.4	1275	9.0	17.1	108	1435	9.3	19.3	112	2646	7.8	35.5	94
Home Owned	60417	44454	103	73.6	69.9	10511	73.9	17.4	109	10949	71.0	18.1	105	22993	67.7	38.1	100

Source: Medimark Research, Inc., 1997.

FIGURE 5–25   Ice Cream Consumption

	Ice Cream—Bulk	Ice Milk and Sherbet	Frozen Yogurt
Penetration	87.1	24.7	26.2
Purchase cycle (days)	27.0	46.0	33.0
% $ on Deal	37.3	23.3	32.8
% $ Manufacturer coupons	3.5	1.4	4.4
% Repeat buyer	88.3	44.0	51.0
% by Store Type			
Food outlet	97.9	98.9	98.9
Drug outlet	2.0	1.1	1.1
Age of Head of Household			
< 35	89	78	65
35–44	103	106	74
45–54	102	88	106
55–64	108	118	141
65 +	100	118	135
Household Size			
1	64	72	102
2	107	120	128
3–4	108	101	82
5 +	142	106	64
Children Under 18			
None	91	100	118
Any under 18	116	99	68
Any under 6	106	83	65
Any 6–12	121	108	58
Any 13–17	129	108	77
Household Income			
< 12,000	82	85	88
12,000–19,000	87	97	83
20,000–29,000	96	98	90
30,000–39,000	101	97	97
40,000–49,000	108	105	92
50,000–59,000	106	85	118
60,000 +	115	120	127
Occupation of Head of Household			
Professional / mgr.	97	100	100
Clerical / sales	93	97	106
Blue collar	104	85	70
Not in work force	102	112	122
Household Lifestyle			
Young single	49	35	57
Middle-aged childless couple	80	75	91
New family	94	64	83
Maturing family	121	107	56
Established family	119	103	90
Middle-aged single	58	53	92
Childless couple	102	116	92
Aged empty-nester	120	133	158
Older single	72	94	120
Race			
Caucasian	103	104	110
African-American	81	85	59
Asian	77	65	37
Hispanic	102	114	80

Source: Consumer Decisions 2000; AC Nielsen Homescan Panel, 1997.

Focusing on super-premium, we see (Figure 5–26) evidence that consumption is highest in the young, upscale, college-educated market, both in general and in comparison to Dreyers' current customers, although 20 percent of households buy super-premium at least once a year. Interestingly consumers are also predominantly (67 percent) male.

What They Buy
- Sales by Category: Super Premium   10.1%
  - Premium   45.0%
  - Regular   20.1%
  - Private Label   23.7%
- Sales by Flavor: A large number of flavors are consumed, with vanilla (29.0%) and chocolate (8.9%) the top two choices (see Figure 5–27). Dreyers' top 10 flavors in 1999 are shown in Figure 5–28.
- Sales by Brand: Data based on IRI's Marketing Fact Book for 1997 show supermarket sales by brand as well as price paid and dealing activity (Figure 5–29).

When They Buy
Consumption is related to temperature (and therefore seasonal). For example, using data from the early 1950s, a regression of consumption over four weeks versus temperature showed ($R^2 = 60\%$): per capita consumption in pints = .21 + .0031 (temperature).

Where They Buy
In general, since 1992 more food has been purchased at restaurants than at supermarkets. The two main sources of super-premium ice cream sales are on-premise outlets and supermarkets.

The top five cities in sales of ice cream per capita in 1999 were Portland, Baltimore, Omaha, Buffalo/Rochester, and Seattle, while New York and Los Angeles led in total consumption. More generally, the Northeast and West are heavy consumption areas.

Personal Digital Assistants

Who the Customers Are
The customers for PDAs are primarily upscale mobile professionals. The current general profile of users shows that they are predominantly male, analytical and quantitative in nature, well educated, and over 21 years of age.

Mobile professionals, the key target market, can be segmented as in Figure 5–30. These labels do not help the product manager locate these people, of course. However, early adopters of PDAs have a high incidence of purchasing other high-tech consumer products such as personal and laptop computers, home fax machines, cellular phones, and so forth.

FIGURE 5–26 Ice Cream Sales by Brand

Base: Female Homemakers	Total U.S. '000	Edy's Grand				Häagen-Dazs			
		A '000	B % Down	C % Across	D Index	A '000	B % Down	C % Across	D Index
All Female Homemaker's	89443	4703	100.0	5.3	100	6157	100.0	6.9	100
Men	—	—	—	—	—	—	—	—	—
Women	89443	4703	100.0	5.3	100	6157	100.0	6.9	100
Household Heads	38147	1575	33.5	4.1	79	2563	41.6	6.7	98
Homemakers	89443	4703	100.0	5.3	100	6157	100.0	6.9	100
Graduated College	17169	1285	27.3	7.5	142	2160	35.1	12.6	183
Attended College	23736	1366	29.0	5.8	109	1789	29.1	7.5	110
Graduated High School	31977	1588	33.8	5.0	94	1656	26.9	5.2	75
Did not Graduate High School	16562	*463	9.9	2.8	53	552	9.0	3.3	48
18–24	7845	*399	8.5	5.1	97	779	12.7	9.9	144
25–34	19184	799	17.0	4.2	79	1654	26.9	8.6	125
35–44	20154	1358	28.9	6.7	128	1524	24.8	7.6	110
45–54	14824	764	16.2	5.2	98	927	15.1	6.3	91
55–64	10381	580	12.3	5.6	106	639	10.4	6.2	89
65 or over	17055	803	17.1	4.7	90	634	10.3	3.7	54
18–34	27029	1198	25.5	4.4	84	2433	39.5	9.0	131
18–49	55545	2960	62.9	5.3	101	4441	72.1	8.0	116
25–54	54163	2921	62.1	5.4	103	4105	66.7	7.6	110
Employed Full Time	40050	2197	46.7	5.5	104	3285	53.4	8.2	119
Part-time	10670	697	14.8	6.5	124	699	11.4	6.6	95
Sole Wage Earner	13368	544	11.6	4.1	77	993	16.1	7.4	108
Not Employed	38723	1810	38.5	4.7	89	2173	35.3	5.6	82
Professional	9157	770	16.4	8.4	160	933	15.2	10.2	148
Executive/Admin./Managerial	6777	*429	9.1	6.3	120	787	12.8	11.6	169
Clerical/Sales/Technical	20244	1104	23.5	5.5	104	1515	24.6	7.5	109
Precision/Crafts/Repair	1058	*11	0.2	1.0	19	*45	0.7	4.2	61
Other Employed	13484	580	12.3	4.3	82	705	11.4	5.2	76
H/D Income $75,000 or More	13615	1129	24.0	8.3	158	1348	21.9	9.9	144
$60,000 - 74,999	8572	694	14.8	8.1	154	926	15.0	10.8	157
$50,000 - 59,999	7341	482	10.3	6.6	125	463	7.5	6.3	92
$40,000 - 49,999	9283	549	11.7	5.9	112	766	12.4	8.3	120
$30,000 - 39,999	11776	529	11.3	4.5	85	597	9.7	5.1	74
$20,000 - 29,999	13159	537	11.4	4.1	78	855	13.9	6.5	94
$10,000 - 19,999	14645	*322	6.8	2.2	42	710	11.5	4.9	70
Less than $10,000	11051	461	9.8	4.2	79	491	8.0	4.4	65
Census Region: North East	17920	1532	32.6	8.5	163	2114	34.3	11.8	171
North Central	20997	2011	42.7	9.6	182	960	15.6	4.6	66
South	32866	1120	23.8	3.4	65	1393	22.6	4.2	62
West	17660	*41	0.9	0.2	4	1690	27.4	9.6	139
Marketing Reg.: New England	4683	355	7.5	7.6	144	334	5.4	7.1	104
Middle Atlantic	15091	1318	28.0	8.7	166	1866	30.3	12.4	180
East Central	12106	964	20.5	8.0	151	*291	4.7	2.4	35
West Central	13576	1110	23.6	8.2	156	916	14.9	6.7	98
South East	18186	843	17.9	4.6	88	802	13.0	4.4	64
South West	10325	*73	1.5	0.7	13	498	8.1	4.8	70
Pacific	15477	*41	0.9	0.3	5	1449	23.5	9.4	136

	Breyer's				Dreyer's Grand				Ben & Jerry's		
A	B	C	D	A	B	C	D	A	B	C	D
	%	%			%	%			%	%	
'000	Down	Across	Index	'000	Down	Across	Index	'000	Down	Across	Index
14713	100.0	16.4	100	2889	100.0	3.2	100	5918	100.0	6.6	100
—	—	—	—	—	—	—	—	—	—	—	—
14713	100.0	16.4	100	2889	100.0	3.2	100	5918	100.0	6.6	100
5806	39.5	15.2	93	1269	43.9	3.3	103	2380	40.2	6.2	94
14713	100.0	16.4	100	2889	100.0	3.2	100	5918	100.0	6.6	100
3730	25.4	21.7	132	1047	36.2	6.1	189	2016	34.1	11.7	177
4265	29.0	18.0	109	858	29.7	3.6	112	2027	34.3	8.5	129
4692	31.9	14.7	89	732	25.3	2.3	71	1352	22.8	4.2	64
2024	13.8	12.2	74	*251	8.7	1.5	47	523	8.8	3.2	48
1226	8.3	15.6	95	*280	9.7	3.6	110	893	15.1	11.4	172
3579	24.3	18.7	113	715	24.8	3.7	115	1618	27.3	8.4	127
3991	27.1	19.8	120	575	19.9	2.9	88	1743	29.4	8.6	131
2259	15.4	15.2	93	510	17.6	3.4	106	964	16.3	6.5	98
1418	9.6	13.7	83	*346	12.0	3.3	103	358	6.1	3.5	52
2239	15.2	13.1	80	464	16.0	2.7	84	342	5.8	2.0	30
4806	32.7	17.8	108	995	34.4	3.7	114	2511	42.4	9.3	140
10070	68.4	18.1	110	1888	65.4	3.4	105	4789	80.9	8.6	130
9829	66.8	18.1	110	1800	62.3	3.3	103	4325	73.1	8.0	121
6743	45.8	16.8	102	1400	48.5	3.5	108	3462	58.5	8.6	131
1969	13.4	18.5	112	*377	13.0	3.5	109	809	13.7	7.6	115
1721	11.7	12.9	78	302	10.4	2.3	70	1070	18.1	8.0	121
6000	40.8	15.5	94	1112	38.5	2.9	89	1647	27.8	4.3	64
1916	13.0	20.9	127	*338	11.7	3.7	114	860	14.5	9.4	142
1410	9.6	20.8	127	*255	8.8	3.8	116	900	15.2	13.3	201
3270	22.2	16.2	98	722	25.0	3.6	110	1692	28.6	8.4	126
*203	1.4	19.2	117	*106	3.7	10.0	310	*34	0.6	3.2	48
1913	13.0	14.2	86	*356	12.3	2.6	82	786	13.3	5.8	88
2903	19.7	21.3	130	718	24.9	5.3	163	1522	25.7	11.2	169
2068	14.1	24.1	147	*339	11.7	3.9	122	775	13.1	9.0	137
1373	9.3	18.7	114	*249	8.6	3.4	105	615	10.4	8.4	127
1551	10.5	16.7	102	*313	10.8	3.4	104	715	12.1	7.7	116
1781	12.1	15.1	92	464	16.1	3.9	122	825	13.9	7.0	106
2004	13.6	15.2	93	*307	10.6	2.3	72	614	10.4	4.7	70
1580	10.7	10.8	66	*302	10.5	2.1	64	518	8.8	3.5	53
1453	9.9	13.1	80	*197	6.8	1.8	55	*333	5.6	3.0	45
4508	30.6	25.2	153	*58	2.0	0.3	10	1865	31.5	10.4	157
3258	22.1	15.5	94	*22	0.8	0.1	3	918	15.5	4.4	66
4581	31.1	13.9	85	*247	8.5	0.8	23	1167	19.7	3.6	54.
2367	16.1	13.4	81	2563	88.;7	14.5	449	1968	33.3	11.1	168
840	5.7	17.9	109	*10	0.3	0.2	6	643	10.9	13.7	208
4056	27.6	26.9	163	*48	1.7	0.3	10	1357	22.9	9.0	136
1787	12.1	14.8	90	—	—	—	—	470	7.9	3.9	59
2109	14.3	15.5	94	*175	6.1	1.3	40	714	12.1	5.3	79
2945	20.0	16.2	98	*76	2.6	0.4	13	627	10.6	3.4	52
1023	7.0	9.9	60	*170	5.9	1.7	51	*394	6.7	3.8	58
1953	13.3	12.6	77	2410	83.4	15.6	482	1713	28.9	11.1	167

(continued)

FIGURE 5–26   Ice Cream Sales by Brand (Continued)

	Total U.S. '000	Edy's Grand				Häagen-Dazs			
Base: Female Homemakers		A '000	B % Down	C % Across	D Index	A '000	B % Down	C % Across	D Index
County Size A	35180	2850	60.6	8.1	154	4095	66.5	11.6	169
County Size B	27427	1166	24.8	4.3	81	1199	19.5	4.4	64
County Size C	12976	*413	8.8	3.2	60	577	9.4	4.4	65
County Size D	13861	*275	5.8	2.0	38	*286	4.6	2.1	30
MSA Central City	30121	1381	29.4	4.6	87	2396	38.9	8.0	116
MSA Suburban	40932	3005	63.9	7.3	140	3359	54.5	8.2	119
Non-MSA	18391	*317	6.7	1.7	33	*403	6.5	2.2	32
Single	13825	763	16.2	5.5	105	1609	26.1	11.6	169
Married	52777	3124	66.4	5.9	113	3503	56.9	6.6	96
Other	22842	817	17.4	3.6	68	1045	17.0	4.6	66
Parents	36556	2096	44.6	5.7	109	2491	40.5	6.8	99
Working Parents	24493	1568	33.3	6.4	122	1693	27.5	6.9	100
Household Size: 1 Person	14703	528	11.2	3.6	68	657	10.7	4.5	65
2 Persons	28180	1523	32.4	5.4	103	2180	35.4	7.7	112
3 or More	46561	2653	56.4	5.7	108	3320	53.9	7.1	104
Any Child in Household	40040	2205	46.9	5.5	105	2717	44.1	6.8	99
Under 2 Years	7574	443	9.4	5.8	111	659	10.7	8.7	126
2–5 Years	16305	839	17.8	5.1	98	1163	18.9	7.1	104
6–11 Years	18883	1020	21.7	5.4	103	1174	19.1	6.2	90
12–17 Years	16883	947	20.1	5.6	107	1048	17.0	6.2	90
White	76161	4102	87.2	5.4	102	4944	80.3	6.5	94
Black	10317	*469	10.0	4.5	87	579	9.4	5.6	82
Spanish Speaking	7447	*237	5.0	3.2	60	673	10.9	9.0	131
Home Owned	60417	3600	76.5	6.0	113	3455	56.1	5.7	84

Source: Mediamark Research, Inc., 1997.

What They Buy

Buyers and potential buyers of PDAs seek the following features in decreasing order of importance:

Small size/light weight.

PC connectivity.

E-mail communications capability.

Phone/address book.

Appointment book/calendar/alarm.

One-way paging.

PDAs were initially valued primarily as organizers and less as communications devices by current users (Figure 5–31). This implies that two benefit segments are emerging: (1) those who value PDAs solely for their

	Breyer's				Dreyer's Grand				Ben & Jerry's		
A	B %	C %	D	A	B %	C %	D	A	B %	C %	D
'000	Down	Across	Index	'000	Down	Across	Index	'000	Down	Across	Index
7084	48.1	20.1	122	1666	57.7	4.7	147	3424	57.9	9.7	147
4349	29.6	15.9	96	998	34.5	3.6	113	1404	23.7	5.1	77
2067	14.1	15.9	97	*97	3.4	0.7	23	680	11.5	5.2	79
1212	8.2	8.7	53	*129	4.5	0.9	29	*410	6.9	3.0	45
4639	31.5	15.4	94	1172	40.6	3.9	120	1992	33.7	6.6	100
7823	53.2	19.1	116	1555	53.8	3.8	118	3343	56.5	8.2	123
2251	15.3	12.2	74	*163	5.6	0.9	27	583	9.9	3.2	48
2292	15.6	16.6	101	521	18.0	3.8	117	1645	27.8	11.9	180
9285	63.1	17.6	107	1796	62.2	3.4	105	3226	54.5	6.1	92
3136	21.3	13.7	83	573	19.8	2.5	78	1047	17.7	4.6	69
7195	48.9	19.7	120	1170	40.5	3.2	99	2409	40.7	6.6	100
4758	32.3	19.4	118	835	28.9	3.4	106	1754	29.6	7.2	108
1959	13.3	13.3	81	382	13.2	2.6	80	801	13.5	5.4	82
4279	29.1	15.2	92	989	34.2	3.5	109	1885	31.8	6.7	101
8475	57.6	18.2	111	1518	52.5	3.3	101	3233	54.6	6.9	105
7593	51.6	19.0	115	1382	47.8	3.5	107	2563	43.3	6.4	97
1573	10.7	20.8	126	*247	8.5	3.3	101	526	8.9	6.9	105
3308	22.5	20.3	123	659	22.8	4.0	125	990	16.7	6.1	92
3641	24.7	19.3	117	624	21.6	3.3	102	1081	18.3	5.7	87
2917	19.8	17.3	105	567	19.6	3.4	104	1037	17.5	6.1	93
12602	85.7	16.5	101	2349	81.3	3.1	95	5194	87.8	6.8	103
1454	9.9	14.1	86	*133	4.6	1.3	40	*326	5.5	3.2	48
1213	8.2	16.3	99	*373	12.9	5.0	155	*365	6.2	4.9	74
10311	70.1	17.1	104	2058	71.2	3.4	105	3526	59.6	5.8	88

organizer features and (2) a smaller but growing group who value them for communications. According to a Forrester Brief, 63 percent of buyers use PDAs both at home and at work, 31 percent for only personal use, and 6 percent solely for work. As communications capabilities improve, this latter group will grow. At the present time, demand drops to essentially zero when the price of a PDA exceeds $500 and appears to increase steeply as it drops below $500. Also the Palm operating system still has a greater share than Windows CE.

How They Buy

Advertising and marketing have not been key influencers in PDA purchase decisions to this point. Current users sought out the devices themselves. Again, this is not unusual for a product at the early stage of the product life cycle. Later users, however, will rely more on information-based advertising and recommendations from colleagues and friends.

FIGURE 5–27   **Popular Ice Cream Flavors**

Flavor	Percent Preference
Vanilla	29.0%
Chocolate	8.9
Butter pecan	5.3
Strawberry	5.3
Neapolitan	4.2
Chocolate chip	3.9
French Vanilla	3.8
Cookies and cream	3.6
Vanilla fudge ripple	2.6
Praline pecan	1.7
Cherry	1.6
Chocolate almond	1.6
Coffee	1.9
Rocky road	1.5
Chocolate marshmallow	1.3
All others	
(each below 1.3%)	23.7%

Source: www.gigaplex.com (2)

FIGURE 5–28   **Top Dreyer's Grand Ice Cream Flavors (based on year-end 1999)**

1. Vanilla (including Vanilla Bean and French Vanilla)
2. Rocky Road
3. Mint Chocolate Chips!
4. Cookies 'N Cream
5. Mocha Almond Fudge
6. Cookie Dough
7. Chocolate (including Double Fudge Brownie)
8. Chocolate Chips!
9. Butter Pecan/Almond Praline
10. Real Strawberry

Source: Dreyer's Ice Cream Web Site, www.dreyers.com/scoop/main_cold_topten.html, 2000.

Where They Buy

Customers buy lower-priced, low-feature devices from consumer electronics stores and office supply superstores (e.g., Office Max, Office Depot). Higher-end PDAs are purchased from computer stores, through mail order, or via the Internet.

Motorcycles

For those readers who find ice cream and PDAs too tame to be interesting, Figures 5–32 and 5–33 show a segmentation scheme for motorcycle riders.

FIGURE 5-29   **What They Buy: Supermarket Ice Cream Purchases by Brand/Brands**

Brand	Type Vol. Share	% HH Buying	Volume/ Purchase	Share of Type Requirements	Price/ Unit Volume	% Volume Trade Deals	% Store Features	% Store Display	% Price Reduction	% Manufacturer's Coupons	% Off Price Deals
Agway/Hood	1.89	3.37	5.23	33.09	0.67	62.59	55.83	11.17	16.57	10.97	21.60
Ben & Jerry's	0.53	6.57	1.38	7.03	2.68	33.78	17.75	7.25	24.82	2.55	27.54
Blue Bell	3.12	6.44	4.38	45.84	0.97	58.79	38.96	12.36	43.90	0.50	29.41
Kemps	3.87	6.29	6.51	35.67	0.55	64.31	36.13	22.46	55.62	2.22	25.83
Healthy Choice	3.02	10.62	3.77	20.44	0.96	48.03	23.58	7.86	41.50	37.31	33.13
Dean's (Mayfield)	3.68	9.03	4.61	28.66	0.74	42.63	27.07	6.32	36.76	5.15	31.04
Dryer's	14.29	35.29	4.87	28.63	0.90	69.06	45.14	14.77	50.86	10.40	35.07
Häagen-Dazs	0.93	9.25	1.52	9.74	2.64	39.48	22.14	4.57	32.47	11.94	28.25
Starbucks	0.25	1.99	2.18	10.18	1.93	23.40	7.82	1.93	19.61	8.05	18.41
Friendly's	2.60	6.82	5.66	22.79	0.83	73.66	66.06	15.53	33.00	15.89	35.62
Turkey Hill	2.35	5.84	5.18	25.19	0.76	81.62	69.68	10.56	47.49	9.31	40.40
Breyer's	10.89	31.02	4.76	25.38	0.89	63.56	39.77	11.82	49.02	7.07	31.92
Wells	2.67	5.72	5.52	27.56	0.63	49.50	28.05	6.99	40.56	8.46	26.32
Private Label	36.45	53.79	5.56	51.67	0.53	57.55	33.54	10.20	44.45	0.16	29.20

Average Volume / Household = 36.83
Source: 1997 IRI Marketing Fact Book; Brands greater than 1% share plus Ben & Jerry's, Häagen-Dazs, Starbucks.

Figure 5–30 PDA Market Segments

Segment	Size	Characteristics	Distinctive Attribute
Wide Area Travelers:			
Globetrotters	10%	Age 45–54; mostly male Employed in senior positions	Innovators, have modems installed in their portable PCs
Road Warriors	20%	Mostly in corporate management and sales, property management and real estate	High cellular phone usage Overall computer usage lower than for other mobile pros
Corporate Wanderers	12%	Travel less than Globetrotters or Road Warriors; spend most time visiting employees within their own companies	Employ portable PCs least Heaviest fax users (on PCs) High e-mail users Longest owners of cellular phones
Local Area Travelers:			
Collaborators	8%	Age 25–44 Well-educated young professionals, tend to hold advanced degrees Team leaders, project managers	Innovators High use of pagers (20% of segment) Not very mobile but need mobile products
Corridor Cruisers	15%	Similar profile to Collaborators	Not as likely to adopt new products as collaborators
Hermits	8%	Least mobile Youngest segment (many under 35) Seldom work with others Mostly finance and telemarketing	Heavy e-mail users Virtually all are PC users but not portable users
Solo Practitioners	16%	Like Hermits but older Diverse collection of technical professionals in small to medium-size companies	Typically connect to corporate network when traveling Highest connect times of any group
Small-Site Bosses	11%	Run small businesses	Highest portable PC purchase intention in next 12 months; shifting to portable PC as primary computer

FIGURE 5–31

Important PDA functions

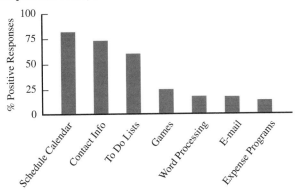

Source: Forrester Research, Inc., July 1999.

FIGURE 5–32 Motorcycle Segment Lifestyle Descriptors

Segment	Description
Tour Gliders (13.8%)	I like long-distance touring bikes. I use my bike for touring. My bike is made more for comfort than for speed. I love to ride long distances . . . to me, 500 miles is a short trip. I like bikes with plastic farings and engine covers.
Dream Riders (39.8%)	Most of the time, my motorcycle is just parked. I like wearing a helmet when I ride. I don't know many other people that ride motorcycles. My bike is pretty much stock. I mainly use my bike for short trips around town.
Hard Core (9.7%)	Some people would call me and my friends "outlaws." I have spent lots on speed modifications for my bike. Sometimes I feel like an "outlaw." Some people would call me a "dirty biker." I think it's true that "real men wear black."
Hog Heaven (8.7%)	When I'm on my bike, people seem to be admiring me. I really believe that cars are confining, like a "cage." Women admire my motorcycle. When I ride I feel like an Old Wild West cowboy. I feel close to other motorcyclists I see on the road.
Zen Riders (20.3%)	I like dirt bikes. When I'm on my bike, people seem to be admiring me. I like the attention I get when I'm on my bike. Most of the time, my motorcycle is just parked. I get excited about motocross or scrambling.
Live to Ride (7.6%)	I love to ride long distances . . . to me, 500 miles is a short trip. Motorcycles are a total lifestyle to me. Riding, to me, is often a magical experience. It's true that "I live to ride and ride to live." My bike is everything to me.

Source: William R. Swinyard, "The Hard Core and Zen Riders of Harley Davidson: A Market-Driven Segmentation Analysis," *Journal of Targeting, Measurement and Analysis for Marketing,* Vol. 4, June 1996, pp. 349–50.

FIGURE 5–33   **Summary of Demographic and Motorcycle
Ownership Characteristics, by Segment**

	Tour Gliders	Dream Riders	Hard Core	Hog Heaven	Zen Riders	Live to Ride
Demographics						
Average owner age	42.6	42.9	36.2	39.2	36.9	36.6
Sex male	93.8%	95.1%	93.5%	85.4%	94.7%	91.7%
Married	60.0%	68.5%	51.1%	56.1%	75.0%	58.3%
Number of children at home	1.3	1.2	1.0	1.2	1.2	1.2
Education: college graduate	15.4%	24.7%	8.7%	7.3%	19.8%	25.0%
Income of $50,000 and over . . .						
Personal	29.7%	30.2%	4.4%	31.7%	26.3%	25.0%
Household	50.8%	52.0%	26.6%	41.0%	55.4%	55.5%
Average income:						
Personal	$40,438	$40,087	$27,389	$34,744	$38,816	$33,667
Household	$46,563	$46,500	$34,944	$40,397	$47,435	$44,222
Occupation: Professional/ managerial	21.5%	30.1%	0.0%	26.8%	19.8%	29.4%
Motorcycle Ownership						
Motorcycle is 1991 or newer	24.6%	30.7%	7.3%	22.0%	28.7%	15.2%
Owned motorcycle under 2 years	16.7%	22.7%	10.3%	35.5%	30.4%	30.3%
Bought motorcycle new	40.0%	50.0%	15.2%	45.0%	33.0%	55.9%
Model year of principal Harley	1985.9	1985.8	1980.5	1986.2	1983.6	1985.7
This is their first motorcycle	1.5%	9.0%	15.9%	19.5%	9.4%	2.8%
No. of motorcycles owned	9.06	5.34	6.3	6.82	5.7	9.77
No. of Harleys owned	4.74	1.63	2.85	2.13	1.44	2.12
Money spent on motorcycle for . . .						
Purchase of motorcycle	$9,048	$7,460	$5,082	$6,631	$6,966	$8,976
Parts/accessories this year	$ 690	$ 322	$1,260	$ 321	$ 767	$ 860
Parts/accessories in total	$1,571	$1,426	$3,233	$2,419	$1,734	$2,483
Estimated value of motorcycle today	$10,066	$8,414	$8,062	$8,591	$8,827	$10,342
Riding per year . . .						
Number of miles	7351	3675	7099	5051	4169	9662
Number of days	188	109	187	148	112	214
Number years riding	24.1	20.2	16.5	16.9	18	17.7
Type of motorcycle they ride:						
Touring	39.0%	16.4%	0.0%	7.9%	12.6%	31.3%
Full dress	18.6%	18.6%	11.4%	10.5%	14.9%	18.9%
Cruiser	23.8%	26.0%	36.4%	29.0%	28.7%	31.3%
Sportster	5.1%	30.5%	29.5%	52.6%	35.6%	0.0%
Other type	13.6%	8.5%	22.7%	0.0%	8.0%	18.8%

Source: William R. Swinyard, "The Hard Core and Zen Riders of Harley Davidson: A Market-Driven Segmentation Analysis," *Journal of Targeting, Measurement and Analysis for Marketing,* Vol. 4, June 1996, p. 351.

Summary

All phases of customer analysis provide potentially useful information. However, a tremendous amount of this information can be summarized in a figure that includes segments across the top and the various aspects of customer analysis as the rows of the figure to describe the segments.

The process of arriving at a useful version of such a figure is likely to be messy, imprecise, and involve trial and error. The best approach is to try several different schemes for defining the segments (e.g., versions of who or why, possibly in combination). The choice of which segmentation scheme to use often depends on the insight gained and the potential for the segmentation scheme to lead to useful strategies (e.g., selecting which segments to serve) and efficient program (e.g., advertising, distribution) determination.

In analyzing customers, it is both natural and useful to look at history. Nonetheless, the reason for doing so is not to be a good historian, but to be a good forecaster. Put differently, one needs to make judgments about what might cause behavior to change (including both your actions and outside influences such as culture, competition, economic conditions, and regulation). In addition, some assessment is needed of the likelihood that these causal influences will in fact change. Finally, the impact of likely changes on customer behavior, and consequently sales, must be analyzed. Then and only then will customer analysis be useful for deciding what to do in the future and what trends to monitor most closely.

References

Aaker, David A. (1996) *Building Strong Brands.* New York: The Free Press.

Aaker, David A. (1991) *Managing Brand Equity.* New York: The Free Press.

Anderson, Eugene W. and Mary W. Sullivan (1993) "The Antecedents and Consequences of Customer Satisfaction for Firms," *Marketing Science,* 12, Spring, 125–43.

Anderson, Eugene, Claes Fornell, and Donald R. Lehmann (1994) "Customer Satisfaction, Market Share, and Profitability," *Journal of Marketing,* 58, July, 53–66.

Bettman, James R. (1979) *An Information Processing Theory of Consumer Choice.* Reading, MA: Addison-Wesley.

Boulding, William, Richard Staelin, Ajay Kalra, and Valerie A. Zeithaml (1992) "Conceptualizing and Testing a Dynamic Process Model of Service Quality." Cambridge, MA: Marketing Science Institute Working Paper, 92–127.

Corfman, Kim P., Donald R. Lehmann, and Sundar Narayanan (1991) "The Role of Consumer Values in the Utility and Ownership of Durables," *Journal of Retailing,* Summer, 184–204.

DeBruicker, F. Steward (1974) "Ocean Spray Cranberries (A)" and "Ocean Spray Cranberries (B)," Harvard Business School cases #9-575-039 and #9-575-040.

Fornell, Claes (1992) "A National Customer Satisfaction Barometer: The Swedish Experience," *Journal of Marketing,* 56, January, 6–21.

Green, Paul E. and Yoram Wind (1975) "New Way to Measure Consumers' Judgments," *Harvard Business Review,* July–August, 107–17.

Grover, Rajiv and V. Srinivasan (1987) "A Simultaneous Approach to Market Segmentation and Market Structuring," *Journal of Marketing Research,* 24, May, 139–52.

Howard, John A. (1989) *Consumer Behavior in Marketing Strategy.* Englewood Cliffs, NJ: Prentice Hall.

Johnston, Wesley J. and Jeffrey E. Lewin (1996) "Organizational Buying Behavior: Toward an Integrative Framework," *Journal of Business Research,* 35, 1–15.

Kahle, Lynn P., Sharon E. Beatty, and Pamela Homer (1986) "Alternative Measurement Approaches to Customer Values: The List of Values (LOV) and Values and Life Styles (VALS)," *Journal of Consumer Research,* 13:3, December, 405–9.

Kamakura, Wagner A. and Gary J. Russell (1989) "A Probabilistic Choice Model for Market Segmentation and Elasticity Structure," *Journal of Marketing Research,* 26, November, 379–90.

Keller, Kevin L. (1998) *Strategic Brand Management.* Upper Saddle River, NJ: Prentice-Hall.

Lehmann, Donald R., Sunil Gupta, and Joel Steckel (1998) *Marketing Research.* Boston: Addison-Wesley.

Lovelock, Christopher H. (1979) "Federal Express (B)," HBS Case Services #9-579-040, Harvard Business School, Boston, MA 02163.

Lynes, Russell (1949) "Highbrow, Lowbrow, Middlebrow," *Harper's.*

Martin, Justin (1994) "Make Them Drink Beer," *FORECAST,* July–August, 34–40.

Parasuraman, A., Valerie A. Zeithaml, and Leonard L. Berry (1988) "SERVQUAL: A Multiple-Item Scale for Measuring Consumer Perceptions of Service Quality," *Journal of Retailing,* 64, Spring, 12–37.

Patterson, Gregory A. (1995) "'Target 'Micromarkets' Its Way to Success: No 2 Stores Are Alike," *The Wall Street Journal,* May 31, A-1.

Pessemier, Edgar A. (1963) *Experimental Methods of Analyzing Demand for Branded Consumer Goods with Applications to Problems in Marketing Strategy,* Bulletin #39, Pullman, WA: Washington State University Bureau of Economic and Business Research, June.

Pine, B. Joseph II, Bart Victor, and Andrew C. Boynton (1993) "Making Mass Customization Work," *Harvard Business Review,* September–October, 108–19.

Rangan, Kasturi, Rowland R. Moriarty, and Gordon S. Swartz (1992) "Segmenting Customers in Mature Industrial Markets," *Journal of Marketing,* 56:4, October, 72–82.

Sullivan, Allanna (1995) "Mobil Bets Drivers Pick Cappuccino over Low Prices," *The Wall Street Journal,* January 30, B-1.

Urban, Glen L. and Eric von Hippel (1988) "Lead User Analyses for the Development of New Industrial Products," *Management Science,* 34:5, May, 569–82.

Wilkie, William L. (1990) *Consumer Behavior,* 2d ed. New York: John Wiley & Sons.

APPENDIX 5A
ECONOMIC VALUE TO THE CUSTOMER (EVC)

Basic Concept

The economic value to the customer is the net dollar value (savings) from using a particular product (often a new one) instead of a relevant substitute (often the one currently used). That is, it is the difference in the total direct cost of using two competing products. Total cost is measured either for a particular time period (e.g., month, year) or activity (job). Since it is frequently used as a means to set price for a new product, it often is computed using the price of the comparison/old product as part of its cost but no price for the new product. At the most general level, the calculation looks like Figure 5A–1 where the difference in total costs ($TC_A - TC_N$) is the economic (cash) value of switching from the old to the new product for the time period or activity level used as a basis of calculation. (For example, if the monthly EVC is $10,000, then the yearly savings is $120,000; similarly, if the EVC is $5,000 per job and the firm completes 40 jobs per year, the yearly EVC is $200,000.)

Example

Improved Lubricant: A new synthetic motor oil is about to be introduced with the primary benefit that it needs to be changed less frequently, specifically once every two years regardless of mileage. Assume current oils need to be changed every 6,000 miles at a cost of $30 per change (oil at $1 a quart or a total of $5, labor $20, disposal of oil $5) for an average car. What is the EVC of the new oil to a car/driver who drives 15,000 miles per year?

This is a straightforward problem where it is relatively easy to get the EVC for a given mileage. First set up Figure 5A–2 similar to Figure 5A–1. We use a two-year basis because it makes the calculation easy. The key distinction between the old and the new is the number of oil changes needed in the two-year period: 1 for the new product and $(2)(15,000/6,000) = 5$ for the old product.

Therefore the economic value (benefit) to using the new product versus the old is $150 − $25 = $125 over the two-year period. Converting this to a per-quart basis means the value of the new oil is $125/5 = $25 per quart.

FIGURE 5–A1   Total Cost Comparison

	(New) Product N	Current (old) Product A	EVC for New Product
Product (Part) Price	?	P_A	
Labor Costs			
Related (e.g., Parts) Costs			
TOTAL COST	TC_N	TC_A	$TC_A - TC_N$

FIGURE 5–A2 Total Cost: Two Years

	New Synthetic Oil	Old Oil
Product Price	?	5 changes × $5/change = $25
Labor Costs	1 change × $20 = $20	5 changes × $20/change = $100
Other Costs (oil disposal)	$5	5 change × $5 = $25
TOTAL	$25	$150

FIGURE 5–A3 The Relation of EVC to Usage Rate

New Product		Old Product		
		Low Mileage (3,000)	Average Mileage (15,000)	High Mileage (45,000)
Product Price	?	1 × $5 = $5	$25	15 × $5 = $75
Labor Costs	$20	1 × $20 = $20	$100	15 × $20 = $300
Other Costs	$5	1 × $5 = $5	$25	15 × $5 = $75
TOTAL COSTS	$25	$30	$150	$450
EVC		$5	$125	$425
EVC/Quart of New Product		$1	$5	$85

Implications

One of the major implications of an EVC calculation is for setting prices. For example, consider the improved lubricant example in Figure 5A–2. For such an "industrial" product (i.e., one without important functional/performance or psychological benefits), the maximum price rational average drivers would be willing to pay would be $25 per quart. However at that price drivers have no incentive to switch to the synthetic (i.e., they are indifferent). In order to give them an incentive to switch, therefore, you must pick a price below $25 (but hopefully above cost). If direct costs are $8 per quart, one then selects a price between $8 and $25. Generally the greater the competition (i.e., number of producers of synthetic oil), the need to quickly capture customers, and available production capacity, the lower the price.

Issues

First, the calculation assumes that customers believe the benefits exist, optimally use the new product, and perform the calculation correctly. One can deal with the calculation aspect by providing it to potential customers (e.g., in ads, sales pitches, etc.). In terms of beliefs, those "trained" to change oil frequently will doubt that the synthetic oil can go two years without changing. If they change it more frequently, the EVC drops. Therefore educating customers is a relevant activity both so they believe the claims and so they use the product correctly.

Second, EVC depends on the usage rate. In this example, heavy users will find the product much more valuable. Consider two drivers, one who drives 3,000 miles per year and one who drives 45,000. The low mileage (3,000 miles) driver only needs one change every two years anyway, while the high mileage driver would need 15. As Figure 5A–3 shows, the low mileage driver should be willing to pay at most $1 per quart (the same as for regular oil) whereas the high mileage driver might pay up to $85. The point of this is that economic value to the customer depends on the particular customer in question.

APPENDIX 5B
MEASURING THE VALUE OF CUSTOMERS

Consistent with the view of a customer as an asset, the value of an individual customer is simply the net discounted margin over time derived from that customer. The expected value depends on the retention probability (r) and margin (m) over time as well as the annual cost to maintain that customer as an account (A). This can easily be set up as a standard spreadsheet (Figure 5B–1) and the value calculated accordingly.

In addition to the value of the customer's direct relationship to a firm, of course, there is value in the nature of the customer (who serves as an ad, in particular when they are celebrities) and what the customer communicates to other customers (word-of-mouth and, now, critically, word-of-web) and to influentials (e.g., government regulators, watchdog groups). These intangibles can obviously overwhelm the direct margin results of a particular company–customer relationship. They are mentioned here as a "heads-up" but not formally factored into the analysis that follows.

The aggregate value of customers is simply the value of an average customer multiplied by the number of customers. More generally, the net aggregate value is

> Value of customers = Sum over time of :
> (Number of Customers in Time t)(Average Net Margin in Time t) −
> (Acquisition Costs$_t$) − (Retention Costs$_t$) − (Expansion Costs$_t$)

In a *very* special case, the value of a customer can be reduced to a simple formula. Specifically, if (1) the retention rate is constant over time and (2) the growth/expansion rate is constant over time (a generally untenable assumption if the growth rate is positive since growth eventually slows), the value of a customer reduces to a formula. For an infinite time horizon[10]

$$\text{VOC} = \sum_{K=1}^{\infty} \frac{(M-A)\, r^{K-1}(1+g)^{K-1}}{(1+d)^{K-1}} = \frac{(M-A)}{1 - \dfrac{r(1+g)}{1+d}} = \frac{(M-A)(1+d)}{1+d-r(1+g)}$$

where:

- M = margin
- A = constant annual account maintenance (retention) cost
- r = (constant) retention rate
- g = (constant) growth in margin rate
- d = constant discount rate

---

[10]Note: These formulas only work when $\dfrac{r(1+g)}{1+d}$ is less than 1.

FIGURE 5B-1   Calculating the Value of a Customer: Spreadsheet Format

	Value in Year					
	1 (current)	2	3	4	...	n
Retention probability (r)	1	r_2	$r_2 r_3$	$r_2 r_3 r_4$	...	$r_2 r_3 \ldots r_n$
Gross margin (m)	m_1	m_2	m_3	m_4	...	m_n
Expected margin (r)(m)	m_1	$r_2 m_2$	$r_2 r_3 m_3$	$r_2 r_3 r_4 m_4$	...	$r_2 r_3 \ldots r_n m_n$
Annual account maintenance cost	A_1	A_2	A_3	A_4	...	A_n
Net Margin	$m_1 - A_1$	$r_2(m_2 - A_2)$	...			
Discount Factor	1	$\dfrac{1}{1+d}$	$\left(\dfrac{1}{1+d}\right)^2$	$\left(\dfrac{1}{1+d}\right)^3$	...	$\left(\dfrac{1}{1+d}\right)^{n-1}$
Discounted Value						

For a finite time horizon (n years) this becomes:

$$\text{VOC} = \sum_{K=1}^{n} \frac{(M-A)\, r^{K-1}(1+g)^{K-1}}{(1+d)^{K-1}} = (M-A)\frac{1 - \left[\dfrac{r(1+g)}{1+d}\right]^K}{1 - \left[\dfrac{r(1+g)}{1+d}\right]}$$

In the case when the growth rate is 0 (i.e., margin is constant over time) over an infinite horizon, this reduces to the simple formula for an annuity:

$$\text{Value of a customer} = \frac{(M-A)(1+d)}{1+d-r}$$

Example

For an interesting example, consider Federal Express's introduction of Courier-Pak. (The figures here are based on Lovelock, 1979.) In the dark old days of 1976, Federal Express sold courier-paks for $12.50 and had a variable cost of $4.00 for a margin per pak of $8.50. One type of account was firms in the advertising business. Specifically, the company had 140 advertising accounts that purchased 2,285 paks per month. To these facts we add the following assumptions:

1. Margin remains constant (i.e., the number of paks per account times the margin per pak stays the same).

FIGURE 5B–2   Value of Advertising Account: Spreadsheet Approach

	Margin	Retention	Discount Factor $\left(\dfrac{1}{1.12}\right)$	Present Value
1	1,617	1	1	1617
2	1,617	.9	.89	1299
3	1,617	.81	.80	1037
4	1,617	.729	.71	840
5	1,617	...	...	...
6	1,617			
7	1,617			
8	1,617			
9	1,617			
10	1,617	.387	.360	225
Total				

   2. The retention rate is 90 percent (which seems reasonable for satisfied customers).

   3. The appropriate discount rate is 12 percent.

The typical advertising account thus generates 2285/140 = 16.32 paks per month or (16.32)(12) = 196 paks per year. This translates into a margin per year of (196)(8.50) = $1,617. Using the spreadsheet approach and a 10-year horizon would then produce Figure 5B–2, and thus a value of about $7,200. Of course we could use an infinite horizon, but since the margin is constant, this will add little to the total discounted value as the following shows:

   1. Infinite Horizon: VOC $= \left(\dfrac{1617}{1 - \dfrac{0.9}{1.12}}\right) = \$8,085$

   2. 10-Year Horizon: VOC $= 1,617\dfrac{1 - \left(\dfrac{0.19}{1.12}\right)^{10}}{\left(1 - \dfrac{0.9}{1.12}\right)} = 1,617\left(\dfrac{1 - .11}{.20}\right) = \$7,196$

Drivers of Value

The key drivers of the value of a particular customer are (1) the retention rate and (2) expansion (i.e., the growth rate). In the previous example, assume the retention rate were 80 percent instead of 90 percent. Using an infinite horizon, the value decreases to

$$\dfrac{1,617}{1 - \dfrac{0.8}{1.12}} = 5,660$$

or 70 percent of the value at a 90 percent retention rate.

Similarly if retention could be increased to 95 percent, the value becomes:

$$\frac{1,617}{1 - \dfrac{0.95}{1.12}} = 10,653$$

which is 32 percent greater than its former value. Thus the value of a customer is very sensitive to the retention rate.

The expansion (or contraction) rate similarly has a major impact on the value of the customer. For example, if we assume a negative 10 percent growth rate, the infinite horizon value becomes

$$\frac{1,617}{1 - \dfrac{(.9)(.9)}{1.12}} = \$5,842$$

or 28 percent less.

Similarly at the aggregate (firm) level expansion comes from a combination of (1) new customer acquisitions and (2) expansion of same-customers' sales (margin).

There is both good news and bad news in these sensitivities. The good news is that it is clear what can be done to improve value: increase retention (e.g., through satisfaction if not barriers to exit) and expand relations with customers (e.g., cross-sell or improve the product mix). Further, small changes make a big difference, thus potentially justifying marketing activity as cost effective. On the other hand, the bad news is that since small changes in the parameters lead to big changes in valuation, there is an obvious opportunity to alter the numbers to justify a particular decision.

APPENDIX 5C
LATENT CLASS METHODS

Advances in both computer power and methods have made feasible a different approach to segment construction and interpreting. Most methods discussed in the chapter basically attempt to take individuals and aggregate them into segments. By contrast, latent class methods simultaneously estimate segment sizes and their behavior. These methods make use of the simple fact that aggregate market behavior is the sum of individual or segment level behavior:

$$\text{Total Market Behavior} = \sum_{\text{segments}} (\text{Size of Segment } i)(\text{Behavior of Segment } i)$$

$$= \sum_{\text{segments}} W_i B_i$$

The latent class approach *simultaneously* estimates segment sizes (W_i s) and segment behavior (B_i s). Segment membership is not known in advance (i.e., there is not a high income or nonresponsive-to-promotion segment specified in advance), and individual customers are not assigned to particular segments.

A key issue involves deciding on the number of segments. Basically this decision involves trading off between better describing a market (which allowing for more segments always does since it increases the number of parameters estimated) and keeping only important or "significant" segments. This trade-off is often accomplished with statistical tests on results of allowing for an additional segment (e.g., five versus four segments) or by comparing the abilities of the more and less parsimonious models to forecast behavior of a holdout sample (that is, customers who were not used to estimate the parameters).

When there is enough data to get an estimate of behavior at the individual customer level, latent class methods often incorporate probabilities of segment membership for each customer:

$$\text{Market Behavior} = \sum_{\text{customers}} \sum_{\text{segments}} P_{ij} B_i$$

where P_{ij} = probability person j is a member of segment i

In interpreting such analyses, it is desirable to describe segments in terms of descriptor variables (demographics, firm characteristics). This can be done separately from the latent class analysis by relating individuals' estimated probabilities of being in each segment to other characteristics (i.e., letting $P_{ij} = f$ [characteristics of customer j]). This two-step approach then becomes

Step 1:
$$\text{Market Behavior} = \sum_{\text{customers}} \sum_{\text{segments}} P_{ij} B_i$$

Step 2:
$$P_{ij} = \sum_{\text{characteristics}} C_{li} X_{li}$$

Occasionally the two steps are combined in a single step:

$$\text{Market Behavior} = \sum_{\text{customers}} \sum_{\text{segments}} \sum_{\text{characteristics}} (C_{li} X_{ij} B_i)$$

Currently latent class methods have not been widely applied in commercial settings. It is a good bet, however, that their use will increase substantially.

CHAPTER

6 Market Potential and Sales Forecasting

Overview

In this chapter, we describe methods for forecasting future results, namely sales or market share. Of course, other forecasts such as costs are also required. Since sales forecasts are the most visible and widespread forecasts made by marketing managers, we focus on them here. Fortunately most of the methods described here (e.g., time series extrapolation) apply to other types of forecasts as well.

A critical part of forecasting is the specification of key assumptions. Often managers make assumptions about factors beyond their control. Most of these are environmentally related factors, such as those covered in Chapter 3. For example, the product manager for Healthy Choice must make assumptions about the likelihood of continuing interest in low-calorie entreés. The product manager for Fuji film must make assumptions about the worldwide supply of silver as well as the demand for digital photography. Marketing personnel in the home construction business make assumptions about future home mortgage interest rates. These assumptions both summarize earlier analyses and establish the basis for potential estimates and forecasts.

Definitions

The terms *potential* and *forecast* are used in many contexts, and are frequently confused. We use the following definitions:

> *Potential:* The maximum sales reasonably attainable under a given set of conditions within a specified period of time (i.e., what you might or could achieve).

FIGURE 6–1   Forecasts versus Potential

	Expectations	Possibilities
Firm / brand	Sales forecast	Sales potential
Category	Market forecast	Market potential

Forecast: The amount of sales expected to be achieved under a set of conditions within a specified period of time (i.e., what you probably will achieve).

Quota: A related term referring to a target typically set by senior managers. Quotas are what an individual in the company, for example a salesperson, is expected to achieve (i.e., what you should or are expected to achieve).

Figure 6–1 shows the distinction between potential and forecast in a sales context. The key difference between the concepts is that *potential* represents what *could* happen in a category if all the competitors (market potential) or the product in question (sales potential) had full distribution, heavy advertising and promotion, and appeal to all the customers who could possibly purchase the product. Alternatively, *forecasts* represent expectations, which (usually) fall far below the potential in a market. Both potentials and forecasts depend on a set of conditions. These conditions can be divided into the four major categories of what customers do, what the firm does, what competitors do, and what occurs in the general environment (economy, culture).

Potentials and forecasts are time dependent. Stated differently, what may not be possible in the short run may be quite attainable in the longer term. While strategic plans depend on long-term potentials, annual plans focus primarily on short-run potentials and forecasts. This suggests a trap into which a firm can fall. By optimizing short-run decisions, the firm may make what in the long run is a less than optimal series of decisions. That is one reason why products are often assigned different objectives, such as increasing sales (when the long-term potential seems large and increasing) or maximizing cash flow (when the long-term potential appears low).

Market Potential

Overview

Market potential is a difficult concept to grasp. In particular, it is hard to estimate the upper limit or maximum of sales. In addition, although managers may perceive potential as a fixed number, it is in fact a dynamic concept and can change dramatically over time. The key to understanding this point is the clause "under a given set of conditions within a specified period of time." In other words, market or sales potential change depending on market factors such as average category price or general economic conditions.

For example, when Texas Instruments introduced its first handheld calculator, the SR10, which made slide rules largely obsolete, it had four functions (add, subtract, multiply, divide), no memory, and cost over $100. Now calculators and even computers far better than the SR10 are given away as promotions. The market potential of the original calculator was limited to those individuals, usually scientists or college students, who needed to make math calculations and could afford the price. When the number of functions offered dramatically increased and the price rapidly fell, more people could both use and afford one. Consequently both market potential and sales increased.

What They Are Used For

There are five major uses of potential estimates:

1. *To make entry/exit decisions.* Potentials (both market and sales) are key numbers in the strategic decisions of what markets to be in.
2. *To make resource-level decisions.* One key aspect of allocation decisions relates to stage in the life cycle. Generally firms are more willing to allocate resources during growth phases. Of course just because sales have plateaued does not mean sales have reached potential. An interesting illustration of the differences between conventional product life cycle thinking and market potential thinking can be found in the running shoe category. In the 1960s, a buyer could get sneakers cut either high or low and in either black or white. The major brands were Keds and Converse. The product life cycle indicated maturity. In the 1970s, the market shot up with the introduction of performance shoes such as Nike, Adidas, and Puma. It became commonplace to wear running shoes to work and then change into work shoes. However, the market again became mature. What happened in the 1980s? Brands such as Reebok and L.A. Gear appealed to different segments (e.g., aerobics and fashion), and again the market jumped. Now a stupefying array of walking shoes, running shoes (for different mileages, degree of pronation, etc.) trail running shoes, cross-trainers, and court shoes are available. One manager's mature market is another's growth market in which growth (actually potential growth) is defined as the gap between actual sales and market potential. Thus, as many writers have warned (Dhalla and Yuspeh, 1976), the product life cycle concept must be used carefully.
3. *To make location and other resource allocation decisions.* Both manufacturing plants and distribution facilities tend to be located based on potential estimates as do retail stores. Similarly sales force efforts and advertising are often allocated across products or regions based on potential.

FIGURE 6–2

Deriving potential estimates

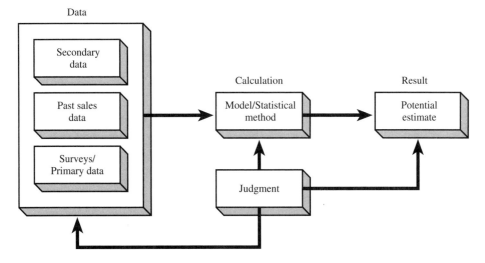

4. *To set objectives and evaluate performance.* Potentials provide a standard to try to achieve. When actual sales fall below potential, a key question is "Why is there such a difference?" Examining this often leads to changes in market strategy and programs. For example, sales managers use market (or more accurately, area) potential in two ways. First, sales territories are often designed to have equal market potential so that different salespersons can be better judged on the basis of actual sales. Second, sales quotas are sometimes set based on the potential sales in a territory.
5. *As an input to forecasts.* A major use of potentials in annual planning is as a basis for the sales forecast. In this case, a forecast is viewed as the product of potential times the percent of potential expected to be achieved.

Information Sources

Market potential may be estimated in a variety of ways. While the details involved depend on the particular industry and product under consideration, this section suggests some general approaches to assessing potential. Past sales data are useful, and for a stable market provide the necessary information for both a potential estimate and a sales forecast. In new markets (including most Internet businesses), however, such data may be unavailable, inaccurate, or unduly influenced by isolated events. Even when such data are available, other data should *not* be ignored. Figure 6–2 summarizes a general process for deriving potential estimates (which is also useful for forecast development). The exact data collected and calculations used depend on the situation. Some of the sources useful for potential estimates (and forecasts) are already familiar to readers.

Government Sources
Market size estimates are available for many industries from sources such as the U.S. Department of Commerce and the Bureau of the Census (e.g., *Survey of Current Business, Current Industrial Reports*). Even when specific size estimates for an industry or a product are not available, government data may be useful as inputs to the potential estimate. Examples include breakdowns of industry by location, size, and SIC code and forecasts of general economic conditions.

Trade Associations
These groups are a good source of information for particular industries or product categories, although they may be a bit optimistic.

Private Companies
A number of private companies track and forecast sales for various industries (e.g., FIND/SVP). Some also survey capital spending plans (e.g., McGraw-Hill), consumer sentiment, and durable purchasing plans (e.g., the Survey Research Center at the University of Michigan).

Financial and Industry Analysts
Industry specialists often provide forecasts or potential estimates for various industries (e.g., Forrester, Gartner for computers).

Popular Press
A substantial amount of material finds its way into the business press (e.g., *Fortune, Forbes, Business Week*) or specialty publications.

The Internet
As in most areas, the Internet provides access to a wide and increasing pool of information.

While many sources often exist, their competency and accuracy may not be very high. (Although it is comforting to assume that published potential estimates and forecasts are accurate and done by experts, both the accuracy and expertise are often suspect. Think of it this way: The person who prepared the forecast may have been a classmate of yours!) To understand or assess the value of a forecast (whether provided by an outsider or a subordinate), it is important to have at least a rudimentary knowledge of how forecasts are constructed. This chapter therefore goes into some detail on forecasting methods in the hope that the reader will become a more intelligent consumer of forecasts.

New or Growing Product Potential

In considering both the saturation level (ultimate potential) and the time pattern of market development, it is useful to compare the product to its major (and typically older) competitors. This can be accomplished by considering three major dimensions: relative advantage, compatibility, and risk.

Relative Advantage

In terms of benefits provided, is the new product superior in key respects and, if so, to what degree? Noticeably superior benefits increase both the saturation level and the rate at which the level is achieved. Also, in general, the relative advantage of a new product increases over time as various modifications and line extensions appear.

Compatibility

The fewer and less important the changes required to adopt a new product, the faster it will be adopted. Compatibility issues relate not only to customers but also to intermediaries, the company itself (e.g., sales staff), and, if customers use a certain product as a component in another product, their customers as well. Therefore, if a chemical company is planning to manufacture a new product, issues of manufacturing compatibility and sales staff effort arise within the company along with potential problems regarding the behavior of wholesalers (assuming the product is sold through that channel), customer problems (is retooling required?), and eventual customer acceptance. Incompatibility tends to decrease over time. Finally, while incompatibility may be primarily psychological (i.e., "We just don't do things that way here"), failure to consider psychological barriers to adoption is often disastrous, at least in assessing short-term potential.

Risk

The greater the risk involved (financial, possible impact on product quality if a new component fails, and so on), the lower the probability that someone will buy the new product. Typically, risk—at least in terms of price—tends to drop over time, thus increasing the potential.

Overall, the higher the relative advantage (benefits) and the lower the costs (incompatibility, risk), the greater the potential and the faster it is likely to be achieved.

Role of Analogous Products

Examining the pattern of use and adoption of analogous products or services is often quite useful, especially for growing or new products. For either, the previous adoption patterns of similar products provide a clue to the likely pattern and rate of adoption and the eventual saturation level. As will be seen later in this chapter, analogies are also useful for sales forecasting.

The problem with using analogies is that two products are rarely perfectly comparable. To be reasonably comparable, both the newer product and its older analogue should be targeted to a similar market; be similar in perceived value, both in toto and in terms of the major benefits provided; and be similar in price. Under these criteria, a microwave oven could be compared to a dishwasher in that both are targeted at households, stress convenience and time savings, and cost about the same. In contrast, a mainframe computer from 1960, a microcomputer from 1984, and a wireless device linked to the Internet are not analogous, even though one is a direct descendant of the other, because the target market (a company versus individuals), perceived value (number crunching and billing versus convenience and word processing or entertainment and information), and price (a million dollars versus a few hundred) all differ dramatically.

Mature Product Potentials

The more mature products are, the more sales come from reorders from past customers. Reorders in a mature market are of two types. For a consumable product, repurchasing will be in proportion to the market need (if an industrial product) or usage rate (if a consumer product). For a durable product, repurchasing will occur to replace a worn-out product, to upgrade to get new features, or, importantly, to add an additional model (e.g., a second TV; see Bayus, Hong, and Labe, 1989, for an example).

Methods of Estimating Market and Sales Potential

The role of managerial judgment in deriving potential is crucial and ubiquitous. It influences the type of data examined, the model used to derive the estimate, and often the estimate itself. Although statistical knowledge is useful, logic or common sense is much more important. Therefore, after estimating market potential, a manager should step back and ask, "Does this estimate make sense?"

Analysis-Based Estimates

A formula-based method can be developed based largely on the potential users or buyers of the product in question in a three-step process.

   1. *Determine the potential buyers or users of the product.* Buyers should be interpreted broadly as customers who have the need, the resources necessary to use the product, and the ability to pay. This often results in the manager assessing that almost all customers are in the potential market (and maybe they are). An alternative approach is to work backward: Who *cannot* qualify as a potential customer? This might include apartment dwellers for lawn mowers, diabetics for regular ice

cream, and so on. The manager can determine potential customers judgmentally. In addition, other data sources that could be useful are surveys, commercial sources such as data from Simmons Market Research Bureau or MRI, and government documents.

As an example, consider the problem of estimating the market potential for laptop computers. One judgmental approach for determining the number of potential adult employed users is to divide the market into categories such as: (1) "fleet workers" who are not in an office but need portable computing capabilities in a warehouse or manufacturing line, (2) "road warriors" who are on the road full time and need a virtual office, (3) "office functionalists" who work mainly out of the office but sometimes from home, (4) "corridor cruisers" who need their office computers when they go to business meetings, and (5) "road runners" who need a second office but less intensively than "road warriors" do (Beeh, 1994).

2. *Determine how many are in each potential group of buyers defined by step 1.* Often steps 1 and 2 are done simultaneously. If defined in terms of a particular demographic group, for example, people above age 60, sources such as the *Statistical Abstract of the United States* can help determine how many people are in the group. For the previous example of laptop computers, the estimated group sizes were 15 million "fleet workers," 10 million "road warriors," 8 million "office functionalists," 6 million "corridor cruisers," and 5 million "road runners."

The potential U.S. market for ice cream includes most individuals. If we start with a population of 280 million, we need to remove diabetics and individuals with lactose intolerance or other reasons not to consume dairy products. Based on the percent of the population who have these conditions, that would eliminate approximately 16 million diabetics and 30 million with lactose intolerance, leaving about 234 million as the potential market. Of course many of these are young children, so the size of the buying market is smaller. The real issue is how long growth in super-premium sales will continue given obvious health issues.

3. *Estimate the purchasing or usage rate.* This can be done either by taking the average purchasing rate determined by surveys or other research or by assuming that the potential usage rate is characterized by the heaviest buyers. The latter notion would be based on the assumption that all buyers could be convinced to purchase at that heavy rate. Market potential is then calculated by simply multiplying the number obtained from step 2 by the number from step 3, that is, the number of potential customers times their potential usage rate. For example, if we assume one laptop computer per potential user, the U.S. installed base market potential is simply 44 million units. The market potential estimate derived in this manner usually results in a

large number when compared to current industry sales. To get an annual potential, the installed base potential of 44 million must be multiplied by the percent who buy each year. Assuming purchases are made every four years, this leads to an annual potential of 11 million. This method is often referred to as the successive ratio or chain ratio method. However, the number itself is often not as important as the process of trying to get the number. Estimating market potential using this kind of analysis forces the manager to think about who the potential customers for the product are, which can often result in new thinking about untapped segments. A second impact of the market potential estimate is that it usually reveals a significant amount of untapped purchasing power in the market that is waiting for a new strategy, a new product formulation, or perhaps a new competitor.

Two examples help illustrate this method. The first illustration is from the infant/toddler disposable diaper category. The potential users are rather obvious in this case. During the 1990s, an average 4 million babies were born annually in the United States. The average child goes through 7,800 diapers in the first 130 weeks of life (2.5 years) until toilet training, or 60 per week (Deveny, 1990). To compute potential sales, this 7,800 figure can be used to represent a mix of children at different ages. Thus, the annual market potential for disposable diapers is 31.2 million [(2.3)(4 million) babies][60 diapers/week][52 weeks/year]. This figure includes babies who are allergic to the diapers as well as households using cloth diapers or diaper services. Importantly, households using cloth diapers are still potential customers.

A second application shown in Figure 6–3 is typical of estimates of market potential for industrial products (Cox, 1979, Chapter 7). In this case, the potential customers are identified by SIC code. How much they can buy is extrapolated from an activity measure, in this case dollars of purchases per employee. A defect of this approach, however, is that current nonbuying SIC codes that are potential buyers are not included in the analysis.

Now consider again U.S. consumption of ice cream. In 1999, the population was 273,401,000. Of these, 16 million suffer from diabetes (and hence cannot consume regular ice cream) and 30 million are lactose intolerant. Removing these leaves 227,401,000 potential customers (plus those who are both diabetic and lactose intolerant). On average, consumption per person is 46.6 pints per year. This means potential is 10.5 billion pints per year which, at an average price per pint of $3.19, translates into a $33.5 billion market.

For handheld devices (PDAs), market potential is based on the total population of 278.1 million. From this we eliminate children under 13 (56.2 million) and those who live below the poverty level (21.1 million) for a potential market size of 200.8 million. Note that

FIGURE 6–3   **Market Potential: Electric Coil**

SIC	Industry	Purchases of Product	Number of Workers	Average Purchase/ Worker	National Number of Workers	Estimated Potential
3611	Electrical measuring	$160	3,200	$ .05	34,913	$1,746
3612	Power transformers	5,015	4,616	1.09	42,587	46,249
3621	Motors and generators	2,840	10,896	.26	119,330	31,145
3622	Electrical industry controls	4,010	4,678	.86	46,805	40,112
		$12,025				$119,252

this potential assumes each person buys only one and that purchases occur annually, so potential can vary widely as these assumptions are altered.

Analysis-based estimates have to be used carefully for durable consumer products or industrial products with long interpurchase cycles. In those cases, buyers not in the market because they recently purchased the good must be subtracted from the total. However, sometimes multiple purchases of such products occur; for example, many households have two or three VCRs.

This approach to estimating market potential has implications for increasing the sales volume in a category or for a brand. There are two ways to increase sales. First, the manager can increase the number of customers—by pursuing new segments, developing new products, or just getting more customers in existing segments (see Chapter 7). Second, the purchase rate can be increased; that is, the manager can attempt to get customers to buy more through promotions, package size changes, and other tactics. These approaches have been used successfully at General Mills, which has a large stable of mature products (e.g., Hamburger Helper, Betty Crocker cake mixes; Sellers, 1991).

Area Potential

Area potential is often derived by breaking down total sales by area. When sales data are available for a variety of regions, along with some data on characteristics of the regions, it is common to use a weighted index that combines these characteristics to indicate the relative potential in the area. Many consumer goods companies use the general *Sales and Marketing Management* buying power index, which is 0.2 × (percentage of the population of the area compared to the United States) + 0.3 × (percentage of retail sales of the area of the U.S. total) + 0.5 × (percentage of disposable income of the area of the U.S. total). When population, retail sales, and disposable income are input as a percentage of the total United States, this index projects the percentage of the product sold in the various regions. For established products, these weights may be estimated from the actual sales data by, for example, running a regression of sales versus various factors such as the number of schools in the region. Product-related data, such as sales of analogous products, might also be used. In fact, as noted earlier in this chapter, sales of truly analogous products are often the best indicators of potential. An index approach for a hypothetical new copying system might be as follows:

Bases: Percent population in the region (P).

Percent schools in the region (S).

Percent retail businesses in the region (RB).

Percent banks in the region (B).

Percent offices in the region (O).

Percent warehouses in the region (WH).

Percent manufacturing facilities in the region (MF).

Percent other businesses in the region (OB).

Percent Xerox sales in the region (XS).

Percent other copier sales in the region (CS).

$$\text{Index} = W_1\,P + W_2\,S + W_3\,RB + W_4\,B + W_5\,O + W_6\,WH + W_7\,MF + W_8\,OB + W_9\,XS + W_{10}\,CS$$

Here the Ws are the weights assigned to each factor.

Sales Potential

Sales potential is the firm-level analogy to market potential. An obvious approach to calculating sales potential is to multiply the estimated potential of the market by some market share figure. This share figure should represent potential share, which the firm could achieve under optimal conditions (but usually not 100 percent).

Sales Forecasting

Overview

As noted earlier, forecasting deals with expectations of the future, that is, what the manager thinks will happen. The most obvious things to be concerned about, and the focus of this chapter, are results such as sales, market share, and profits.

Other quantities are of course important to forecast as well. *Resources* used as a factor of production must be forecast (note the earlier discussion about general planning assumptions). Sometimes the key resources are human, making it important to forecast the needed labor pool. *Costs* are also an important factor to forecast. If the product is manufactured and follows the experience curve, costs are somewhat more predictable than in other situations. For many product managers, accurate forecasts of the rate of change of *technology* are critical to keeping an edge on competitors. General *economic conditions* have important effects on many types of businesses. Finally, in global businesses currency exchange rates have a major impact on profits.

Forecasts are used in several ways.

1. *To answer "what if" questions.* In considering which strategy and tactics to follow, the key is an estimate of the outcomes of the various strategies and tactics, typically the sales and profit levels. The simplest "what if" question is what will happen next year if everything remains as it has been in the past, which makes the forecast basically an extrapolation.

2. *To help set budgets.* Sales forecasts become the basis of a budget because they specify both sales levels to be attained and, by implication, the resources needed. All pro forma income statements are based on a sales forecast.

3. *To provide a basis for a monitoring system.* Deviations from forecasts serve as warnings to product management to reexamine a market and their strategy in it. Both positive and negative deviations from forecasts can lead to a better understanding of the marketplace through an examination of the underlying causes.

4. *To aid in production planning.* With more companies and their channels moving to just-in-time production and distribution systems with low levels of inventory, accurate forecasting is becoming even more critical. This is particularly important in the personal computer industry. Mistakes in forecasting demand for personal computers cost Compaq $50 million and IBM much more in 1994 (McWilliams, 1995). For several years Apple Computer underestimated the demand for its Powerbook laptop computers, which exacerbated its financial problems.

5. *By financial analysts to value a company.* The huge valuations of the "dot.com" companies at the end of 1999 could be justified only on the basis of large growth rates. Further, deviations from forecasts have a major impact on stock prices (e.g., missing sales or earnings targets).

A good forecast takes into account four major categories of variables, all of which either have been or will be discussed in this book: customer behavior (Chapter 5), past and planned product strategies (Chapter 7), competitor actions (Chapter 4), and the environment (Chapter 3). Company actions are predictable and/or under the control of the manager. In contrast, customer and competitive actions are much harder to forecast. The general environment consists of such elements as the state of the economy, key industries in it, demographic changes in the population, and costs of basic resources. Although

FIGURE 6–4

Scenario-based forecasts

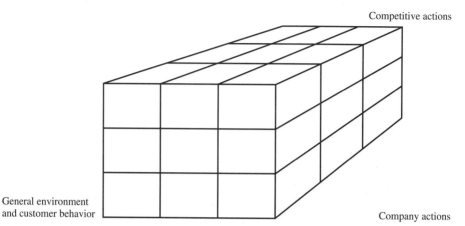

some of these elements can be forecast by the manager, they are generally derived from secondary sources, such as government projections, and appear in the category analysis or the planning assumptions section of a marketing plan. While environmental changes affect the plan mainly through their impact on competitor and customer behavior, they can be so crucial that we treat them separately here.

Forecasting can be thought of as the process of assessing the possible outcomes under reasonably likely combinations (sometimes called scenarios) of the four basic determinants of outcome. This suggests forecasting without considering competitive reactions is, unless the competitors are asleep, insufficient. The forecasting process can be viewed as a process of filling out a three-dimensional grid such as that shown in Figure 6–4, with the likely outcomes contingent on values of the three sets of independent variables.

The forecast in each cell should not be a single number but rather a range of possible outcomes. While a forecast of 787.51 may sound better than 800 ± 50, it may be misleading and an example of foolish precision (which puts you out on a limb with your boss). Do not expect forecasts to six decimal places, especially when such precision is not crucial to making a sound decision.

Knowing the range of likely results is crucial for strategy selection. A manager may be unwilling to undertake a strategy with a high expected result (e.g., a profit of $8 million) that also has a reasonably likely disastrous result (e.g., a loss of $5 million). Conversely, a manager may be willing to gamble on a possible large return even if the likely result is a small profit or even a loss. It is also useful to know the likely range of outcomes for purposes of monitoring and control. For example, in one situation, a drop of 30 percent below the forecast may be well within the expected range and therefore not necessarily cause for a major reanalysis, whereas in a different situation, a 15 percent drop below the forecast may signal a serious problem.

At this point, it should be clear that producing a forecast for each possible combination of factors is a tedious task at best. Consequently, it is desirable to limit the task to, say, three environments (expected, benign, and hostile) and a limited number of competitive postures (e.g., status quo, more/less aggressive). This limitation should, however, be made with two points in mind. First, the initial forecasts may suggest a promising avenue or a potential disaster that may lead to refining the scenarios. Second, the assumptions made in forecasting are crucial; therefore, it is desirable to designate them formally as *planning assumptions*.

Level of Accuracy Needed

Obviously, more accuracy in a forecast is better than less. Also, assuming a reasonably intelligent forecasting procedure is being employed (something one should *not* generally assume), then the only way to get a better forecast is to spend more time, effort, and money. Since increasing forecast accuracy has severely diminishing marginal returns (to make the range of a forecast half as large will generally at least quadruple its cost), at some point the cost of improving the forecast will exceed the benefit.

The benefit of a better forecast usually is greater when (1) the price of the product is high in either absolute or relative terms ($40,000 may not be much to IBM but it is to the authors); (2) the product demand is relatively volatile; and (3) the cost of an error in forecasting (including reorder cost and the cost of being out of stock—which may include the long-term loss of a disenchanted customer) is high. The cost of a better forecast increases as (1) the number of items or product forms increases (e.g., machine tool A with feature X, with features X and Z, and so on); (2) the method becomes more complicated to use; and (3) the forecast (and its basis) is difficult to communicate to others in the organization. (Generally speaking, review committees prefer not to hear about Fourier series, correlated errors, and so on.)

Judgment-Based Methods

A large number of methods have been developed for forecasting (Chambers, Mullick, and Smith, 1971; Georgoff and Murdick, 1986; Wheelwright and Makridakis, 1985). Figure 6–5 compares a number of methods. Here we discuss four basic approaches: judgment based, customer based, sales extrapolation, and model based. The first set of methods is referred to as *judgment-based* methods because, unsurprisingly, they rely solely on judgments.

Naive Extrapolation
One method of naive extrapolation uses the last-period sales level and adds x percent, the estimated percentage change in sales. For example, dishwasher sales could be forecast to be last year's plus 6 percent. A related approach might

184

FIGURE 6-5 Summary of Forecasting Methods

	Dimensions	1. Time span	2. Urgency	3. Quantitative skills needed	4. Financial resources needed	5. Past data needed	6. Accuracy
Judgment	*Naive Extrapolation*	Short/ medium term	Rapid turnaround	Minimal	Very low	Some	Limited
	Sales Force	Short/ medium term	Fast turnaround	Minimal	Low	Not necessary	Highly variable
	Executive Opinion	Short/ medium term	Depends on whether inside or outside company	Minimal	Could be high if outside experts used	Not necessary	Poor if one individual; better if a group
	Delphi	Medium/ long	Needs time	Minimal	Could get high	Not necessary	Best under dynamic conditions
Counting	*Market Testing*	Medium	Needs time	Moderate level	High	Not necessary	Good for new products
	Market Survey	Medium	Needs time	Yes	High	Not necessary	Limited

Time Series						
Moving Average	Short/medium	Fast turnaround	Minimal	Low	Necessary	Good only in stable environment
Exponential Smoothing	Short/medium	Fast turnaround	Minimal	Low	Necessary	Good in short run
Extrapolation	Short/medium/long	Fast turnaround	Basic skills	Low	Necessary	Good for trends, stable time series
Association/Causal						
Correlation	Short/medium/long	Fast turnaround	Basic skills	Moderate	Necessary	Highly variable
Regression	Short/medium/long	Moderately fast	Basic skills	Moderate/high	Necessary	Can be accurate if explained variance is high
Leading Indicators	Short/medium/long	Moderately fast	Basic skills	Moderate	Necessary	Moderately accruate at best
Econometric	Short/medium/long	Needs time	High level	High	Necessary	Best in stable environment

Source: David M. Georgoff and Robert G. Murdick, "Manager's Guide to Forecasting," *Harvard Business Review*, January–February, 1986, pp. 110–20.

FIGURE 6–6

Graphical eyeball forecasting

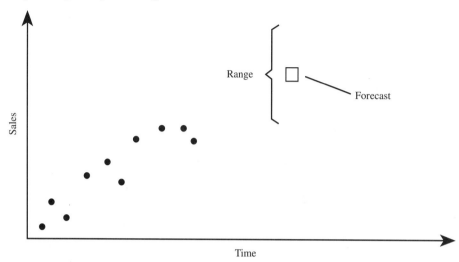

be termed "graphical eyeball." This requires plotting the past sales series and then "eyeballing" the next value to match the past pattern (see Figure 6–6).

Sales Force Composite

Salespeople are often asked to make sales forecasts. Their forecasts can then be aggregated to create a sales forecast for the product or product line. The advantage of this approach is that salespeople are close to customers and thus in an excellent position to understand their purchasing plans. Unfortunately, when the forecast is used to set quotas, such forecasts are naturally on the low side. Alternatively, salespeople can be overly optimistic in an attempt to impress the sales manager.

Jury of Expert Opinion

An extreme example of this method relies on a single expert's opinion. If the expert happens to know the Delphic oracle or be a mystic, the forecast can be excellent. Unfortunately, it is hard to know ahead of time whether someone can predict the future.

Many studies have been published deriding expert forecasts. Consider the following business-related predictions made by "experts" (Cerf and Navasky, 1984):

- With over 50 foreign cars already on sale here, the Japanese auto industry isn't likely to carve out a big slice of the U.S. market for itself. (*Business Week,* August 2, 1968).
- A severe depression like that of 1920–1921 is outside the range of probability. (Harvard Economic Society, November 16, 1929).

- The phonograph . . . is not of any commercial value. (Thomas Edison, ca. 1880).

TRW sponsored a major technological forecasting project back in the mid-1960s. Some of their predictions were

- A manned lunar base by 1977.
- Commercial passenger rockets by 1980.
- Undersea mining and farming by 1981.

Despite examples like these, expert forecasts can be useful. The key to the value of expert judgment is the ability of the expert to recall and assimilate relevant data in making a guess. While judgment is often unsystematic, it is an important supplement to other methods and can overcome some of the limitations of quantitative techniques.

The jury approach collects forecasts from a number of experts. The forecasts are then combined in a particular manner, such as a simple or weighted average, in which the weights can be assigned by the level of expertise. A variant of the jury approach is the panel consensus method, in which a group of experts is put in a room where they attempt to develop a forecast. Unfortunately the result is often driven by a strong, vocal member of the group.

An example of the jury approach is provided every month by *Wired* magazine. In each issue, a group of experts in an area are asked for the year in which certain phenomena are likely to occur. The forecasted year is the average across the experts. For example, in 1995 five experts were asked about the year in which we could expect to be able to purchase custom clothing overnight. The average of the experts was 1999 (*Wired*, 1995).

Delphi Method
A variation of the panel consensus is called the *Delphi* method. The process begins by asking a number of individuals to independently produce a forecast. An outside person then collects the forecasts and calculates the average. Next, the outside person returns to each participant both the original forecast and the average and asks the participants to reconsider their initial forecasts. Typically, the participants then change their forecasts to more nearly conform to the average. If the process is repeated several times, consensus is generally achieved. Delphi panels are often established to forecast sales of new technologies (e.g., videotext) for which historical data do not exist.

Customer-Based Methods

A second set of methods relies on customer data.

Market Testing
This category includes a large set of methods involving primary market research. The methods include mall intercept surveys, focus group, or at-home

or at-work situations in which potential customers are asked to respond to a product concept. Methods such as conjoint analysis, discussed in Chapter 5, are widely used to assess desired product features and ultimate market share.

Market Surveys

Market surveys are a specific form of primary market research in which potential customers are asked to give some indication of their likelihood of purchasing the product. A common approach is to use a 1 to 10 scale, with a 10 implying certainty of purchase. Customers frequently overstate their likelihood of purchase (although for really new products they often underestimate their eventual purchase likelihood). Researchers often use either a "top box" approach (i.e., count only the 10s as purchasing) or some other method based on the past relation between intent and purchase as the basis for the forecast. Alternatively, respondents are asked to indicate the quantity of a product they expect to purchase. These purchase intention surveys are then extrapolated to the population to form demand forecasts. Purchasing agents, for example, are often surveyed to determine demand for industrial products. Many of the problems typical with surveys, such as nonresponse bias (are the people who do not respond to the survey different from those who do?) and inaccurate responses, exist with this method.

Whom to Survey.   When conducting surveys for industrial products, it is not clear whom to talk to within a company even if the company is known. For example, when the Federal Communications Commission (FCC) invited bids for cellular mobile phone licenses in various cities, it required a study of market potential as part of the application. Most applicants attempted to address this by phone surveys, contacting the manager of telecommunications (or someone having a similar title) and asking about how many phones the company would use. However, it is not clear that these managers knew how many were needed or had much authority over such acquisitions.

To determine which companies to survey, first specify the potential segments and then ensure enough of each type are included to get a reasonable estimate. Unfortunately, if there are 10 target groups and five size variations per group, the overall sample size will be large.

Consider Figure 6–7, which shows the number of firms by employee number in several SIC codes. How would you apportion the sample and still be able to represent each segment accurately? The answer requires a balance between a stratified sample based on assumed variability of demand and getting a reasonable number in each cell.

How to Deal with the Results.   Considering again the example in Figure 6–7, it would be preferable if the results "made sense," but sometimes they are inconsistent. For example, assume that the average firm sales for the five

FIGURE 6-7   Potential Customers by Industry and Size

SIC	Industry	Percent of 1981 Demand Accounted for	Total Number of Firms	Number of Employees				
				50-99	100-249	250-499	500-999	1,000 or more
28	Chemical	20	7,012	754	610	293	193	123
29	Petroleum	20	444	57	73	53	42	22
33	Primary metals	10	1,889	266	352	181	74	108
12	Bituminous	2	4,050	295	272	166	80	11
20	Food	5	10,032	1,114	957	393	153	57
22	Textile	2	1,786	207	229	187	160	50
26	Paper and allied products	10	1,314	184	235	116	104	58
34	Fabricated metal	3	4,568	310	111	16	2	—
36	Electrical equipment	3	942	90	109	94	43	35
49	Electricity, gas	25	5,250	766	588	214	97	69
	Total		37,287	4,043	3,536	1,713	948	533

Expected Maximum Spending by Size Category

Employee Size	Maximum Spending
50 to 99	$ 100,000
100 to 249	200,000
250 to 499	500,000
500 to 999	750,000
1,000 or more	1,000,000

size categories in Figure 6–7 were as follows: 192, 181, 490, 360, and 2,000. Do you treat those figures as "truth," or do you smooth them so bigger firms spend more? Moreover, what do you do if total demand comes out three times expected? Do you scale every estimate down by one-third?

In summary, then, while surveys may produce a useful number, they are equally likely to produce numbers that, without "creative" manipulation, appear on the surface to be wrong.

Sales Extrapolation Methods

A third set of methods utilizes historical sales data and is referred to as *time-series* methods.

Moving Averages

Moving averages, an old forecasting standby, are widely used to reduce the "noise" in data to uncover the underlying pattern. In doing so, it is important to recognize that past data have at least four major components:

1. Base value
2. Trend
3. Cycle(s) (seasonality)
4. Random

Moving averages essentially smooth out random variations to make the patterns (trends and cycles) more apparent.

For purposes of introduction, consider the simple moving-average approach. A three-period moving average of sales at time t is given by

$$\bar{S}_t = (S_{t-1} + S_t + S_{t+1})/3$$

Note that (1) each data point used is weighted equally and (2) no trend or cycle is accounted for. To see how this method works, consider the three-month moving average for the eight periods of sales given in Figure 6–8. The moving average for the first three periods of data is 105, the simple average of 100, 110, and 105. The moving average for periods 2 through 4 is 115, the average of 110, 105, and 130. As can be readily seen by comparing the moving averages to the Raw Changes column, the fluctuation in values is much less in moving averages than in the raw data, and a consistent trend of increase of about 10 units per period becomes quite apparent. Forecasts can now be based on the pattern of moving averages rather than on the raw data.

The basic moving-average method just described can be extended to track trends and seasonal patterns as well. For example, to smooth a trend, simply calculate the period-to-period changes and average them as in Figure 6–8. While other methods, such as regression, are more sophisticated means of developing forecasts, moving averages remain a popular approach.

FIGURE 6–8 **Sample Data**

Period	Sales	Three-Period Moving Average	Raw Changes	Average Change
1	100	—	—	—
2	110	105	+10	—
3	105	115	−5	10
4	130	125	+25	10
5	140	130	+10	5
6	120	140	−20	10
7	160	152	+40	11.33
8	175	—	+15	—

Exponential Smoothing

A second time-series approach is called *exponential smoothing*. The formula for a simple exponentially smoothed forecast is

$$\hat{S}_{t+1} = aS_t + (1 - a)\hat{S}_t$$

where "^" refers to a forecast. In other words, an exponentially smoothed forecast for period $t + 1$ is a combination of the current period's sales and the current period's forecast. The parameter a is between 0 and 1 and can be determined from historical sales data. In reality, exponentially smoothed forecasts are close relatives to moving-average forecasts in that the former weight past sales using exponentially declining weights.[1] As in the case of moving averages, this approach literally smooths out the random variation in period-to-period values. Trends and cycles are estimated separately.

Regression Analysis

A simple and popular form of extrapolation uses regression analysis with time (period) as the independent variable. Time-series regression produces estimates of the base level (intercept) and the trend (slope). Seasonal patterns can either be removed a priori from the data or estimated in the model using dummy variables (see Chapter 6). Ignoring seasonality, the model is simply

$$\text{Sales} = a + b \,(\text{time}).$$

Addressing the same eight-period example from Figure 6–8 produces the graph in Figure 6–9 and the predicted results in Figure 6–10. The forecast for period 9 based on this model would be

$$S_9 = 85.4 + 9.9(9) = 174.5$$

---

[1]To see this, simply rewrite the equation in terms of period t, that is, $\hat{S}_t = aS_{t-1} + (1 - a)\hat{S}_{t-1}$, and substitute repeatedly for S_t in the equation in the text.

FIGURE 6–9

Time-series extrapolation

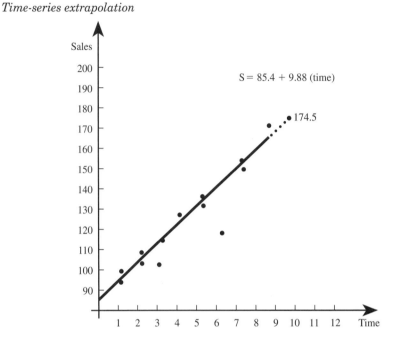

FIGURE 6–10

Time-series regression example

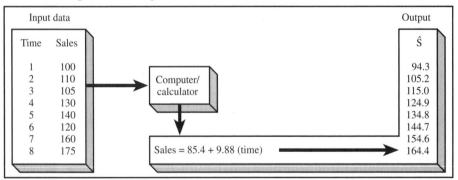

This is represented by the dotted extension to the fitted line in Figure 6–9. Two other useful statistics produced are the R^2, a measure of fit that is the percentage variance in the dependent variable (sales) explained by the independent variable (time), and the standard error of the estimate, which is a measure of the variance of the errors (the differences between the predicted values of sales based on the preceding equation and the actual values) about the line. Rather than just using the point forecast, 174.5, a confidence interval or a

FIGURE 6-11

Trial over time for a new product

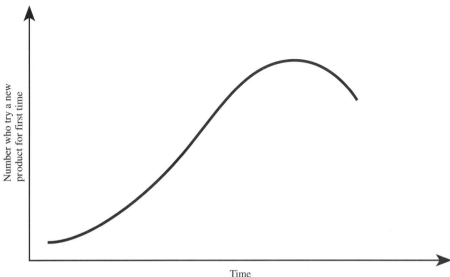

range of likely outcomes should be placed around it. This is often done by multiplying the standard error of the estimate (in this case, 12.3) by 2 to approximate a 95 percent confidence interval. The forecast then becomes 174.5 ± 24.6. In addition, longer-term forecasts can be developed simply by plugging in values for time periods later than 9, extending the line farther out in time.

Sometimes sales data are highly nonlinear, as in Figure 6-11. This product life cycle curve is clearly not a straight regression line. Figure 6-11 can be estimated using a variety of functional forms. We discuss one, the Bass model (Bass, 1969), later in this chapter.

Model-Based Methods

The fourth category of forecasting methods is often termed *association* or *causal* because the techniques utilize one or more variables other than time to predict sales (e.g., advertising).

Regression Analysis
This method is explained in more detail later in the chapter. Basically it is a generalization of the time-series model: Instead of having only time as the independent variable, other variables that could affect sales are included. For example, a regression model to predict sales of Pepsi might be the following:

$$\text{Sales} = a + b \text{ (advertising)} + c \text{ (price)} + d \text{ (population age 13–25)}$$

Given historical data on sales, advertising, price, and population, the coefficients a, b, c, and d can be estimated and used to develop a forecast.

Leading Indicators

Economists use certain macroeconomic variables to forecast changes in the economy. When changes in these variables occur before changes in the economy and they are thought to be linked, they are termed *leading indicators*. For example, changes in employment, housing starts, interest rates, and retail sales often are associated with changes in the economy. The construction and real estate industries use leading indicators to forecast demand. Industry-specific leading indicators also exist, such as retail auto dealer inventories for the automobile industry.

Econometric Models

These are essentially large-scale, multiple-equation regression models. During the 1970s they were extremely popular, and companies such as Data Resources, Inc. (subsequently bought by McGraw-Hill) sold these models to companies seeking to develop better forecasts of industry sales. They are less popular today as companies strive to keep their expenditures down in all areas. In addition, they never forecasted as well as advertised. A noteworthy failure came during the Arab oil embargo of the early 1970s when the models predicted less damage to the U.S. economy than actually occurred.

What Methods Are Used?

Figure 6–12 shows the results of a survey of 96 companies examining which forecasting methods are actually used in practice (Sanders and Manrodt, 1994). For the short and medium term, judgmental approaches are heavily used. The most frequently used quantitative method is a moving average. This is rather discouraging given the length of time more sophisticated methods have been available. However, regression is used quite frequently, particularly for long-run forecasts. Since regression is sufficient for most situations and widely available (e.g., in Excel), we concentrate on it.

Using Regression Models for Forecasting

Given the results from Figure 6–12 and the wide applicability of regression to other marketing contexts (see the application to segmentation research in Chapter 5), we devote significant space in this chapter to show how it is used in forecasting contexts. Regression models are generally developed in three stages. First, the variables assumed to affect dependent variables are specified. The variables selected might be

$$\text{Sales} = f(\text{our price, competitors' prices, our advertising, competitors'} \\ \text{advertising, disposable income})$$

Next, a model is specified indicating the form of the relation between the independent variables and sales. Most often the nature of the relationship is linear, such as

FIGURE 6–12   **Forecasting Method Usage**

	Forecast Period			
Forecasting Technique	*Immediate* (<1 month)	*Short* (1 month–<6 months)	*Medium* (6 months–1 year)	*Long* (>1 year)
Judgmental				
Manager's opinion	27.9%	39.8	37.1	9.3
Jury of executive opinion	17.5	28.9	40.1	26.2
Sales force composite	28.6	17.5	33.1	8.7
Quantitative				
Moving average	17.7	33.5	28.3	8.7
Straight-line projection	7.6	13.2	12.5	8.2
Naive	16.0	18.5	13.8	0
Exponential smoothing	12.9	19.6	16.8	4.2
Regression	13.4	25.1	26.4	16.5
Simulation	3.4	7.8	11.2	8.3
Classical decomposition	0	6.8	11.9	9.3
Box-Jenkins	2.4	2.4	4.9	3.4

Source: Reprinted by permission. Nada R. Sanders and Karl B. Manrodt, "Forecasting Practices in the U.S. Corporations: Survey Results," INTERFACES. March-Aril, 1994. Copyright 1994. The Institute of Management Sciences and the Operations Research Society of America (currently INFORMS). 2 Charles Street, Suite 300, Providence, RI 02904 USA.

$$\text{Sales} = b_0 + b_1 \text{ (our price)} + b_2 \text{ (competitors' prices)} + b_3 \text{ (our advertising)} + b_4 \text{ (competitors' advertising)} + b_5 \text{ (disposable income)}.$$

Finally, the model is estimated by means of regression analysis, usually using commonly available computer programs:

$$\text{Sales} = 1.2 - .3 \text{ (our price)} + .4 \text{ (competitors' prices)} + 1.1 \text{ (our advertising)}$$

$$- .3 \text{ (competitors' advertising)} + .2 \text{ (disposable income)}$$

This estimated model serves two useful purposes. First, a regression model can be used to forecast sales. Notice that to use this regression model to forecast, one must first forecast the values of the independent variables. This is because all the variables are *contemporaneous;* that is, current (say, 2001) sales are determined by current (2001) prices, advertising, and disposable income. We use data from some point in the past through 2000 to estimate the model. However, to forecast sales for 2001, we need 2001 values for the independent variables. While some of the variables may be under the manager's control (price, advertising), several others must be forecasted. If this is difficult, regression becomes less useful as a forecasting device. Put differently, try to use predictor variables that are themselves easy to forecast.

Second, a regression model can answer "what if" questions. In the preceding example, b_1 is the marginal effect of changing our price and b_3 is the

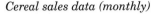

FIGURE 6–13

Cereal sales data (monthly)

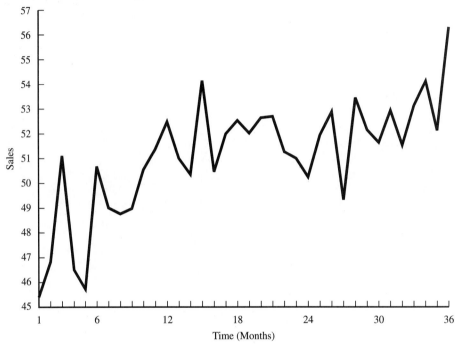

Source: Scott A. Neslin and Robert W. Shoemaker, "Using a Natural Experiment to Estimate Price
Elasticity: the 1974 Sugar Shortage and the Ready-to-Eat Cereal Market," *Journal of Marketing,* Winter
1983, pp. 44–57.

marginal effect of changing our advertising. If we are willing to assume the
relationships between price and advertising and sales are causal rather than
just correlational, the manager can answer a question such as "What if I
increase my price by $5?" In this case, based on the model, an increase in
price would be predicted to lead to a decrease in sales of $(5)(-.3) = 1.5$.

Developing Regression Models

While developing regression forecasting models is largely a trial-and-error
process, certain steps can make the process more systematic and efficient.

1. *Plot the sales data over time.* It is useful to get a feel for the sales series
   by simply plotting sales versus time. An important use of this plot is
   as an aid for identifying key variables that might be useful in predicting changes in sales. Any peaks or valleys in the sales series can
   prompt the manager to try to uncover the factor that may have caused
   that sharp change.

   As an illustration, Figure 6–13 shows the (deseasonalized) monthly
   sales series from 1973 to 1975 of presweetened breakfast cereal pur-

chases made by a sample of households on a diary panel (Neslin and Shoemaker, 1983). A significant price increase for sugar occurred during 1974 and resulted in a sharp increase in cereal prices. It is difficult to pick out the effect of price alone from the graph. However, it is clear that an overall positive trend in purchases occurred over the three-year period. Thus, some variable accounting for that trend must be included in the regression model.

2. *Consider the variables that are relevant to predicting sales.* The manager or a team of managers familiar with the product category should brainstorm to develop a set of factors that affect sales. At this stage, the list of variables should be long, allowing for as much creativity as possible. In terms of the type of variables to include, it is generally useful to consider which variables in each of the following categories might be most appropriate:

   1. Customer status and traits (e.g., the size of the population in a particular age category).
   2. "Our" marketing programs (e.g., advertising).
   3. Competitive behavior (e.g., new product introductions).
   4. General environment (e.g., gross domestic product).

   In the case of presweetened cereals, two major factors affecting sales are price and advertising. As noted above, the data are already deseasonalized, so any winter versus summer consumption factors for cold cereals have already been eliminated from the sales series. For simplicity, the upward trend of the data can be accounted for by a trend variable that assumes the values 1 through 36. Finally, it is possible that advertising has what is called a lagged effect on sales. In other words, not only may current advertising affect current sales but last month's advertising may also affect current sales through consumer recall. Thus, the general form of the model is

   Cereal sales $= f$(price, advertising, lagged advertising, trend).

3. *Collect data.* Once the variables have been specified, historical values for those variables must be collected. There must be as many historical values for the independent variables as there are for the sales variable. Thus, since there are 36 observations on cereal sales, the analyst needs 36 observations on price and advertising (lagged advertising can be computed directly from the advertising series). Figure 6–14 shows the data for this example.

4. *Analyze the data.* There are several aspects to the data analysis step of the model-building process.

   First, it is important to examine the *correlations among the independent variables.* Many time series variables are highly correlated because they tend to change over time at the same rate. For example, if the economy is expanding, employment and GDP are highly correlated.

FIGURE 6–14   Cereal Data

Sales	Price	Advertising	Time	Lagged Advertising
45.4	29.0	6803	1	—
46.8	28.7	6136	2	6803
51.1	28.1	8850	3	6136
46.5	27.9	6689	4	8850
45.7	27.9	7004	5	6689
50.7	27.6	7801	6	7004
49.0	27.0	7091	7	7801
48.8	26.7	6958	8	7091
49.0	26.6	7357	9	6958
50.6	26.7	7010	10	7357
51.4	26.7	6627	11	7010
52.5	26.7	7350	12	6627
51.0	26.6	6952	13	7350
50.4	26.6	7441	14	6952
54.2	26.8	7519	15	7441
50.5	27.1	8409	16	7519
52.0	27.6	8084	17	8409
52.6	28.3	7830	18	8084
52.1	28.6	7399	19	7830
52.7	28.9	7566	20	7399
52.7	29.3	7076	21	7566
51.3	29.8	7310	22	7076
51.0	30.9	7604	23	7310
50.3	31.6	6793	24	7604
52.0	31.6	7038	25	6793
52.9	31.6	6514	26	7038
49.4	31.7	6439	27	6514
53.5	31.7	6056	28	6439
52.2	31.7	6148	29	6056
51.7	31.1	5787	30	6148
53.0	30.9	6043	31	5787
51.6	30.5	6191	32	6043
53.2	30.3	8034	33	6191
54.2	29.7	8404	34	8034
52.2	29.8	9524	35	8404
56.4	29.9	8973	36	9524

If a product is being rolled out nationally, the number of distribution outlets and advertising may be highly correlated. If two or more independent variables are highly correlated, computational and interpretation problems can arise. Therefore, an important first step after the data have been collected is to construct a correlation matrix among the variables (remember, we want high correlations between the independent variables and sales, the dependent variable). Note that the diagonal of the matrix (Figure 6–15) contains 1s; the correlation of a variable with itself is obviously 1. The matrix is also symmetric; that is, the correlation between price and advertising is the same as the correlation between advertising and price. The analyst should be on guard

FIGURE 6–15   Cereal Data Correlation Matrix*

	Price	Advertising	Time	Lagged Advertising
Price	1.0	−.28	.76	−.26
	(35)	(35)	(35)	(35)
	.00	.10	.00	.13
Advertising	−.28	1.00	.05	.55
	(35)	(35)	(35)	(35)
	.10	.00	.76	.00
Time	.76	.05	1.00	−.02
	(35)	(35)	(35)	(35)
	.00	.76	.00	.90
Lagged advertising	−.26	.55	−.02	1.00
	(35)	(35)	(35)	(35)
	.13	.00	.90	.00

*The numbers in each cell are presented as: correlation, sample size, significant level.

against any correlations with high absolute values (i.e., above .90, although this number should not be considered a rigid threshold).[2] More generally, you want the correlations between the independent and dependent variables to be larger than the correlations among the independent variables. High negative correlations are as harmful as positive ones but are not a major problem here, although time and price are closely related.

Second, *run the regression.* The regression results from the cereal illustration are shown in Figure 6–16, assuming the simple linear form of the model.

Third, determine the *significant predictors* of the dependent variable (i.e., sales). Even when care is taken to choose only those variables thought to be excellent predictors of sales, some often turn out to have little effect. To assess the strength of the effect of an independent variable on sales, look at the ratio of the absolute value of the regression coefficient to its standard error (given on all regression printouts), otherwise known as the t statistic. Generally speaking, if this ratio is greater than 2, the variable is referred to as a significant predictor of sales. Examining the first cereal regression results in Figure 6–16, we can see that price is marginally significant ($t = 1.92$), advertising is insignificant ($t = 1.21$), time is very significant ($t = 5.02$), and lagged advertising is very insignificant ($t = .41$) at the 5 percent significance level. A decision to be made here is whether to

---

[2]Actually, this is a complex area of econometrics in which academics are continually searching for a simple rule to determine when the correlation problem, termed *multicollinearity,* is severe.

FIGURE 6–16   **Regression Results: Cereal Data***

1. Model: Sales = 58.528 − .461 (price) + .00044 (advertising) − .00015 (lagged advertising) + .211 (time)
                (.242)   (.00037)   (.00037)   (.042)
    Standard error of the estimate = 1.479
    Adjusted R^2 = .60

2. Model: Sales = 60.041 − .538 (price) + .00033 (advertising) + .230 (time)
                (.244)   (.00032)   (.038)
    Standard error of the estimate = 1.468
    Adjusted R^2 = .65

3. Model: In Sales = 3.193 − .053 (In price) + .090 (In advertising) + .044 (In time)
                  (.095)   (.043)   (.007)
    Standard error of the estimate = .028
    Adjusted R^2 = .68

*Numbers in parentheses are standard errors.

rerun the regression after dropping insignificant variables. *Parsimony* is important in forecasting models, because fewer independent variables must be predicted to develop the ultimate forecast for a "smaller" model, that is, one with fewer independent variables. Since lagged advertising is relatively unimportant, regression 2 in Figure 6–16 repeats the regression with that variable eliminated. Price is now firmly significant ($t = 2.45$), as is the time trend, although advertising is still insignificant.

Fourth, check the *signs* of the significant independent variables. This is a logic check and is perhaps the most important test of all. The manager *must* ensure that the signs on the regression coefficients make sense. For example, a significant positive sign on a price coefficient is a problem; most of the time, these kinds of sign flip-flops are due to what is called *specification error,* the omission of one or more key variables from the model. In the breakfast cereal example, the signs are all in the appropriate direction for the significant variables.

Fifth, check the R^2 of the equation. This is what most analysts gravitate toward first; most people believe that a high degree of fit ensures that the forecasting model is a good one. However, a high R^2 does not guarantee a good forecasting model. This is due to the fact that regression is basically a correlational procedure and it is possible to choose variables that are nonsensical but do explain variance in sales. That is why we stress the combination of spending time *a priori* in choosing independent variables, checking the signs on the coefficients, *and* looking at the R^2. The R^2 of the breakfast cereal model is .65, as shown in Figure 6–16. This is not particularly high for a time-series model and implies that the forecast confidence interval will be relatively wide.

Finally, develop the forecast and confidence interval. As noted earlier, the forecast is developed by plugging in the appropriate values of the independent variables. In addition, a confidence interval can be constructed using the standard error of the estimate. This produces three forecasts: best guess (the point forecast), optimistic (the high end of the confidence interval), and pessimistic (the low end of the confidence interval).

Thus, taking the results of the second cereal regression from Figure 6–16, we can develop a forecast for the first out-of-sample period, January 1976. If we assume the price will be 30 cents per 10 ounces (remember, this is over 20 years ago) and category advertising will be $9 million, then, given that the value of the time is 37, the forecast is 55,400 ounces purchased for the panel members (55.4 in the units of Figure 6–14). Given a standard error of the estimate of 1.47, a 95 percent confidence interval around the forecast is ± 2,940 ounces, or a range of 52,460 to 58,340 ounces. Thus, 55,400 becomes the best guess, 52,460 the pessimistic forecast, and 58,340 the optimistic forecast. Note this can and generally should be repeated for different scenarios (e.g., assumptions about price), as we discuss later.

Recognizing Uncertainty

In order to make forecasts with a regression model, it is necessary to know or forecast the values of the predictor variables (e.g., GDP, advertising) in the next period. When these are known, a reasonable forecast includes a best guess obtained by substituting the known values, a pessimistic forecast (typically the best guess minus two standard errors of estimate), and an optimistic forecast (the best guess plus two standard errors of estimate). Since the predictor variables are rarely known with certainty, it is useful to construct both optimistic and pessimistic scenarios and to generate forecasts based on them. The resulting table (see Figure 6–17) gives a much clearer picture of the uncertainty inherent in the market (and what it depends on). While managers like to have *the* forecast, they *should* be given information like that in Figure 6–17. (Of course, that is easier for the authors, both of whom have tenure, to say than it is for a junior person facing a demanding boss.)

The impact of uncertainty about predictor variables can be shown more dramatically graphically (Figure 6–18). Notice here that the true range is considerably larger than the range implied by using the standard error of the regression as a basis for estimating uncertainty. What this means is that unless you are fairly certain of what the value of the predictor variable will be, it doesn't help forecast very much. Hence, variables that are easy to predict (e.g., year, GDP) are, *ceteris paribus,* more useful as predictors than variables that are themselves unpredictable (e.g., consumer sentiment, commodity prices).

FIGURE 6–17   **Format Matrix for Reporting a Regression Model Based Forecast**

	Forecast		
Scenario	*Pessimistic Forecast – 2S$_{YX}$*	*Best Guess Forecast*	*Optimistic Forecast + 2S$_{YX}$*
Pessimistic: No change in GDP Advertising down 10 percent			
Best guess: GDP up 3 percent Advertising up 10 percent			
Optimistic: GDP up 5 percent Advertising up 25 percent			

Nonlinear Relations

Most regression forecasting models are linear; that is, they are of the form

$$\text{Sales} = b_0 + b_1 X_1 + b_2 X_2 + \ldots,$$

where X_1 and X_2 are the independent or predictor variables and sales is the dependent variable.

In some cases, there is a nonlinear relationship between the Xs and sales. For example, there may be diminishing returns to advertising. In the linear framework, each dollar of advertising is equally effective. If there are diminishing returns to advertising, the impact of the millionth dollar is less than that of the tenth. This can be handled in the regression framework by, for example, using a logarithmic function:

$$\text{Sales} = b_0 + b_1 \,(\log \text{advertising})$$

One model, which has been used fairly extensively, is a multiplicative model (in economics, referred to as a Cobb-Douglas function):

$$\text{Sales} = b_0 X_1^{b1} X_2^{b2}$$

which can be written and estimated with a standard regression program by using a logarithmic transformation of the Xs:

$$\log \text{Sales} = b_0 + b_1(\log X_1) + b_2(\log X_2)$$

An interesting implication of this formula is that the coefficients are interpreted as *elasticities* rather than slopes. Thus, b_1 would be interpreted as the percentage change in sales due to a 1 percent change in X_1.

FIGURE 6–18

The impact of uncertain predictors on forecasting

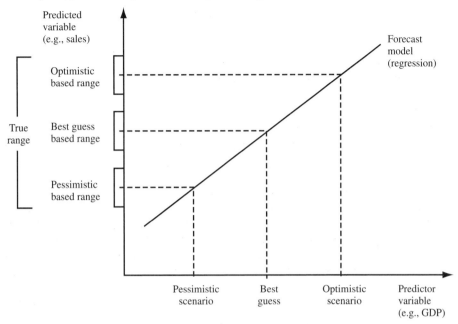

The results of a logarithmic model of the breakfast cereal data appear in Figure 6–15 (regression number 3). It is interesting that the results differ from those of the linear model. Here the price elasticity is insignificant ($t = .56$), whereas the advertising elasticity is significant ($t = 2.09$), as is the trend. The slope results for price and advertising from the linear model were the opposite. This can happen when two different theories about how sales are created are specified. It also suggests that a third model, using a linear function of price and a logarithmic one for advertising, might be the best.

Share Forecasts

To this point we have focused on volume forecasts. In stable markets, share is critical. Share forecasts are typically based largely on the impact of marketing mix components (price, promotion, advertising) on sales or share. In fact for share models in consumer products, the so-called logit model is now widely applied. Its basic form is

$$\text{Share Brand } i = \frac{\exp{(BX_i)}}{\sum_{\text{all brands}} \exp{(BX_j)}}$$

where $\exp(BX)$ means e to the power BX, and BX is a linear function such as $B_0 + B_1 (\text{Advertising \$}) + B_2 (\text{Price})$.

Logit models can be used to answer "what if?" questions such as, "What will happen if I increase advertising 20 percent?"

Forecasting Innovations and New Products

For many products, the requirement that regression models have a large number of years (or other time period) of data is unrealistic. This is particularly the case for technological innovations or new durable goods. In addition, the demand in the early stages of the product life cycle does not necessarily look very linear. Figure 6–11 demonstrates such a sales curve. For example, the manager for a PDA in 1995 did not face the same forecasting environment as the product manager for Quaker Oatmeal. PDAs had not been for sale for many years (mainly since 1992), and were in the early growth stage of the product life cycle.

To handle these situations, models of the diffusion of an innovation have been developed to forecast first purchases of products. The most popular model in marketing is the Bass model (1969). The model assumes two kinds of customers for a durable good: innovators, who purchase the product early in the life cycle, and imitators, who rely on word of mouth from other purchasers. This results in what is called a *diffusion* process. The model used by Bass has the following form:

$$P_t = p + [q/M]Y(t - 1)$$

where

P_t	=	Probability of purchase given no previous purchase.
$Y(t - 1)$	=	Total number who have purchased the product through period $t - 1$.
M	=	The market potential (saturation level).
q	=	Parameter representing the rate of diffusion of the product reflecting the influence of others (also called the *coefficient of imitation*).
p	=	Initial probability of purchase (also called the *coefficient of innovation*).

Sales in period t are

$$S(t) = [M - Y(t - 1)] P_t$$

Substituting P_t from the first equation into the sales equation, we obtain

$$S(t) = pM + [q - p]Y(t - 1) - q/M [Y(t - 1)]^2$$

If q is greater than p (the rate of imitation is greater than the rate of innovation), the sales curve will rise and then fall. If q is less than p (the rate of imitation is less than the rate of innovation), the sales curve will fall from its initial level.

The model can be estimated running a regression of the form

$$\text{Sales} = c_0 + c_1 Y(t - 1) + c_2 [Y(t - 1)]^2$$

that is simply using sales as the dependent variable, with the independent variable being the cumulative number of previous adopters and that quantity squared. In other words, all that is needed are historical sales data. Once the c coefficients are estimated, the quantities p, q, and M can be solved for by the following identities:

$$c_0 = pM, \; c_1 = [q - p]; \text{ and } c_2 = - q/M$$

There are three equations and three unknowns, so p, q, and M have unique solutions.[3] Forecasts of sales can be developed directly from the sales equation, if desired.

The Bass model has fit past adoption patterns well. For example, it correctly forecast a downturn in sales of color TVs in the late 1960s, something the "expert" forecasts at the major manufacturers failed to do because they used essentially linear extrapolation. Unfortunately, the model is sensitive to the number of periods of data that are available and can be unreliable when only four or five years of data exist.[4] Also, for example, the market saturation level, M, is probably affected by price, and the imitation parameter, q, is affected by advertising (Horsky and Simon, 1983; Jones and Ritz, 1991). While the preceding model includes no marketing variables, an extended model incorporating these variables has been developed (Bass, Krishnan, and Jain, 1994).

Illustrations

Super-Premium Ice Cream Sales

Regression analysis was used to forecast super-premium ice cream sales as a function of previous sales, GDP, and change in the number of flavors in the category, using data from 1986 through 1998. The resulting model was

Market Sales (in millions) = −32.64 + 0.043 (GDP)
+ 160.3 (% change in number of flavors)

While GDP is relatively easy to forecast, change in flavors is not. On the assumption flavors increase by 26 percent and 31 percent respectively in

---

[3] If c_2 is less than zero, p must be solved for using the quadratic formula. It has two solutions, one negative and the positive one that is used.

[4] Reasonable forecasts are obtainable when the results of past studies—essentially the average values of p and q—are combined with data (Sultan, Farley, and Lehmann, 1990).

FIGURE 6–19   **Bass Model: PDA Actual versus Predicted**

Year	PDA Sales (000s)	Predicted	Percent Error
1992	63	78.123	24.0%
1993	150	124.674	16.9
1994	200	213.144	6.6
1995	285	282.104	1.1
1996	?	283.614	?

1999 and 2000, the best-guess forecasts become 396.0 and 423.3 million. While the model had an R^2 of 88 percent and a standard error of 33.9, uncertainty over the predictor variables means the range for the forecast is substantially above ± 2 standard deviations (i.e., 67.8).

PDA Sales

Consider the problem of forecasting PDA sales in 1995. The four years of data available at that time (Figure 6–19) provide a limited basis for illustrating the basic Bass model. The results of running the Bass model are

$$\text{Sales} = 78.123 + .783Y(t) - .0007Y(t)^2$$

The model predicts historical sales quite well. In addition, q is much greater than p ($q = .798$ and $p = .065$), indicating that the product has favorable word of mouth. The forecast for 1996 is for 284,000 units, or essentially no growth. As we now know, sales have continued to grow. However, a large part of this growth is due to decreased prices and increased quality (i.e., communication capabilities) as well as the explosion of the Internet. In particular, the Palm Pilot was introduced in 1996. This emphasizes the difficulty in forecasting sales early in a life cycle; clearly estimating the Bass model using all data to the present would produce a much higher forecast for future sales.

Forecasts made in early 2000 are much more bullish:

- IDC (via CNETNews.com) suggests sales will increase from 5.4 million in 1999 to 18.9 million in 2000.
- *Industry Standard* (using analysis by Forester Research) suggested that by 2000 there could be 15 million PDAs in use and that by 2002 handhelds will outsell PCs.
- *Mobile Insights* (via Field Force Automation) suggested sales of "mobile information appliances" would be over 25 million and surpass sales of notebooks.

Whether these forecasts are more accurate remains to be seen.

Using Forecasts

As noted earlier in this chapter, it is difficult to say which techniques are good and which are bad because success often depends on the circumstances. Accuracy depends on factors such as time horizon, how much money is spent on the forecast, how much time was spent developing the forecast, the volatility of the category, and the like.

While using quantitative procedures may at times seem tedious, two major reasons encourage their use: (1) they simplify routine, repetitive situations, and (2) they force explicit statements of assumptions. When using quantitative methods, it is best to take the following supplementary steps:

1. *Do sensitivity analysis.* Only when a result seems to be stable over method and data points (e.g., drop one or two years of data and rerun the analysis) can the forecast be advanced with much conviction.

2. *Examine large residuals.* Residuals are individual forecasting errors made for each period. By examining the characteristics of those periods when the forecast was bad, omitted variables can often be uncovered.

3. *Avoid silly precision.* This means round off the forecast and give an honest plus or minus range.

4. *Be tolerant of errors.* Expect the methods to improve one's odds of making a good forecast, not guarantee them. Be suspicious of forecasts with very narrow ranges.

5. *Remember that you will generally miss the turning points.* Quantitative (as well as qualitative) forecasting methods work well as long as the patterns that occurred in the past extend into the future. Whenever a major change occurs, however, most forecasts will be way off. Stated another way, most forecasting methods are relatively useless for predicting major changes in the way the world operates, and consequently most forecasts do not include the effects of these changes.

Combining Forecasts

So far this chapter has described a number of forecasting methods and their strengths and weaknesses. When making an important forecast, it is both common and prudent to make several forecasts and then combine them, perhaps using some averaging method. An average of a set of forecasts using disparate methods will tend to be better than a forecast using only one method that is susceptible to its own particular weaknesses.

The results of several methods can be summarized in a table such as that in Figure 6–20. The range of these forecasts provides a useful indication of

FIGURE 6–20   **Sample Format for Summarizing Forecasts**

	Forecast		
Method	*Pessimistic*	*Best Guess*	*Optimistic*
1. Time-series extrapolation			
2. Regression model:			
Version A			
Version B			
3. Expert judgment:			
Expert A			
Expert B			
4. Own judgment			
5. Bottom-up forecast			
Average			

the uncertainty faced. Moreover, deciding how to combine these forecasts forces one to make explicit assumptions. In Figure 6–20, a simple average is used as the combination rule (that is, equal weighting), but weights could also be assigned, for example, in inverse proportion to the size of the confidence interval (Wilton and Gupta, 1987).

Gaining Agreement

The previous discussion implies that only one person is involved with developing a forecast. Sometimes forecasts are "top down": a higher-level manager develops a forecast for various products' sales. Alternatively, forecasts can be "bottom up," an aggregation of several forecasts made by regional salespeople, country managers, or others. Unfortunately, top-down and bottom-up forecasts rarely agree either with each other or growth targets established for the product. The process of reaching agreement is both useful and frustrating.

In understanding bottom-up forecasts, it is useful to recognize that both personal incomes and budgets depend on the forecast. Personal incomes, especially salespeople's, are tied to quotas, which in turn are derived from forecasts. Therefore, a salesperson will tend to be conservative in his or her forecast to make the sales goal or quota easier to attain. In contrast, certain managers may overstate sales potential to gain a larger budget. Thus, the bottom-up process, though based on the knowledge of those closest to the customer, may well produce a biased estimate. Total reliance on either bottom-up or top-down methods is generally a mistake.

Why Not Just Go to the Web?

An increasingly common approach to forecasting is to search the Internet for forecasts and then combine them, typified by averaging the estimates. This is expeditious but somewhat naive. First, ask yourself where their forecasts came from. Chances are they are influenced by earlier forecasts, creating a snowball or cascade effect in which early forecasts have a big impact. Second, consider who did the forecasts and how: Often the person has less training than you do as a result of reading this chapter. If that makes you uneasy, good. The point is that, if the forecast is important, you need to understand the process used to make it and either make it yourself or find a reliable (as opposed to convenient) source.

Summary

Market potential is generally poorly understood, yet very important for different reasons. Low estimates of market potential result in marketing managers declaring categories mature too soon. This tends to create opportunities for ambitious competitors who have different views on the amount of untapped potential. The mere act of trying to calculate potential market size often gives a manager ideas about how to extend the product or service into new segments, a topic we consider further in the next chapter.

Forecasting is one of the most important jobs facing a manager. The forecast is an input to aspects of marketing strategy. It is also critical to production planning. When forecasts are substantially off on the high side, objectives are overly ambitious, inventories are too large, and senior managers, production personnel, and channel members become upset. When the forecast is much lower than actual, the losses are opportunity costs: lost sales. Multiple methods and logic, plus some knowledge of regression analysis, provide a good basis for forecasts.

References

Bass, Frank M. (1969) "A New Product Growth Model for Consumer Durables," *Management Science,* 15:5, January, 215–27.

Bass, Frank M., Trichy V. Krishnan, and Deepak C. Jain (1994) "Why the Bass Model Fits without Decision Variables," *Marketing Science,* 13 (Summer), 203–23.

Bayus, Barry L., Saman Hong, and Russell P. Labe, Jr. (1989) "Developing and Using Forecasting Models of Consumer Durables: The Case of Color Television," *Journal of Product Innovation Management,* 6, 5–19.

Beeh, Jenny E. (1994) "PCs Are Taking to the Streets," *Advertising Age,* October 31, 28.

Cerf, C. and V. Navasky (1984) *The Experts Speak.* New York: Pantheon Books.

Chambers, John C., Satinder K. Mullick, and Donald D. Smith (1971) "How to Choose the Right Forecasting Technique," *Harvard Business Review,* July–August.

Cox, William E. (1979) *Industrial Marketing Research.* New York: John Wiley & Sons.

Deveny, Kathleen (1990) "States Mull Rash of Diaper Regulations," *The Wall Street Journal,* June 15, B–1.

Dhalla, Nariman K. and Sonia Yuspeh (1976) "Forget the Product Life Cycle Concept!" *Harvard Business Review,* January–February, 102–12.

Georgoff, David M. and Robert G. Murdick (1986) "Manager's Guide to Forecasting," *Harvard Business Review,* January–February.

Horsky, Dan and Leonard S. Simon (1983) "Advertising and the Diffusion of New Products," *Marketing Science,* 2:1, Winter, 1–18.

Jones, J. Morgan and Christopher J. Ritz (1991) "Incorporating Distribution into New Product Diffusion Models," *International Journal of Research in Marketing,* 8, June, 91–112.

McWilliams, Gary (1995) "At Compaq, a Desktop Crystal Ball," *Business Week,* March 20, 96.

Neslin, Scott A. and Robert W. Shoemaker (1983) "Using a Natural Experiment to Estimate Price Elasticity: the 1974 Sugar Shortage and the Ready-to-Eat Cereal Market," *Journal of Marketing,* 47:1, Winter, 44–57.

Sanders, Nada R. and Karl B. Manrodt (1994) "Forecasting Practices in US Corporations: Survey Results," *INTERFACES,* March–April, 92–100.

Sellers, Patricia (1991) "A Boring Brand Can Be Beautiful," *Fortune,* November 18, 169.

Sultan, Fareena, John U. Farley, and Donald R. Lehmann (1990) "A Meta-Analysis of Applications of Diffusion Models," *Journal of Marketing Research,* 27, February, 70–77.

Wheelwright, Steven C. and Spyros Makridakis (1985) *Forecasting Methods for Management.* New York: John Wiley & Sons.

Wilton, Peter C. and Sunil Gupta (1987) "Combination of Forecasts: An Extension," *Management Science,* 33:3, March, 356–72

Wired, November 1995, p. 76.

APPENDIX 6A:
TIME SERIES REGRESSION WITH SEASONAL FACTORS

Consider the following data on quarterly fuel oil shipments to the United Kingdom in 1964–66 (Figure 6A–1). In plotting these data, we see that there is, as expected, a very strong seasonal effect (Figure 6A–2). Clearly, ignoring the seasonal component would be a major error. (It would also produce significant autocorrelation.)Running four separate regressions is impractical because there would only be three observations per regression. It would be possible to deseasonalize the data before performing the regression, using an adjustment factor for each quarter such as

$$\frac{\text{Average sales for the particular quarter}}{\text{Average sales for all quarters}}$$

FIGURE 6A–1   Fuel Oil Shipments to the United Kingdom

Quarter	Year	Sales
1	1964	210
2		120
3		140
4		260
1	1965	220
2		125
3		145
4		270
1	1966	225
2		128
3		149
4		275

FIGURE 6A–2

Graph of fuel oil shipments

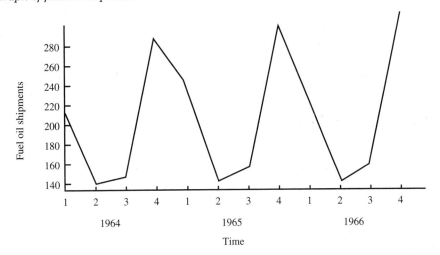

Possibly the most appealing approach, however, is to employ dummy variables. This would consist of first creating ("dummying up") a variable for each of the four quarters (Figure 6A–3). The following equation would then be estimated by regression:

$$\text{Shipments} = B_0 + B_1\,(\text{Time}) + B_2\,(\text{Winter}) + B_3\,(\text{Spring}) + B_4\,(\text{Summer})$$

Note that one of the possible dummy variables must be left out so the computer program will run. If all the independent variables are included, the independent variables are perfectly multicollinear. In this case it is impossible to invert a key matrix,

FIGURE 6A–3   Seasonal Dummy Variables

		Dummy Variables			
Shipments	Time	Winter	Spring	Summer	Fall
210	1	1	0	0	0
120	2	0	1	0	0
140	3	0	0	1	0
260	4	0	0	0	1
220	5	1	0	0	0
125	6	0	1	0	0
145	7	0	0	1	0
270	8	0	0	0	1
225	9	1	0	0	0
128	10	0	1	0	0
149	11	0	0	1	0
275	12	0	0	0	1

and the program will bomb. (Alternatively, we could drop the constant B_0 and retain all four dummy variables, if that were an option of the computer program being used.) In general, if a categorical variable has c categories, $c - 1$ dummy variables must be employed. Here, fall was excluded. This does not affect the forecasts, which are independent of the variable deleted. The results were

$$B_0 = 256.5$$
$$B_1 = 1.468$$
$$B_2 = -45.6$$
$$B_3 = -141.1$$
$$B_4 = -122.2$$

Predictions for each of the quarters are thus

$$
\begin{aligned}
\text{Winter:} \quad \text{Shipments} &= B_0 + B_1(\text{Time}) + B_2(1) + B_3(0) + B_4(0) \\
&= (B_0 + B_2) + B_1(\text{Time}) \\
&= 210 + 1.468\,(\text{Time}) \\
\text{Spring:} \quad \text{Shipments} &= (B_0 + B_3) + B_1(\text{Time}) \\
&= 115.5 + 1.468\,(\text{Time}) \\
\text{Summer:} \quad \text{Shipments} &= (B_0 + B_4) + B_1(\text{Time}) \\
&= 134.4 + 1.468\,(\text{Time}) \\
\text{Fall:} \quad \text{Shipments} &= (B_0 + B_1) + B_1(\text{Time}) \\
&= 256.6 + 1.468\,(\text{Time})
\end{aligned}
$$

The results are shown graphically as Figure 6A–4. The coefficients of the dummy variables are interpreted as the difference in the average value of the dependent vari-

FIGURE 6A–4

Predicted shipments by season

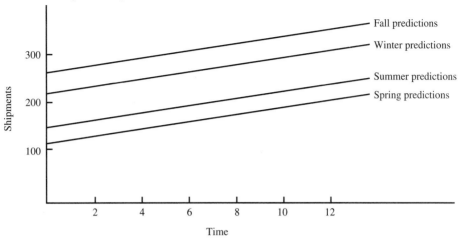

able between the category of the dummy variable and the category of the variable that has no dummy variable (in this example, fall). Thus,

$$B_2 = \frac{210 + 220 + 225}{3} - \frac{260 + 270 + 275}{3} + 3(1.468)$$

$$= -50 + 3(1.468) = -45.6$$

If this model were used to predict shipments in the second quarter of 1968, the "best guess" prediction would then be

$$\text{Predicted shipments} = 155.5 + 1.468(18) = 142$$

7 Developing Product Strategy

Overview

The previous chapters gave a detailed view of the background analysis necessary to develop a marketing plan. The purpose of background analysis (homework), of course, is to provide a sound basis for action.[1] That action plan should address three related questions:

1. *Where are we headed?* Here the focus is on basic objectives such as growth versus profits.

2. *How will we get there?* This is the core of marketing/product strategy that addresses issues such as whether to focus on existing versus new customers. It is summarized in a Targeting and Positioning Statement defining (1) customer targets, (2) competitive targets, and (3) the proposition (general offering) that will enable the firm to succeed in capturing the targeted customers in the face of competition.

3. *What will we do?* This addresses specific programs/tactics to be employed in order to carry out the core strategy. Basically it entails describing the marketing mix (product, pricing, promotion, distribution, service).

In this chapter, we focus primarily on number 2 in the list above, the strategy. Specific programs are covered in the following chapters.

---

[1] Much of our thinking about marketing strategy has been influenced by James "Mac" Hulbert, Columbia Business School; William Brandt, Impact Planning Group; and the late Abraham Schuchman, long-time marketing professor at Columbia.

Benefits of Strategy

A successful strategy leads to at least three key outcomes:

First, it helps *achieve coordination* among functional areas of the organization as well as within marketing. Different areas of the organization have different perspectives on how to make a product successful. Product managers often like to increase advertising spending. Sales managers like (more) flexible pricing policies. Production personnel typically like longer production runs and fewer products. Financial/accounting analysts require quantitative justification of all expenditures.

For example, suppose a computer manufacturer wishes to target a specific industry with unique product features. The image or "positioning" of the product is high quality and technological superiority. In such a case, a sales manager's flexible pricing orientation is inconsistent with the strategy. The production people may be upset with the segmentation approach because it means lower volume and more customization. The image-building activities of the advertising agency are difficult to evaluate in financial terms for the accounting personnel. A strategy that is not accepted, poorly articulated, or not well understood cannot provide the necessary coordination. One purpose of strategy is to ensure that all members of the team are working together.

Second, strategy *defines how resources are to be allocated.* At any level of the organization, resources are limited. Typically some resources, such as manufacturing or service capacity, sales force time, money, and so forth, will be more limited than others. In addition, these resources are often shared. For example, a single sales force often sells many different products. The lower the level of the organization, the more resources are typically shared. Therefore, at the product level it is essential that the strategy provide clear guidance for the allocation of resources across activities and other products.

Third, strategy should *lead to a superior market position.* A good strategy takes cognizance of existing and potential competitors and their strengths and weaknesses (see Chapter 4). A *competitively sensible* marketing strategy has at least one of four main characteristics:

a. It is something a competitor *cannot* do. A competitor's inability could be based on patent protection (e.g., the pharmaceutical industry), extra capacity, or some other proprietary or technological advantage. For example, until the release of Windows 95, Apple Computer was the only personal computer supplier with a truly easy-to-use graphical user interface. Other competitor operating systems, notably DOS and earlier versions of Windows, could not match the Apple interface.

b. It is something a competitor *will choose not to do.* Often smaller companies pursue small segments of the market in the hope that large companies will ignore them due to financial criteria. For example, Silicon Graphics, Inc., a manufacturer of computer workstations, specialized in computers that manipulate three-dimensional images on screen for jet design, movie special effects, and other applications. The other major suppliers of workstations, Sun, IBM, and Hewlett-Packard, built more general-purpose computers that did not perform as well as those made by Silicon Graphics for the segment's needs.

c. Competitors *would be at a disadvantage if they do it*. Sears's marketing strategy of "everyday low pricing" was an unsuccessful attempt to emulate the success of Wal-Mart and K mart because the company was not prepared to fully integrate a low-cost and low-price orientation in the entire organization.

d. *It causes us to gain if the competitor does it*. Campbell Soup Company ran an advertising campaign around the theme "Soup is good food." Such a theme is clearly generic and is aimed at increasing soup consumption in general. Since Campbell has a dominant position in the market, it benefits from such generic promotion. However, Heinz or Lipton could not afford such a strategy because it would likely primarily cause Campbell's sales to increase.

In sum, a good marketing strategy coordinates functional areas of the organization, helps allocate resources efficiently, and helps the product attain the market position management desires. It also identifies an advantage over the other products and services pursuing the same customers.

Elements of a Product Strategy

A more complete statement of marketing strategy for a product consists of seven parts (Hulbert, 1985):

1. Statement of the objective(s) the product should attain.
2. Selection of strategic alternative(s).
3. Selection of customer targets.
4. Choice of competitor targets.
5. Statement of the core strategy.
6. Description of supporting marketing mix.
7. Description of supporting functional programs.

The first two elements, objectives and strategic alternatives, establish the general direction of the strategy. The next three elements, selection of customer and competitor targets and description of the core strategy, are the essence of marketing strategy.[2] Taken together, they are often referred to as positioning, that is, how the product is to be differentiated from the competition in the minds of the target customers. Finally, the supporting marketing mix and functional programs relate to the implementation of the strategy.

---

[2]Product selection—that is, "which products" to "which markets?"—is also part of the marketing strategy.

A systematic approach to developing strategy helps to achieve the coordination and integration referred to earlier. There is a logical order to the aspects of the strategy: It is clear that marketing mix decisions such as price and advertising logically depend on the basic strategy. For example, the strategy of a high-quality positioning to upscale customers, such as Ralph Lauren's Polo clothing line, must be implemented by high price, exclusive distribution, and classy advertising to obtain consistency between the strategy and implementation.

Setting Objectives

An organization has a variety of objectives, beginning with mission or vision and ranging from corporate to product to human resource objectives. The type of objective that is our concern addresses the question "Where do we want to go?" Clearly, the answer to such a question will differ depending on the level of the organization. At the corporate level, objectives related to return on investment, stock share price, and business mix are common. However, they are not very useful for the marketing manager because they give little guidance at the product level for how to proceed.

Figure 7–1 represents the different levels of objectives and strategies in an organization, referred to as a *hierarchy of objectives*. Objectives at different levels of the organization should mesh to achieve overall corporate objectives. The job of ensuring that individual product objectives add up to the organization objective usually falls to corporate personnel who are responsible for negotiating both business unit and product objectives to achieve the overall objective.

In this chapter, we are concerned primarily with level III, product objectives. The two objectives most commonly set for specific products or services are growth—in terms of sales revenues or market share—and profitability. It is usually not possible to optimize both simultaneously during the time span of an annual marketing plan. The kinds of activities necessary to achieve an ambitious market share objective work against satisfying an ambitious profit objective.

For example, to reach a market share objective, the usual actions include price reductions, increased spending on advertising, increasing the size of the sales force, and so forth. Significant growth in share is, at the margin, achievable only by increasing expenditures or lowering profit margins per unit. This trade-off between profits and share is exemplified by Japanese auto manufacturers that shifted to a profit orientation from a share objective, partly due to losses suffered when the yen rose to 80 to the dollar in 1995. The result was the introduction of upscale cars (e.g., Lexus) and SUVs (*Business Week,* Feb. 26, 1996).

Few managers employ a growth objective without some consideration of its impact on the product's profits (although certain Internet firms seem to

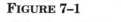

FIGURE 7–1

Hierarchy of objectives

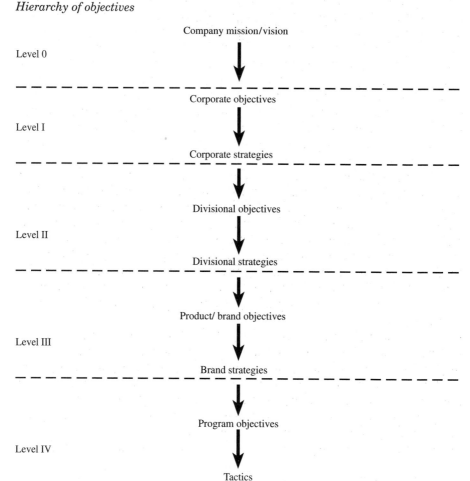

ignore profits). Likewise, profitability may be the main goal but subject to share maintenance or controlled decline (i.e., harvesting). The objective to be maximized might be called the *primary* objective and the objective acting as the constraint the *secondary* objective. A third objective that can be set for a product is cash flow. When a company is bought through a leveraged buyout (as was the rage in the 1980s), cash flow to pay down debt is a primary concern, and thus the company's products are often charged with generating cash.

Other characteristics of good objectives are the following:

1. They should have *quantified standards* of performance. In other words, every objective statement should include language such as "increase market share two share points."

2. They should be ambitious enough to be *challenging,* subject to internal and external constraints. Objectives act as motivators. If regularly set too high, employees treat them as meaningless. If set too low, the organization does not achieve its potential. For example, Floating Point Systems, a manufacturer of scientific computers, consistently disappointed stock analysts with earnings that did not reach projections. As a result, the CEO set objectives so low that they could not be missed (Levine and Anderson, 1986). Clearly, such an objective-setting mechanism is inconsistent with what objectives are supposed to accomplish.

3. They should have a *time frame* within which to achieve the objectives. Objectives are not open-ended; for proper motivation and evaluation, a time frame must be set. For annual planning purposes, the planning period serves as an adequate time frame, with perhaps quarterly checkpoints.

Two key questions with respect to objectives are (1) which one should be pursued and (2) how high a target should I set?

To answer the first question, product managers should consider information from industry, competitor, and customer analyses and consider the company's current and anticipated financial resources. For growth objectives to be feasible, there must be some competitor vulnerabilities that can be exploited (competitor analysis), a customer segment with remaining potential (customer analysis), or general category growth anticipated (industry analysis).

Some industries have traditional objectives. For example, in consumer products, the focus for many years has been market share and sales volume. Product managers have been under constant pressure to "move cases" of products. However, a recent trend emphasizes profits more heavily over traditional volume targets. This is difficult to implement, for two reasons. First, information systems at most companies do a good job of measuring share and sales volume on a regular basis but not of measuring profits. Second, and perhaps more important, companies do not always reward product managers on the basis of profits; the key to fast-track careers has been to increase volume and share.

The second issue is how much to go for in the objective: If the manager is pursuing an increase in market share, how much is appropriate? In some cases, no growth in share is challenging enough: If the product has had declining share, halting the decline could be considered ambitious. Clearly, the size of the gain to be expected is built on the market size forecasts and the anticipated activities of competitors. If the competitors are going for profits, it can be a good time to gain significant share. If the market increases 10 percent, a 10 percent increase in sales only maintains share.

A number of noneconomic or nonquantitative objectives are also pursued, although not necessarily as primary product objectives. For example, it is difficult to find a U.S. company that has not made a major push for quality. Many firms have set customer satisfaction objectives (e.g., to increase satisfaction from 70 to 75 on a 100-point scale) as a result. Similarly maintenance of brand equity is a concern in a growing number of companies. However, there is an obvious link between these "enabling" objectives and economic objectives: Achieving the former should eventually lead to reaching the latter.

In sum, the task of setting objectives involves choosing the appropriate objective, quantifying the objective with an amount, and setting a time frame for its achievement. It relies on the analyses that provide the background for the marketing plan.

Selection of Strategic Alternatives

The choice of strategic alternatives follows the selection of the primary objective. This is really the first step in developing marketing strategy for the product or service that provides broad guidelines for the ultimate strategy selected. Figure 7–2 presents alternative strategies in a treelike structure. The diagram assumes the long-run objective is to maximize the product's long-run profits (which in turn should maximize shareholder value). We link the description of the alternatives to the selection of whether the primary objective is growth in sales/share and hence long-run profits or short-term profitability. The options available depend on the objective. If a manager chooses growth, the two main ways to achieve it are market development and market penetration strategies, often via the introduction of new products or extensions. Market development strategies are directed toward selling the current product to current noncustomers; market penetration aims at current or past customers of the product category. If the manager chooses the profitability path, the primary focus is on either decreasing inputs (basically cutting costs, also known as denominator management) or increasing outputs (sales revenue from existing units sold).

Increasing Sales/Market Share

Market Development Strategies
These strategies are aimed at noncustomers of the product (i.e., customer acquisition). One approach is to pursue nonusers in segments already being targeted. For example, if an Internet service is targeted to law firms, a development strategy would pursue those law firms that have not yet purchased the product (while, of course, continuing to pursue current customers with value-added services such as productivity seminars). Essentially, this approach tries to tap remaining market potential from those segments identified as prime prospects. Another example is the increased attention small business owners received from large banks such as Wells Fargo. While the banks already have customers from that segment, the lack of growth from

FIGURE 7–2

Strategic alternatives

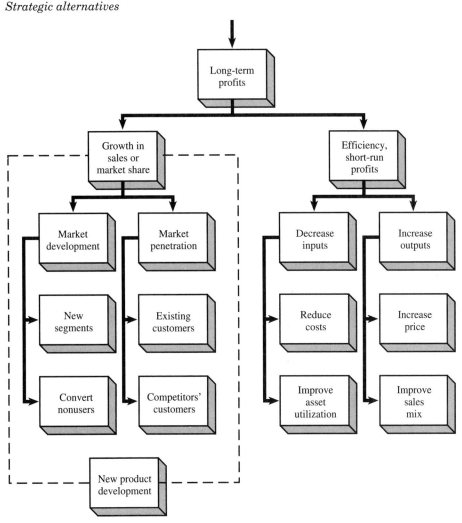

lending to larger clients gave the banks more incentive to expand their marketing efforts to get more customers from entrepreneurial companies.

A second approach is to enter new markets, developing segments previously ignored by the product category. An example of this strategy is the attempt by Kodak and Fuji to attract children to photography using a variety of promotions and special programs (Bounds, 1994). Another example is the seed company that put small containers of vegetable seeds in plastic wheelbarrows at garden supply stores to try to get children to begin gardening at a young age. Similarly, antacids such as Tums have been positioned as not only solving stomach acid problems but also as a calcium additive for the diet.

Market Penetration Strategies

Another, and often overlooked, way to increase market share or sales volume is to increase the usage rate of the brand's existing customers (i.e., customer expansion). The biggest asset the manager owns is the customer base, and it should be leveraged as much as possible. A firm can obtain more volume from existing customers by, for example, using larger package sizes, promoting more frequent use, or getting a larger share of the business if the customer uses several vendors.

Many firms have successfully taken this tack. The classic example is Arm & Hammer baking soda, which has been marketed as useful for several purposes. Banks try to get a larger share of commercial customers' business by selling other services, such as cash management and annuities. Coupons are often used to induce customers to buy larger package sizes in the hope of increasing the consumption rate. In the spirit of the discussion on market potential in Chapter 5, managers should always ask themselves: Is the actual consumption rate equal to the *potential* rate?

A second route to increasing sales or market share is to attract competitors' customers (i.e., customer acquisition), that is, to induce brand switching. This is a difficult strategy when the switching costs are high (e.g., mainframe computers, nuclear generators). In addition, the strategy could be risky. First, it can incur the wrath of a larger, more formidable competitor. Second, it may involve substantial use of sales promotion, which could make the strategy unprofitable. Third, a strategy inducing brand switching may call for comparative advertising, which is not only expensive but also risky; if poorly executed, it may call attention to the competitor's brand, particularly if the brand is the market leader. Because of the increase in credit card issuers (e.g., AT&T, General Electric, "affinity" cards), category participants resorted to stealing the best customers from one another (Pae, 1992). AT&T has been heavily involved in defending its long-distance phone calling business from MCI, which is constantly developing new services (e.g., "Friends and Family") and launching price comparison ads to steal customers from AT&T as well as the Baby Bells, Sprint, and newer entrants.

Increasing Profitability

Decreasing Inputs

One way to increase profits is cost reduction. Obvious candidates for reduction are fixed costs of marketing such as advertising, promotion, selling expenses, marketing research, and so forth. Unfortunately, reducing these inputs may have adverse long-run effects. A possible danger in stressing variable cost reduction is that a reduction in the inputs can cause a commensurate reduction in the outputs if some of the variable cost reduction affects product quality. Aluminum Company of America (Alcoa) restructured its operations in 1992

and reduced its workforce; the result was a rejection rate at one of its can manufacturing facilities of 25 percent and a drop in customer satisfaction to below
50 percent (Milbank, 1992). At the same time, some minor product changes can
save a substantial amount of money. For example, Ford reduced its costs $8 to
$9 million per year by decreasing the number of carpeting options from nine
to three and saved $750,000 by using black screws rather than color-matched
screws on Mustang side mirrors (Schwartz, 1996).

A second way to decrease the inputs is to improve the utilization of the
assets at the disposal of the manager. This might mean keeping down
accounts receivable and, for a manufactured product, the costs of inventories. Other, related activities include running production equipment more
efficiently and, at a more aggregate level, investing idle cash on hand in
overnight interest-bearing securities.

Managers choosing the profit branch of the tree must, of course, also
choose customer targets. The probable approach for this objective would be
to concentrate on current customers. In fact, one of the most obvious ways to
improve profits is to reduce customer turnover/churn, (i.e., increase customer retention).

Increasing Outputs

The easiest way to increase revenues from existing unit sales is to improve
prices. This can be done in a variety of ways, including increasing the list
price, reducing discounts, reducing trade allowances, and so forth. One must
be careful to do this, however, only within a range in which the customer is
relatively insensitive to price, or total revenues can actually fall. There is also
the issue of competitive reaction that has doomed many price increases by
airlines and hurt P&G's attempt to institute everyday low pricing (EDLP).

The other way to increase revenues is to improve the sales mix. The
80/20 rule often holds: 20 percent of the product variants (sizes, colors, etc.)
produce 80 percent of the sales or profits. In such an instance, it may make
sense to reduce the product line and emphasize selling more of the profitable
items. Alternatively, if we apply the rule to customers, the manager may
want to de-emphasize the unprofitable customers and concentrate resources
on those producing 80 percent of the profits (i.e., customer deletion).

Summary

We have presented two broad strategic options available to a marketing
manager in terms of strategic alternatives.[3] This does not mean that a manager is limited to either growth or profits. For example, it is common to seek

---

[3]A similar view of the alternatives in a high-tech context is provided by Kadanoff
(1995), pp. 24–26. She labels current customers in the installed base as "Low-hanging
fruit," new customers in current segments as "Juicy fruit," new customers in "adjacent"
markets as "Ripe fruit," new customers in new segments as "Fruit on the vine," and new
customers in developing segments as "Seedlings."

reductions in variable costs while pursuing market share gains. In addition, a product manager may choose both to increase the consumption rate of current customers and to introduce product-line extensions.

The marketing manager's dilemma is that while several of the options may appear to be equally attractive, it is very difficult and expensive to successfully implement multiple strategic alternatives. The difficulty arises from the multiple positionings different alternatives may require. For example, to simultaneously obtain new customers and get current customers to buy more, different advertising campaigns may have to be run, projecting different images and confusing customers. Multiple strategies prevent economies of scale from advertising copy, increase the use of more expensive media (i.e., spot versus national TV), and so forth, thus increasing expenses. Hence there is pressure on the manager to select a subset of the options available and concentrate resources on them.

Three key criteria for evaluating strategic alternative options are

1. *Size/growth of the segment.* An important part of customer analysis focuses on which customer groups are growing and how fast.
2. *Opportunities for obtaining competitive advantage.* In competitor analysis, we assess which market segments competitors are pursuing and their claimed competitive advantages, the resources they can put into the market, and their likely future marketing strategies.
3. *Resources available to penetrate the segment.* This is covered in the self-analysis part of the assessment of competition analysis.

Positioning: Choice of Customer Targets

As mentioned earlier, positioning entails a specific statement of how the product differs from the competition in the minds of a specific set of customers and encompasses (1) customer targets, (2) competitor targets, and (3) some attribute(s) by which the differentiation will occur. The choice of which customer group(s) to target follows immediately from specification of the strategic alternatives and the segments developed in the customer analysis. If the profit route is taken, the customer targets are generally current ones, for example, "men 18 to 25" or "banks with assets between $100 million and $1 billion." The task is similar for any of the growth alternatives. For a market penetration strategy aimed at the product's own customers or a market development strategy aimed at nonusers, the customers of the current strategy would again be selected. For the market penetration strategy aimed at stealing competitors' customers, the specific descriptors of those customers would be used. Finally, for the market development strategy aimed at new segments, the descriptors from the new segments chosen would be specified.

FIGURE 7–3   **Target Segments for Handspring**

Factor	Price-Sensitive Business Professionals	Nonbusiness Professionals	Nonprofessionals
Benefits, key attributes of PDA	• Functionality, expandability • Status • Design, sleek, small, nice screen • Price • Memory, speed	• Ease of use, convenience • Design, sleek, small, nice screen • Price • Functionality, expandability • Status • Durability	• Ease of use, convenience • Price • Fun/enjoyment (music, games) • Design, nice screen • Battery life • Status, sense of belonging (cool product)
Main factors affecting PDA purchase	• Price • Functionality • Memory	• Ease of use • Functionality • Price	• Ease of use • Price • Design, sleek, small, nice screen
Where do they purchase?	• Through company, possibly buy themselves at consumer electronics retailers • Over Internet	• Through company, possibly buy themselves at consumer electronics retailers • Over Internet	• Consumer electronics retailers • Over Internet
When do they buy?	• When colleagues buy	• When colleagues buy	• When friends, neighbors, or classmates buy • Receive or purchase as gift

Consider Handspring's strategy in the PDA market in 2000. Given that their basic product is strong on convenience and low in price, their target segments differ from the traditional PDA customer: the upscale, price-insensitive business professional. One can identify three segments worth pursuing (Figure 7–3). Obviously the choice of customer targets involves benefit-cost tradeoffs. That is, why choose to serve customers who currently provide little profit? In the case of acquisition strategies, this means ensuring that the value of an acquired customer is greater than their acquisition cost.

Positioning: Choice of Competitor Targets

Even if the competition is not explicitly mentioned in any of the product's communications programs, it is still important to consider which competitors are the primary targets of the strategy. For a penetration strategy that involves stealing competitors' customers, the targeted customers should be identified based on an analysis of which competitor's customers are both valuable and the most easily pried away. However, all strategic alternatives at least implicitly involve competition because of the necessity to position the product *against* major competitors.

Positioning involves some prioritization of the competitors, both direct and indirect. Again, the chief source of information about this choice is the situation analysis in Chapter 4, which details the strengths and weaknesses of the competition. The hope is to identify a weak or docile company with significant sales that can be easily overcome. Unfortunately such targets are not always available (Ries and Trout, 1992; Czepiel, 1992). Market leaders often take defensive steps and therefore focus on the strong second competitor and perhaps the third one. The followers in the market take different competitor stances depending on their market share relative to the leader. A strong second might focus on offensive warfare and target the leader. Weak followers often try to avoid the major competitors and seek market niches that have either few or weak rivals. For example, in banking they might be a "boutique," offering customized services targeted at high net worth individuals, thus avoiding full-scale competition with large banks.

Positioning: The Core Strategy

The core strategy defines the differential advantage to be communicated to the target customers, often referred to as *product positioning*. The advantages that can be employed fall into two basic categories: (1) cost/price (economic) differential advantage and (2) differentiation based on product offering/service features.[4] (Note that this can include psychological as well as functional benefits.) In other words, you either have to have a lower price that can be supported in the long run only with lower costs or be better on some element of the product offering customers recognize as a benefit.

As several examples show, being "stuck in the middle" can be disastrous. In 1991, Compaq Computer was in deep trouble. The previously high-flying computer company, known for its high-priced, high-quality personal computers, showed its first-ever quarterly loss. This arose because it was neither the low-price nor the quality/performance leader in an increasingly competitive market. United Airlines' Shuttle ("express") service failed to significantly affect Southwest Airlines in the large California market since it was not lower priced and was not perceived to be of any higher quality.

In general, the positioning decision has four steps (Day, 1990, Chapter 7):

1. Identify alternative positioning themes by consulting the advertising account team, the product team, and past marketing plans.

---

[4]See, for example, Porter (1985). Porter actually advocates a third basic strategy, market segmentation. However, we believe market segmentation is a necessary part of any strategy.

2. Screen the alternatives according to whether each is (*a*) meaningful to customers, (*b*) feasible given the firm and product resources and customer perceptions, (*c*) competitive (see the definition in the overview of this chapter), or (*d*) helpful for meeting the product objective.

3. Select the position that best satisfies these criteria and is accepted by the marketing organization.

4. Implement the programs (e.g., advertising) consistent with the product position selected.

This systematic approach ensures that alternative positionings are considered and diverse constituents are consulted.

The core strategy should be easy to summarize and communicate in paragraph form. Sometimes this statement of the core strategy is referred to as the *value proposition*. The value proposition for Southwest Airlines, for example, would be the following:

> To provide travelers with the lowest-cost air transportation with an enjoyable, fun atmosphere.

This clearly states that Southwest's differential advantage is price and fun, not food, frills, and nonstop routes.

Cost/Price Strategy

Almost every product category has a competitor that focuses on price or "value," as opposed to product features or on some aspect of the product other than price. Wal-Mart made Sam Walton the richest man in the United States. Charles Schwab invented the discount brokerage business. Private labels have become very popular in many supermarket product categories, often being the number one brands in the categories (e.g., frozen juices/drinks and cookies). Mail-order personal computers stressing price constitute a huge business, and for a time Packard-Bell (now aligned with NEC) became the largest vendor of personal computers in the United States largely through its low-price, mass distribution channel approach.

However, not all products can be the low-price leader. Many firms lack the size, capital, or other resources needed to be the low-cost manufacturer or service provider. To successfully implement a low-cost/low-price core strategy, several activities must be pursued that are consistent with the experience curve. First, a high volume of a single product or family of products should be produced or sold. Focused production hastens cost reduction, which must be continuously pursued. Second, investment should focus on efficient facilities and market share. Again, efficiency does not apply just to production equipment. The lowest-cost companies pay strict attention to corporate overhead, including size of staff, perks such as jets and limousines, fancy offices, and so on. Finally, control should focus on cost in manufacturing products, delivering services, and implementing activities such as advertising and promotion.

In pursuing lower costs, the manager should focus on important activities in which the cost competitiveness is low (i.e., their relative price is high). The important costs involved vary widely over different products. For a personal computer, decreased cost of semiconductors, microchip boards, video screens, cooling fans, and the like can all bring the cost of the product down significantly (and have in recent years). However, for a laundry detergent, the major cost items might be the thickness of the plastic package and the size of the label.

The low-price core strategy poses certain risks. One is that customer tastes shift, and the product being produced in large quantities may no longer be desired (e.g., Atari and other video games before the Nintendo era). A second is that technological shifts can either make it easier for competitors to have the same costs or make the product obsolete. Competitors can also leapfrog in cost cutting, which eliminates the cost differential advantage. One advantage of a low-price strategy is that there is probably always room in a product category for a low-priced, "value" option because some segment of customers will always be price sensitive. The key question, of course, is how large the price-sensitive segment is and how many competitors will target it, and therefore whether it is worth the investments necessary to be a cost leader.

Nonprice Strategy

One way to think about the nonprice differential advantage is as a product characteristic, not necessarily tangible, that allows the manager to obtain a price higher than the price that would be allowed under perfect competition. As every student of microeconomics (and, it is hoped, every reader of this book) knows, with many suppliers of undifferentiated commodities, the market price is marginal cost. Therefore, the differential advantage is intended to create added value in the minds of customers that enables the producer to obtain a higher price than the pure competition case; with a significant differential advantage, customers focus on product benefits other than price.

From where can a differential advantage be obtained? Figure 7–4 portrays what is called the *total product concept* (Levitt, 1986). The *generic* product is the bundle of characteristics—the functional aspects of a product. For example, an automobile could be described by quality of tires, miles per gallon, engine size, and so forth. The *expected* product is described by other benefits delivered by the product that customers have come to take as routine. For cars, the expected product includes some degree of reliability and warranty coverage. The *augmented* and *potential* products are often what give rise to differential advantage. The augmented product includes features or benefits that can be delivered now to go beyond expectations, for example a satellite-based (GPS) tracking system. The potential product contains

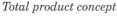

FIGURE 7–4

Total product concept

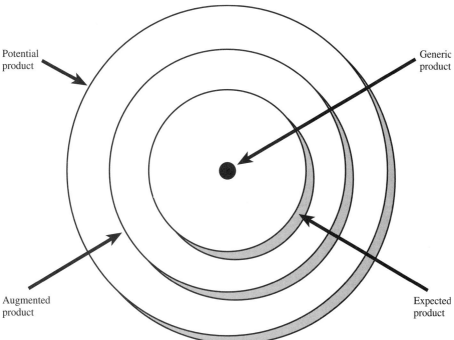

those features or benefits that can be added to a product or service some time in the future. Customers remember restaurants that offer free meals when a customer is dissatisfied or the retail clerk who pays special attention to a customer when the store is busy, and these actions lead to repeat buying.

The point here is that differential advantages are often obtained by going beyond what customers expect to provide unanticipated product benefits. It may take some creative thinking, but the most important aspect of providing differential advantages is to move away from asking, "How can I make this product different?" to asking, "What am I selling?" By focusing on what customers are buying—that is, benefits, and more broadly, customer experience—managers can better determine how to make their products or services different from the competition.

Managers typically use five areas for differentiation (Schnaars, 1991).

1. *Quality*. Product quality has many dimensions. For example, particularly for technologically based products, enhanced quality can mean improved performance. Intel originally differentiated its products by being technologically ahead of other semiconductor companies. Quality can also mean superior design. Automobile brands such as Lexus,

computers such as Apple, stereo manufacturer Bang & Olufsen, and consumer product companies such as Sony emphasize superior design in their products. Customer service is also an area for differentiation based on quality. Manufacturers such as Timken (bearings) and Caterpillar (farm equipment) are well known for their customer service. For service businesses, product quality and customer service are virtually synonymous. Airlines such as Singapore and retailers such as Nordstrom differentiate on this basis. For manufactured products, quality can also mean reliability and durability. Brands marketed by the appliance manufacturer Maytag, for example, are advertised on this dimension (the "lonely repairman").

2. *Status and image.* In the bottled water category brands such as Evian and Perrier have claimed this point of differentiation from other bottled waters. Many consumer fashion brands, such as Rolex watches and Polo clothing, use this approach.

3. *Branding.* A particular aspect of image involves brands. Brand names and their values communicated to customers, brand equity, can serve as a point of differentiation. IBM, McDonald's, and Nestlé are leading brands worldwide. It is particularly interesting when a product that had previously been considered a commodity is differentiated and becomes successful after branding, such as Perdue chickens. A more recent illustration is the campaign by Intel using ads touting "Intel Inside."

Perceptual mapping, described in Chapter 5, has been used by managers to assess the current perceptual positions of brands among customer and competitor targets and to help determine if the current positioning is effective or whether repositioning can help. Figure 7–5 shows what is called a *joint space* because it not only indicates brand locations versus competition on the two axes but also displays *ideal points,* the preferred bundle of attributes of clusters of households. Note that the map incorporates all three aspects of positioning. Customers are represented by the ideal points (the segments are numbered according to size), competitors are located on the map, and the differential advantage can be assessed using the brand attributes represented by the axes.

Consider the joint space figure from the perspective of RC Cola. RC is perceived as a nondiet cola, but it is equidistant from segment 1, which is close to Coke and Pepsi, and segment 3, which seems to want a lower-calorie cola. RC can position itself more within the mainstream, where it would encounter heavy competition from Coke and Pepsi. Alternatively, it can pursue segment 3 with a "lighter" image where it would find fewer competitors, but also fewer potential customers.

4. *Convenience and service.* Given the demographic trends pointed out in Chapter 3, many consumer products are differentiated on the basis

FIGURE 7–5

Joint space for colas

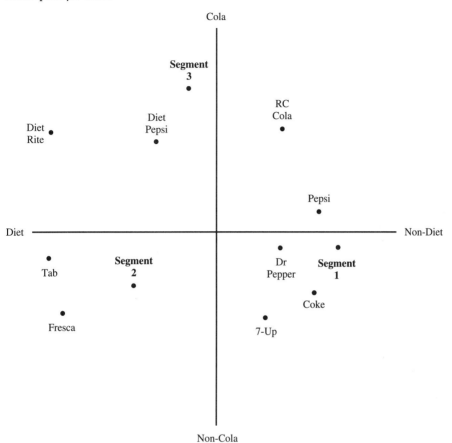

of convenience. Two Japanese luxury car brands, Lexus and Infiniti, differentiated themselves from other luxury car brands by making it easier for customers to have their cars serviced, giving free loaner cars and sometimes making arrangements to pick up the car at the customer's home. The grocery home shopping services focus on convenience to entice people with home computers and modems to change their buying habits and purchase their weekly supermarket orders from home.

5. *Distribution channels.* Firms can sometimes gain differential advantage by reaching customers more efficiently and effectively than competitors. Federal Express, through its Powership terminals, allowed its customers to determine for themselves where their packages are in the system and to order the "product." Thus, Federal Express becomes, in effect, the customers' shipping department.

The requirements for a nonprice differential advantage core strategy are naturally quite different from those for a cost/price strategy. First, the strategy requires searching for continuous product improvements (or improvements in perceptions) to maintain the differential advantage. Second, a differential advantage core strategy requires flexibility in both production and management to keep up with changes in customer tastes and competition.

The risks involved in the differential advantage core strategy are also considerable. First, the cost/price differential may become so great that customers are willing to pay less to get less. Perhaps the biggest problem is that the differential often can disappear due to imitation. Witness the quick adoption of frequent-flier programs by almost all the major airlines. Who remembers—or cares—that American was the first with such a program?

Managing Brand Equity

Managing a product's reputation is one of the most important strategic jobs facing the manager. Like objects owned by a firm such as manufacturing equipment and buildings, a brand name is an asset, and a potentially valuable one.

For several years, the increased growth rates of private label brands and higher spending on price-oriented promotions led pundits to predict the "death" of national and international brands. This belief was given further credence when "Marlboro Friday," the Friday in April 1993 on which Philip Morris reduced the price of its venerable Marlboro brand by 40 cents per pack to combat private label cigarettes, caused sharp drops in the stock prices of manufacturers of national brands. This action was replicated by the cereal manufacturers, led by Post (also owned by Philip Morris) and Kellogg's in April 1996.

Since that date, many companies have decided that the best way to combat lower-priced competitors, whether private labels for supermarket products or clones for computers, is to reemphasize their brand names. Companies such as Coca-Cola, Hewlett-Packard, and Gillette invest in advertising and attempt to reduce harmful price-oriented promotions. These efforts caused the sales of private labels to plateau and made 12 out of the 15 *Fortune* most admired companies household brand names (Morris, 1996). During 1999 and 2000, new Internet companies poured massive dollars into ads designed to attract customers and build brand recognition (the first level of brand equity), although with at best mixed success.

Brand names are also important in the global warfare against counterfeiters and "knockoffs," products that are made almost identical to the originals with very similar brand names and packaging but substantially lower prices. Knockoffs often mislead customers into thinking that the product is the well-known global brand. Counterfeiting is particularly prevalent in the music CD, computer software, and clothing industries (the U.S. government has sent numerous trade missions to China to try to persuade them to crack down on these activities to little effect). The problem is not just the lost revenues but the potential for the reputations of the global brands to be damaged by poorly made substitutes.

The concept of brand equity at the customer level was introduced in Chapter 5. To reiterate, brand equity can be defined as follows (Aaker, 1991, 1996):

> Brand equity is a set of assets (and liabilities) linked to a brand's name and symbol that adds to (or subtracts from) the value provided by the actual (physical) product or service to a firm and/or that firm's customers.

In Chapter 5 we described brand equity in terms of awareness, associations (image), attitude (overall quality), and attachment (loyalty). A slightly different version developed by Aaker (1996) appears in Figure 7–6 and includes five categories:

1. *Brand loyalty.* The strongest measure of a brand's value is the loyalty (repeat buying, word of mouth) it engenders among customers. Sometimes the loyalty is circumstantial: Repeat buying comes from a lack of reasonable alternatives. Circumstantial loyalty includes what are called *proprietary* assets (e.g., patents, copyrights, trademarks, control of an airport) that give a firm at least a temporary monopoly position (the impact of generic drugs when an ethical drug comes off patent suggests that much of the advantage is in fact circumstantial and hence temporary). In other situations, loyalty reflects an *efficiency* motive: The brand is good, so we automatically select it to minimize effort. Notice that an important special case of efficiency loyalty occurs when a customer relies on an "expert" (e.g., a dealer) to make the choice for her or him and the expert has a preferred alternative. In this case, loyalty is really channel-created loyalty.

   The strongest form of loyalty is *attachment.* In this case, the customer doggedly seeks out a product, often out of deference to its role in a previous situation (e.g., "they were there when I needed them") and sometimes in an almost ritualistic manner (e.g., stopping at a certain ice cream store as a rite of summer). This level of loyalty insulates a brand from competitive pressures such as advertising and price promotion and leads to higher margins and profits.

2. *Brand awareness.* The simplest form of brand equity is familiarity. A familiar brand gives the customer a feeling of *confidence* (risk reduction), and hence it is more likely to be both considered and chosen. There is also convincing evidence that, on average, customers *prefer* brands with which they are familiar. Finally, choosing a known brand gives the customer a *justification* for the decision, an explanation for his or her actions. This justification also serves a *social* role, indicating that the person has bought something of value.

FIGURE 7–6

Brand equity

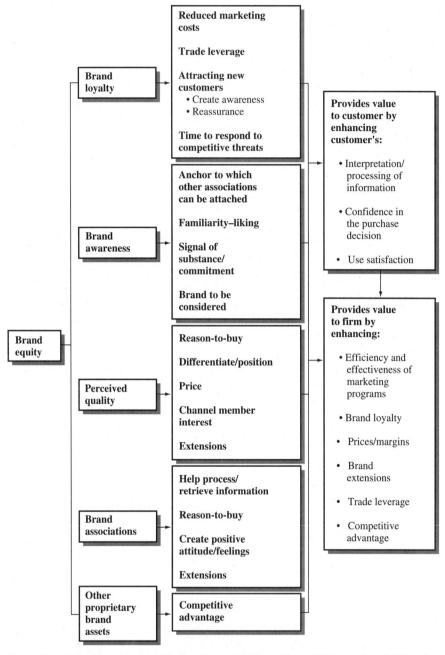

Source: Reprinted with permission of the Free Press, a division of Simon & Schuster from *Building Strong Brands* by David A. Aaker. Copyright 1996 by David A. Aaker.

3. *Perceived quality*. A known brand often conveys an aura of quality (good or bad). A quality association can be of the general halo type; for example, Levi Strauss has an outstanding reputation both for its products and as a place to work. Associations can also be attribute or category specific: Gillette makes fine-quality razors, Apple produces user-friendly products, and Samsonite products last forever. In some cases, a brand becomes synonymous with a category (e.g., Xerox, Kleenex, FedEx). Further, a brand often has strong price associations that influence quality perceptions (e.g., a K mart brand product is expected to be low in price and probably low in quality as well). Thus, strong quality associations exist for many products and brands.

4. *Brand associations*. While quality associations are very important, other, more subjective and emotional associations are also an important part of brand value. These include *personal* associations; Gatorades' "Be Like Mike" campaign was a blatant example, but every celebrity endorsement contains elements of it. Other associations are more emotional, relating to such lifestyle or personality characteristics as *stability* (see many Kodak ads, as well as Prudential's "A piece of the rock"), being *"hip"* or *"with it"* (a standard appeal of fashionable clothing companies; soft drinks, beer, and liquor; and Andre Agassi's "Image is Everything" ads), and being *responsible* (e.g., environmentally conscious, currently both an important issue and the subject of much hype). Other strong associations may be with the type of customer or user of the product (e.g., white shirts and bald heads with business executives) or geographic region (e.g., country of origin for Japanese cars, Swiss watches). Figure 7–7 provides a general list of both product attribute and user images. Taken together, these associations form a *brand personality* that suggests situations for which a brand is (and is not) suitable (Aaker, 1997).

5. *Other brand assets*. Other assets, such as patents and trademarks, are clearly valuable. However, we exclude these from brand equity since they are tied to the physical product or process and not to the brand *per se*.

Brand equity creates value for both customers and the firm. Customers can use brand names as simplifying heuristics for processing large amounts of information. Awareness of the brand name Lexus and the brand associations generated can act as a substitute for reading *Consumer Reports,* talking to friends, and other information sources. Dannon introduced its brand of bottled water under the assumption that consumers who view its yogurt positively will transfer that good feeling to the new product. Over-the-counter cold and headache remedies by well-known companies such as Bayer and Johnson & Johnson command significantly higher prices than

FIGURE 7–7   Some Brand Attributes and Image Dimensions

Attributes	Image Dimensions
Flavor/taste	Reliable—unreliable
Caffeine content	Old—young
Price	Technical—nontechnical
Packaging	Sensible—rash
Size	Interesting—boring
Calories	Creative—noncreative
Brand name	Sentimental—nonsentimental
Sweetness	Impulsive—deliberate
Weight	Trustworthy—untrustworthy
Warranty	Conforming—rebellious
Durability	Daring—cautious
Convenience	Forceful—submissive
Color	Bold—timid
Style	Sociable—unsociable
Comfort	
Freshness	
Construction material	
Availability	
Serviceability	
Compatibility	
Energy efficiency	
Instructions	
Automation	
Ease of use	

Source: Rajeev Batra, Donald R. Lehmann, and Dipinder Singh. "The Brand Personality Component of Brand Goodwill: Some Antecedents and Consequences," in David A. Aaker and Alexander L. Biel, eds., *Brand Equity and Advertising: Advertising's Role in Building Strong Brands* (Hillsdale, NJ: Lawrence Erlbaum Associates, 1993), pp. 83–96.

their private label counterparts because of the trust customers have in those companies. Thus, firms benefit enormously from having strong brand names. Investment in a brand name can be leveraged through brand extensions and increased distribution. High brand equity often allows higher prices to be charged and is therefore a significant competitive advantage.

An example of the power of brand names is the ill-fated Audi 5000, which was accused on a widely viewed edition of TV's *60 Minutes* of having a problem with sudden acceleration. The program claimed the car suddenly lurched forward without the driver's foot being on the gas pedal. Audi failed to view one of its chief marketing jobs as protecting the brand name. As a result, the company handled the problem by accusing U.S. drivers of making mistakes and stepping on the accelerator rather than the brake. Regardless of the truth (it was eventually concluded that the cars did not have a problem), protecting the asset—the company's brand name—should have been Audi's priority. The sales of *all* Audi products dropped two-thirds between 1985 and 1989. As a consequence, the manufacturer introduced new models (Quattro, 100, etc.) and eliminated the problem-ridden 4000 and 5000 lines.[5]

The concept of brand equity raises three important issues. First, it is critical to the long-term success of a product to build brand equity. This is particularly important for packaged goods manufacturers that face increasing competition from supermarkets' "own label" brands. The price difference a national brand can support relative to a private label is a direct function of the level of brand equity of the national brand.

Second, the question of product-line extensions becomes pertinent: How far can a successful brand name be stretched? Clearly Toyota, Nissan, and Honda believed luxury cars could not be sold with cars with a cheaper image; hence the development of Lexus, Infiniti, and Acura, respectively. Not only are the brand names different but the cars are sold in separate dealerships. Mitsubishi believed otherwise. It marketed its new luxury coupe, the Diamante, along with the rest of its product line, with limited success.

Third, the manager must view the management and sustenance of brand equity as an important task. This suggests the desirability of both measuring and setting objectives for brand equity. Aaker (1996) provides 10 guidelines for building strong brands:

1. *Brand identity.* Each brand should have an identity, a personality. It can be modified for different segments.

2. *Value proposition.* Each brand should have a unique value proposition.

3. *Brand position.* The brand's position should provide clear guidance to those implementing a communications program.

4. *Execution.* The communications program needs to implement the identity and position, and should be durable as well.

5. *Consistency over time.* Managers should have a goal of maintaining a consistent identity, position, and execution over time. Changes should be resisted.

6. *Brand system.* The brands in the portfolio should be consistent and synergistic.

7. *Brand leverage.* Extend brands and develop cobranding opportunities only if the brand identity will be both used and reinforced.

8. *Tracking.* The brand's equity should be tracked over time, including awareness, perceived quality, brand loyalty, and brand associations.

---

[5]This problem of how to handle disasters and their impact on the brand name continues to surface. Consider the problems faced by Ford and Firestone over tread separation in Firestone tires on Ford vehicles. Another example is Intel's initial reaction to problems with its Pentium processor.

9. *Brand responsibility.* Someone should be in charge of the brand who will create the identity and positions and coordinate the execution.

10. *Invest.* Continue investing in brands even when the financial goals are not being met.

Measuring Brand Value

Managers can measure overall brand value through a variety of means. Basically, measuring brand value requires answering the question "How much more value does the product have with the brand name attached?" One other method already discussed, conjoint analysis, can also be used. By simply using brand name as an attribute and using the different brand names in the market or fictitious brand names being considered for a new product, the part-worths estimated are quantitative measures of the value of a brand name relative to the others used in the experimental design. (Recall that in the example in Chapter 6, we found different values for Compaq and Gateway.)

A related method relies on so-called hedonic regression. This technique regresses market price (or the amount customers say they are willing to pay for various products) against product features and brand name:

$$\text{Price} = B_0 + B_1 \text{ (Feature 1)} + B_2 \text{ (Feature 2)} + \ldots$$
$$+ C_1 \text{ (Brand A)} + C_2 \text{ (Brand B)} + \ldots$$

The output gives a dollar value for each brand. (Of course, when actual prices are used, this analysis ignores the sales volume of each brand, so it may present a somewhat distorted view of the value to those customers who choose to buy each product.)

The various components of brand value can also be assessed in relatively straightforward ways. Different levels of awareness measurement (e.g., aided or unaided) are possible. Attribute associations can be directly assessed ("If ABC Inc. made a product with X amount of attribute A, how much of attribute B would you expect it to have?").

Given the large amount of attention paid to brand equity in the last few years, it is not surprising that a variety of consulting firms, advertising agencies, and other interested parties have developed their own approaches to measuring the value of brands and, as a result, rankings of relative brand equities (e.g., Research International's Equity Engine, Milward-Brown's Brand Q, and Y&R's Brand Asset Evaluator as well as Interbrand). The board of governors of the United Kingdom's Accounting Standards Board held public hearings on rules to require all companies to value their brands, and some companies in the United Kingdom and the United States carry brands on their balance sheets. Grand Metropolitan, for example, carries specific brand equities for Smirnoff, Pillsbury, and Burger King.

One approach, Valmatrix analysis by Trademark and Licensing Associates (TLA), values a brand by the amount another party will pay to rent or buy the brand name. TLA bases its valuation on comparable sales, licensing, and royalty agreements, as well as on 20 key descriptors of brand strength such as margins, life cycle position, extension potential, and others. Their rank order of brand names in Health and Beauty Aids is Gillette, Johnson & Johnson, Estée Lauder, Chanel, and Avon; for Apparel/Fashion it is Nike, Adidas, Reebok, Dior, and Yves Saint Laurent (Lefton and Anson, 1996).

An example of a survey approach is Total Research's EquiTrend, in which 2,000 households are polled by telephone. Consumers are asked to rate brands on a scale from 0 to 10 where 10 represents extraordinary quality and 0 poor or unacceptable quality. In its 1996 survey, the top five brand names were Kodak, Disney World, National Geographic, The Discovery Channel, and Mercedes-Benz; the bottom five (out of the top 100) were Wal-Mart, Apple Macintosh, The Disney Store, Toyota Landcruiser, and Universal Studios (Mehegan, 1996). In addition to being interesting, the results remind us that reputations can change.

An example from the technology area is a quarterly survey conducted by Techtel Corporation. The firm surveys business buyers of computer equipment including software and hardware on measures such as awareness, trial, purchase, and repurchase intention. The survey also measures the percentage of the buyers who have a positive opinion about a brand. An illustration of the results is shown in Figure 7–8 for IBM notebook computers. The squares represent the opinion measure while the vertical bars represent those who bought recently (within the previous quarter). The obviously high correlation between positive opinion and purchasing measures gives some assurance that brand strength converts into actual buying behavior.

More generally brand equity from the company's perspective relates to the value of a brand to the company (i.e., its worth). Brand worth can be assessed at two levels, product-market and financial market. Financial market valuation methods are based on realized value in sales and franchising/royalty/licensing fees. Given the thinness of these markets (i.e., one buyer and one seller) and their distance from marketing activities, we focus on product-market level measures.

A simple product-market level measure is the extra revenue a brand receives vis-a-vis a private label product of equal quality. It can come in two components: price premium and share premium. Brand equity realized in a particular year is thus simply the additional revenue the brand received, assuming both its share and price are greater than those of the private label. (In cases where only the price of the brand is greater, then equity is the price premium times the sales volume of the branded good.) For example, using the ice cream data in Figure 5–27, Dreyer's price premium versus private label is $0.90 - 0.53 = 0.37$ and its volume is approximately $(14.29\%)(36.83)(100$ million households) so an estimate of its realized equity in 1997 is $(\$0.37)(526.3$ million$) = 194$ million dollars. This measure does not explicitly include additional costs—variable and fixed—associated with the brand or its growth and extension potential. Still it provides a simple measure that is easy to calculate and hence monitor (and serves as the core of the Interbrand method).

FIGURE 7-8

IBM notebook: purchase versus positive opinion

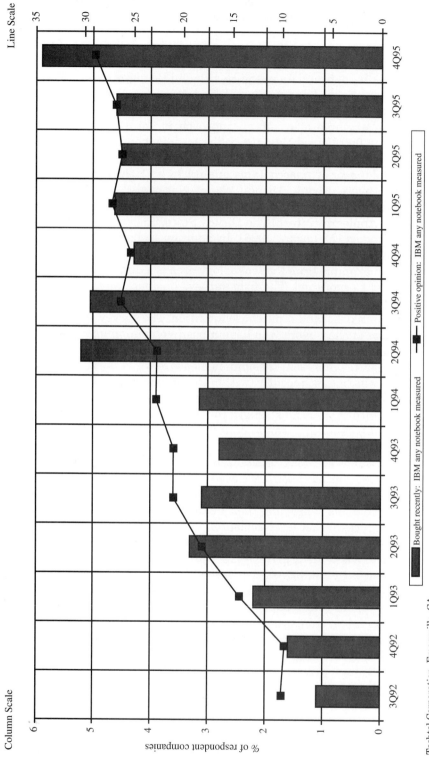

Techtel Corporation, Emeryville, CA.
Source: Developed by Techtel Corp. T-MAS™ © 1992–1996 and data © 1987–1996 by Techtel Corp. and others.

Customer Strategy

Another aspect of strategy involves the most crucial focus in marketing: customers. As suggested earlier, the different strategies suggest different approaches to customers (e.g., market penetration implies acquiring new customers). Four basic customer strategies are available:

1. Customer acquisition (i.e., getting new customers).
2. Customer retention (i.e., keeping current customers satisfied via enhancing brand loyalty or through superior service).
3. Customer expansion, getting customers to either buy more of what they are currently buying (increasing usage) or "cross-selling" other products.
4. Customer deletion, dropping customers that are not profitable (both now and potentially in the future) in such a way as to not generate legal problems or public relations disasters.

Taken together, the results of these activities determine sales and form a high-level implementation of basic strategy (i.e., growth vs. profit).

Product Strategy over the Life Cycle

We have repeatedly mentioned the importance (and weaknesses) of the product life cycle concept. One way the life cycle can be used is to conceptualize different general approaches to developing core strategies and tactics.

Strategies for the Introduction Phase

Up to this point, this book has focused mainly on existing products, but the introductory phase of the life cycle is a useful place to begin this analysis. This stage in the life cycle has several characteristics. First, there are few competitors, perhaps only one. Second, sales volume increases slowly due to the small number of firms marketing the product and the reluctance on the part of customers to purchase it. Early on, selling and advertising focus on selling the generic product; the effort is on product form benefits. Distributors also have the power in the relationship because the product is still unproven with customers, so securing distribution is a major issue. (In the Internet world this means developing links from other sites.) Prices can be high or low depending on the entry strategy of the firm(s) marketing the product.

What are the core strategy options at this stage? There are two well-known options: *skimming* and *penetration*. The skimming strategy assumes a product feature–based differential advantage that allows a firm to enter and stay in the market during the introductory period with a high price. Target segments are narrowly defined to be those customers that are least price sensitive, that is, the pioneers or early adopters of the product. The penetration strategy is just the opposite: The manager uses a low-price core strategy and attempts to get as many customers and establish a significant market share position as quickly as possible.

The skimming strategy is useful when the cost structure of the product is largely variable costs, usually the case when the product is a manufactured good. The ensuing high margin can be sustained because the manager is not under intense pressure to cover large fixed costs. The distribution outlets should be limited to protect the high price. This strategy is most effective when high entry barriers exist because the high price and high margins make the category very attractive to potential competitors. The margins can then be used to fund investment in research and development.

A penetration strategy is more appropriate when fixed costs are high (e.g., many services, general purpose computer software). When a broad segment is being pursued, it is important to obtain wide distribution and thus spend heavily on trade-oriented promotion. The manager is also under pressure to make the market as large as possible, which involves generic or product category marketing. This is the more expensive strategy due to the lower margins and higher marketing costs. The product manager should use a penetration strategy when the lead in the market will likely be short-lived.

There are strategic advantages to being first in a market and establishing a strong position early, consistent with a penetration strategy. Much empirical research shows that the first "mover" (or more precisely, the first to achieve substantial market position) in a category has an advantage (called, not surprisingly, the *first-mover advantage*) in that it tends to maintain its lead through the product life cycle (Urban et al., 1986). Some of this advantage is obvious: Early movers get first access to distribution channels, establish awareness, and have the first opportunity to establish brand loyalty and create preferences (Carpenter and Nakamoto, 1989). However, followers often overtake leaders so first movement itself is no guarantee of success (Golder and Tellis, 1993).

Several examples of this introductory phase illustrate the different core strategies available. Consumer electronics and industrial product companies almost always pursue a skimming strategy. When VCRs, camcorders, digital tape players, and similar products were introduced, they were priced high initially and then fell in price over time. Since usually only one brand was on the market for some months and the early customers for such products (electronics nuts) are very price insensitive, there was little rationale for pricing low initially. In addition, the products needed word of mouth to help spread information about their utility. Alternatively, penetration pricing is often used for consumer packaged goods because market share is very important for retaining shelf space in supermarkets. This is clearly evident in Internet strategies that give away the product for free, hoping (often unreasonably) to recoup costs with advertising revenues and future sales.

Strategies for the Growth Phase

The growth phase of the product life cycle actually encompasses two different kinds of market behavior: early growth—the phase just following the introductory phase—and late growth—the phase in which the rapid increase in sales begins to flatten out. The growth phase has several features beyond the obvious fact that product category sales are still growing. First, the number of competitors increases. This puts pressure on managers to hold distribution channels and changes the focus of sales and communications to the superiority of the product over others in the category. As customers become more knowledgeable about the product and the available options, this puts pressure on price. Finally, with the increased competition, market segmentation begins to be a key issue.

The general strategic options relate to the product's position in the market: whether it is a leader (the brand with the leading market share) or a follower. The leader can choose either to fight, that is, keep the leadership position, or to flee, which cedes market leadership to another product. If the leader chooses to fight, it can attempt to either simply maintain the current position (a dangerous approach, since it is difficult to know exactly what it takes to maintain the position) or keep enhancing the product or service. Why would the leader choose flight? It is possible that the new entrants in the market are just too strong (as indicated by the competitive analysis) and raise the stakes for competing to a level the incumbent cannot sustain. Witness Minnetonka, which established the liquid soap category. When Lever Brothers and Procter & Gamble jumped in, Minnetonka sold out. Thus, exit is always an option. Other options are to attempt to reposition the product so it can be a strong number two or three brand, which can be accomplished through resegmenting the market, or to retreat to a specific niche.

The follower also has a number of options, the choice of which depends on the strength of the leader, its own strength, and market conditions. One option is to simply exit quickly and invest in some product that has better long-term potential. A follower can also be content to be a strong number two or three by fortifying its position. The riskiest move is to try to leapfrog the competition. Some companies do this successfully through pure marketing muscle and an imitative product. For example, Johnson & Johnson often allows another company to establish the market and then becomes number one through its superior marketing. One example is in over-the-counter yeast infection drugs: Schering-Plough established the market and J&J followed with its Monistat 7 brand, which quickly obtained more than half of the market (Weber, 1992). Other companies attempt to leapfrog through technological innovation. While Yahoo was the first "spider" on the World Wide Web, Lycos and Digital Equipment Company's AltaVista offered improved versions that gained share for a time.

A good example is the situation faced by Docutel Corporation in the 1970s (Abel, 1977). Docutel was the first company to develop and market automated teller machines (ATMs) to banks in the United States. The company was very small at the time, with only $25 million in sales in 1974. The market for ATMs grew rapidly during the 1970s as banks discovered they could use ATMs to differentiate themselves from other banks in a geographical area. However, new competitors entered the market, including mainframe computer manufacturers IBM, Burroughs, and NCR, as well as two firms in the bank vault and security information business, Diebold and Mosler. In addition, customers became more concerned about cost savings from the machines as opposed to marketing advantages. Thus, Docutel, the market leader, had to make a fight-or-flight decision. Fighting would mean making substantial investments in marketing and product development, particularly in developing software compatible with banks' computer systems. In addition, the company would have to decide which market segments (defined geographically, by type and size of bank, etc.) it would target. Alternatively, the company could be a strong number two or three given the potential size of the market. Unfortunately, Docutel did not make a clear decision to pursue any strategy and was ultimately surpassed in the market by Diebold.

Strategies for Maturity

The maturity stage of the life cycle, of course, is characteristic of most products, particularly consumer products. Product categories exhibiting fierce battles for market share, access to distribution channels, large amounts of money spent on trade and customer promotion, and competitive pricing policies are often in this stage of the product life cycle.

In the maturity phase, the sales curve has flattened out and relatively few new buyers are in the market. While some untapped market potential usually remains, it is very difficult and/or expensive to reach. Buyers are sophisticated and well versed in product features and benefits. Where differential advantage can be obtained, it is usually through intangible benefits such as image or through the extended product concept discussed earlier (e.g., service, distribution). Market segments are also well defined, and finding new ones that are untapped is a struggle.

The general strategies in mature markets are similar to those in growth markets and depend on the relative market position of the product in question. In this case, however, leaders sometimes look at the time horizon for "cashing out" the product. If the manager is committed to a product for an extended time period, the objective is usually to invest just enough money to maintain share. An alternative objective is to "harvest" the product, that is, set an objective of gradual share decline with minimal investment to maximize short-run profits. Other firms have alternatives that depend on the leader's strategy. If the leader is harvesting the product, the number one position may be left open for an aggressive number two brand. If the leader is intent on maintaining that position for a long time (many leading consumer packaged goods brands have been number one for over 50 years!), the follower may choose to be a profitable number two or to exit the category.

FIGURE 7–9   Strategy over the Life Cycle

	Life Cycle Stage			
	Introduction	*Growth*	*Maturity*	*Decline*
Competitive Position: *Leader/Follower*				
Objective				
Positioning Customer targets Competitor targets Differential advantage				
Programs Product Price Distribution Communications				

Strategies for the Decline Stage

In the decline stage of the life cycle, sales of the category are dropping. So is the number of competitors. Markets reach the decline stage for a variety of reasons. Perhaps the most obvious is technological obsolescence. The demise of the buggy whip is such a case. However, shifts in customer tastes also can create declining categories. The decline of brown alcohol consumption can be related to changing tastes for "white" alcohol such as gin and vodka, and subsequently, for wine and micro-brewed beer.

Perhaps the clearest strategy is to try to be the last in the market. By being last, a product gains monopoly rights to the few customers left. This, of course, results in the ability to charge commensurately high prices. For example, Lansdale Semiconductor was the last firm making the 8080 computer chip introduced by Intel in 1974. While most applications of computer chips are well beyond the 8080, the 8080 is still used in military systems that are typically built to last 20 to 25 years, such as the Hellfire and Pershing 2 missiles and the Aegis radar system for battleships. Where does the Department of Defense go when it needs 8080s? There is only one supplier: Lansdale.

Summary

One way to think about strategic issues over the life cycle is to use a table such as Figure 7–9. The table encourages both an audit of current position (share; leader–follower) and a changing of objectives, positioning, and programs as the industry situation changes.

Illustrations

Dreamery

Objective: To capture 14 percent of the super-premium market, similar to our overall share.

Customer Targets: Primary: Well-educated families in the West and Northeast.

Secondary: The Hispanic market.

Current customers (regular and premium) who can be persuaded to trade up to Dreamery.

Competitive Targets: Primary: Ben and Jerry's, Haagen-Dazs (which have 80 percent of the market)

Core Strategy: Utilize our fleet of trucks and salespeople to get distribution and maintain fresh stock. Provide basic flavors (vanilla, chocolate) plus introduce new flavors that will add to equity and create trial (e.g., Olympic Cinnamon Mint).

Handspring

Objective: To capture 15 percent of the PDA market by the end of year 2.

Customer Targets: As in Figure 7–3, there are three main targets:
1. Price-conscious professionals (including buyers for company salesforces, etc.).
2. Nonbusiness professionals (e.g., teachers).
3. Nonprofessionals (e.g., stay-at-home spouses, students, retired people).

Competitive Targets: 1. Palm
2. Sharp

Core Strategy: Focus on (1) simplicity/convenience, (2) low price, and (3) expandability (via expansion slot).

Summary

This chapter provides the reason for doing the background analyses described in Chapters 2 through 6. The central component of the marketing plan are objectives and strategies for the product that synthesize the current market situation into a recommended plan of action. The strategy then leads

FIGURE 7–10   **Linked Strategic Issues**

		Strategic Alternatives	
		Growth	*Efficiency*
Customer Strategy	Acquire	✓	
	Retain		✓
	Expand	✓	
	Delete		✓
Brand Strategy	Build	✓	
	Leverage	Brand Extensions	Line Extensions
	Milk		License
Product Strategy		New Products	Prune Product Line
Life Cycle Stage	Introduction	✓	
	Growth	✓	
	Maturity		✓

to specific recommendations for marketing programs, such as pricing and advertising. The success of a strategy is largely dependent on the integration of the situation analysis and programs in providing a coherent direction for the product.

Strategy can be organized in multiple ways. Here the focus was on strategic alternative, growth versus efficiency. Other perspectives include customer strategy, brand equity, new products, and stage in the life cycle. While at first this may be confusing, closer inspection reveals a close relationship among them. Growth strategies tend to be preferred during growth states of markets, require new products, focus on customer acquisition and expansion, and involve building brand equity. Efficiency strategies, by contrast, tend to be preferred later in life cycles and involve focusing on retaining and/or expanding current customers, minimal or simple product changes, and leveraging brand equity, often through licensing or selling the name. Figure 7–10 describes these likely contingencies.

References

Aaker, David A. (1996) *Building Strong Brands.* New York: The Free Press.

Aaker, David A. (1991) *Brand Equity.* New York: The Free Press.

Aaker, Jennifer (1977) "Dimensions of Brand Personality," *Journal of Marketing Research,* 34, August, 347–56.

Abel, Derek F. (1977) "Docutel Corporation," Harvard Business School case #9-578-073.

Batra, Rajeev, Donald R. Lehmann, and Dipinder Singh (1993) "The Brand Personality Component of Brand Goodwill: Some Antecedents and Consequences." In *Brand Equity and Advertising: Advertising's Role in Building Strong Brands,* David A. Aaker and Alexander L. Biel, eds., Hillsdale, NJ: Lawrence Erlbaum Associates, 83–96.

Bounds, Wendy (1994) "Photography Companies Try to Click with Children," *The Wall Street Journal,* January 31, B-1.

Business Week, (1996) "Japan Turns a Corner," February 26, 108–9.

Carpenter, Gregory S. and Kent Nakamoto (1989) "Consumer Preference Formation and Pioneering Advantage," *Journal of Marketing Research,* August 26, 285–98.

Czepiel, John A. Czepiel (1992) *Competitive Marketing Strategy.* Englewood Cliffs, NJ: Prentice Hall, Chapter 1.

Day, George S. (1990) *Market Driven Strategy.* New York: The Free Press, Chapter 7.

Golder, Peter N. and Gerard J. Tellis (1993) "Pioneering Advantage: Marketing Logic or Marketing Legend," *Journal of Marketing Research,* 30, May, 158–70.

Hulbert, James M. (1985) *Marketing: A Strategic Perspective.* Katonah, NY: Impact Planning Group.

Kadanoff, Marcia (1995) "Customers Who Are Ripe for the Picking," *Marketing Computers,* December, 24–26.

Lefton, Terry and Weston Anson (1996) "How Much Is Your Brand Worth?" *Brandweek,* January 29, 43–44.

Levine, J. B. and M. A. Anderson (1986) "Floating Point Sets Its Sights— Downward," *Business Week,* September 8, 30–31.

Levitt, Theodore (1986) *The Marketing Imagination.* New York: The Free Press.

Mehegan, Sean (1996) "A Picture of Quality," *Brandweek,* April 8, 38–40.

Milbank, Dana (1992) "Restructured Alcoa Seeks to Juggle Cost and Quality," *The Wall Street Journal,* August 25, B-4.

Morris, Betsy (1996) "The Brand's the Thing," *Fortune,* March 4, 72–86.

Pae, Peter (1992) "Card Issuers Turn to Stealing Customers," *The Wall Street Journal,* August 18, B-1.

Porter, Michael E. (1985) *Competitive Advantage.* New York: Free Press.

Ries, Al, and Jack Trout (1992) *Marketing Warfare.* New York: McGraw-Hill.

Schnaars, Steven P. (1991) *Marketing Strategy: A Customer-Driven Approach.* New York: The Free Press.

Schwartz, Karen (1996) "Pennies Saved, Millions Earned," *San Francisco Chronicle,* March 24 p. D-1.

Urban, Glen L., Theresa Carter, Steven Gaskin, and Zofia Mucha (1986) "Market Share Rewards to Pioneering Brands: An Empirical Analysis and Strategic Implications," *Management Science,* June, 32, 645–59.

Weber, Joseph (1992) "A Big Company That Works," *Business Week,* May 4, 124–29.

Index